TRADITIONS
&
TRANSITIONS

NOTRE DAME PASTORAL LITURGY CONFERENCE
EDITED BY ELEANOR BERNSTEIN, CSJ
AND MARTIN F. CONNELL

LITURGY
TRAINING
PUBLICATIONS

Acknowledgments

Anne Porter, "Leavetaking," from *An Altogether Different Language* (Cambridge, MA: Zoland, 1994): 83–84.

Mark Van Doren, "Morning Worship," from *Morning Worship and Other Poems* (New York: Harcourt Brace, 1960): 13–14.

This book was edited by Martin F. Connell. Audrey Novak Riley was the production editor. The design is by Anna Manhart, and the typesetting was done by Jim Mellody-Pizzato in Sabon and Gill Sans. Cover art: *Left:* Bronze crucifix, Ascension Church, Oak Park, Illinois. Photo by Regina Kuehn. *Right:* "Crucifixion" by Georges Rouault, courtesy of the Philadelphia Museum of Art/Corbis. This book was printed by Bawden Printing in Eldridge, Iowa.

Library of Congress Cataloging-in-Publication Data
Traditions and transitions: culture, church, and worship / edited by
   Eleanor Bernstein and Martin F. Connell.
         p. cm.
      "Notre Dame Center for Pastoral Liturgy."
      Papers from the December 1995 symposium and the June
   1996 conference of the Notre Dame Center for Pastoral Liturgy
   in observance of the Center's 25th anniversary year.
      1. Catholic Church—Liturgy—Congresses. I. Bernstein,
   Eleanor. II. Connell, Martin, 1960– . III. Notre Dame Center
   for Pastoral Liturgy.
BX1970.A1T73   1998
264'.02—dc21   98-3182
                                                            CIP

ISBN 1-56854-024-8
TRTR

To the memory of Pope John XXIII and
Pope Paul VI—strong, loving and wise pastors.
Cherishing the Tradition, they entrusted it to
a new generation.

Contents

Part II
Traditions and Transitions:
Culture, Church and Worship

Eleanor Bernstein, CSJ

Introduction

F rom June 1995 through June 1996, the Notre Dame Center for Pastoral Liturgy observed an anniversary year, celebrating twenty-five years since its founding in 1970. The year included three public events: two pastoral liturgy conferences in June 1995 and June 1996, and a symposium in December 1995. The proceedings of the 1995 conference are available in the volume *The Renewal that Awaits Us* (Chicago: Liturgy Training Publications, 1997). This volume, *Traditions and Traditions,* contains the papers from the second conference in June 1996, as well as the major addresses from the December 1995 symposium, "To Worship the Living God in Spirit and in Truth."

That symposium served as a centerpiece for the year-long celebration. We were honored by the presence of two liturgical scholars who served as *periti* at the Second Vatican Council: Godfrey Diekmann, OSB, and Monsignor Frederick McManus. Former directors of the Center and past recipients of the Mathis award attended as special guests. Together we hailed the remarkable progress made in this first generation of renewal; together we looked to the challenges ahead. The major addresses at that symposium serve as the lead essays in this collection. It was a privilege to welcome as keynote speaker Cardinal Godfried Danneels, primate of Belgium, sacramental theologian and liturgical scholar. His Eminence offered us an assessment of the liturgical reform thirty years after the Council from an international perspective. Sister Mary Collins, OSB, professor of liturgy at The Catholic University of America, proposed issues for the next decade of renewal.

The year-long celebration closed with the 1996 pastoral liturgy conference, "Traditions and Transitions: Culture, Church and Worship." The papers from that conference reflect the dynamic of ambiguity and change inevitable in these decades of transition following Vatican II. How do we hold on to a living and dynamic tradition? How do we keep our balance in this time of transition? We readily identify with the Israelites wandering in the desert; should we go forward to what we don't yet know? Should we return to what is familiar? The pilgrim people of God, tired and dusty, have begun arguing among themselves: "Should we press on? Should we turn back? Are we traveling too fast or too slow?"

The pressure for change increases each year, and the resistance to change increases as well. What change is desirable? What forces affect our culture, our church and our worship? Can we cross over from a time when security and clarity marked Catholic experience to a new time? We admit to divided hearts: Both fear and faith live within us as a church. Having glimpsed a vision of something new ahead, having tasted the new wine, we desire to be attentive to the Spirit's urging and continue the journey.

It is our hope that this volume will make a solid contribution to the ongoing critical conversation so necessary as the church—that's all of us—struggles with the call to conversion and renewal. We move forward, bearing profound respect for what we have received and confidence in the Spirit who inspired this good work. The Council's gift to the church is a gift to be shared with succeeding generations. In that spirit, we hand on what we have received.

Eleanor Bernstein, CSJ
October 11, 1997
35th anniversary of the opening of the Second Vatican Council

Part I

25th Anniversary Celebration of the Center for Pastoral Liturgy: To Worship the Living God in Spirit and in Truth

First Vespers of Advent, 1995

A reading from the First Letter of Paul to the Thessalonians (5:1–5, 14–24):

> Concerning the times and the seasons, brothers and sisters,
> you do not need to have anything written to you.
> For you yourselves know very well
> that the day of the Lord will come like a thief in the night.
> When they say, "There is peace and security,"
> then sudden destruction will come upon them,
> as labor pains come upon a pregnant woman,
> and there will be no escape!
> But you, beloved, are not in darkness,
> for that day to surprise you like a thief;
> for you are all children of light and children of the day;
> we are not of the night or of the darkness.
> We urge you, beloved, to admonish the idlers,
> encourage the faint hearted,
> help the weak, be patient with all of them.
> See that none of you repays evil for evil,
> but always seek to do good to one another and to all.

The word of the Lord.

Sisters and Brothers in Christ:

We have just heard a message from the Church's first and greatest theologian, Paul of Tarsus. We have just heard a message from the earliest of all the New Testament writings. Paul's letters to the Thessalonians provide us with a vivid picture of a young and fervent Christian community just twenty years after the ascension of Christ.

What is in this scripture passage for us? What is the meaning and relevance of Paul's words for us who live in the final years of the second millennium of Christianity? How do these words lead us to happiness and peace? How do these words help us with our own daily life struggles? How do these words motivate us to a deeper discipleship with Christ?

The key concept of this passage is the second coming of Christ, the *parousia* of the Lord. The coming of Christ in glory at the end of time pervades Paul's message to his parishioners, the Thessalonians. Paul presents the *parousia* to these first Christians and to us as the source of courage, the source of patience, the source of hope. Paul says: Focus on the second coming of Christ in glory—this is how you face trials, troubles, temptations, tragedies.

Is this not a timely message for Christians today? I am convinced that the most needed virtue for contemporary Christians is hope. It is difficult in our secular culture to be a follower of Christ. It is difficult to witness to Christ in a society where religious vocations are down, marriage failures are up. It was difficult for the Thessalonians to follow Christ. They faced persecution from without and dissension from within. Paul wrote to encourage them and to help them persevere. We need that same message.

Our hope is based on the resurrection of Christ. Jesus, crucified and buried on Good Friday, was alive and walking around on Easter Sunday morning. The risen Jesus is the absolute of all absolutes. This risen Jesus will return in glory at the end of time.

The End of Time

No theological area more desperately needs Christian rethinking and re-evaluation than the traditional concept of the end of the time, the end of the world. In the *Dogmatic Constitution on the Church*, the council fathers of Vatican II call upon Christians to reform their understanding of the last days. According to Paul, Christians should desire hopefully and joyfully the end of the world. The Christians of the early church impatiently longed for the final day. "Maranatha"—come, Lord Jesus—was their prayer.

Why do today's Christians want to postpone the end of time? Why do today's Christians think exclusively in negative terms about the end of the world: annihilation, fire, hydrogen-bomb holocaust?

For the early church the end of the world signified not a final cosmic catastrophe, but the coming of Christ in glory. Our Nicene Creed professes this fact: "He shall come again *with glory* to judge the living and the dead." The accent must not be on the gloom of a cosmic catastrophe but on the victory day of Christ—the victory day which will reveal the fullness of his triumph and glory.

For too long we have talked about death, judgment, heaven and hell. What is missing from these so-called four last things? Bypassed is the entire notion of *parousia*—the second coming of Christ in glory.

An old Southern preacher looked at his congregation and saw they looked disheartened, disillusioned; maybe it was after a revival-type sermon on sin. He picked up the Bible, thumbed through the pages and waved it above his head, shouting: "I've looked in the back of the book—We win, we win!"

We need to look in the back of the Bible and understand Christ has conquered sin and death: He will come again in glory. Let us be on the side of the winner; we have good reason to persevere. That is what Paul is saying to the Thessalonians and to us in this passage.

Each Day Is the Day of the Lord

Paul wrote: "The day of the Lord will come like a thief at night." Christ's coming will be sudden, unexpected, "like a thief in the night" or like the onset of an expectant mother's labor pains. Paul is stressing that we should live each day as though it were the last. Each day is the day of the Lord. Be prepared, be vigilant.

Paul tells his parishioners: While you are waiting for the Lord to come, "do not quench the Spirit." Do not stifle the Spirit. These are words of the apostle Paul. The holy Spirit was present at Vatican II and gave the universal church new liturgical direction. Liturgical renewal and reform, prompted by the Spirit, came to the pilgrim people of God. Today there are voices calling us to return to a liturgical mentality and practices from prior to Vatican II. "Do not quench the Spirit." *The Constitution on the Sacred Liturgy,* given to us thirty-two years ago this December 4, must continue to breathe life into our worship. Long live the Notre Dame Center for Pastoral Liturgy and all the Center has done to breathe life into our worship. Let us say with Paul: "Do not quench the Spirit."

At the second coming of Christ, there shall be no longer a conflict between the glory of God and the glory of the world. There can be no anxiety or fear about the last day when it is thought of as the glorious return of Christ to take possession of all that is his. Our hope of being with Christ in heaven depends on our being with Christ now. Meanwhile, with hope and courage, let us proclaim "Blessed is He who comes in the name of the Lord" — now and at the *parousia*. Amen.

Liturgy Thirty Years after the Council: High Point or Recession?

Delivered on December 2, 1995,
on the occasion of the 25th anniversary celebration
of the Notre Dame Center for Pastoral Liturgy

A Major Turnabout

It must be difficult for those who have not experienced it for themselves to imagine just how much liturgical praxis has changed in less than half a century. The evolution which has taken place in the last thirty years is barely perceptible nowadays, since the new liturgical model is considered evident practically everywhere. Such a situation is certainly gratifying, but does it mean that the profound intentions of the *Constitution on the Sacred Liturgy* have thereby been realized? Perhaps now is the appropriate moment for an evaluation.

It is evident that the last half-century has brought about a major change in the relationship between the minister and the people in the liturgy. This change, however, was not without consequence for our understanding of the relationship between the sacred and the profane and even between the church and the world. The situation might be roughly stated as follows: Prior to the liturgical reforms, the distance between the minister and the people was clearly designated. This was even given material expression in the ordering of church buildings: the distinct choir area reserved to the priest, the altar oriented to the east, priest and people separated by a communion rail. Even more questionable than the features of church architecture was the parallel configuration of the celebration: It was frequently the case that the priest celebrated the official liturgy while at one and the same time the people set about their personal devotions. The use of Latin, of course, had a significant role to play in this parallel configuration.

The consequence of all this was that the liturgy came to be considered untouchable, an entity regulated by rubrics, to be performed with great obedience and respect. Liturgy was simply a given, and a good liturgist was seen for the most part as an observant performer. The people assisted, of course, but took little part in the liturgy itself.

Active Participation

From its very beginnings, the aim of the liturgical movement, which originated in Belgium in 1909, was to close the gap between the official liturgy of the priest and that of the people. The term "active participation" was borne out of this movement and has since become part of our common usage. It became a key term in the liturgy constitution of Vatican II.

Active participation was first promoted through the circulation of the People's Missals, which contained the Sunday liturgy; the faithful were at least able to follow along. Before long, however, a desire for more than just following in the book emerged: People wanted to participate and join in. Vatican II satisfied this desire by introducing the use of the vernacular, by simplifying liturgical symbolism to make it more transparent, by returning to the praxis of the early church and dropping elements which had later come to overshadow the essentials, and by a correct distribution of roles in the service of the liturgy. The result was far greater involvement of the people, even to the very heart of the liturgy.

From Rubricism to Manipulation

The active involvement of the people in the liturgy is, of course, an unparalleled gift from the council to the people of God. As with every worthy reform, however, there was a shadow side. Active participation in the liturgy, preparing together, and the concern to get as close as possible to the culture and sensitivity of the faithful can lead imperceptibly to a sort of taking possession of the liturgy. Participation and mutual celebration can lead to a subtle form of manipulation.

In such an event the liturgy is not only set free of its untouchable quality—which in itself is not a bad thing—but it becomes in a sense the property of those who celebrate, a terrain given over to their creativity. Those who serve the liturgy—both priests and laity—become its owners. In some cases this can even lead to a sort of liturgical coup in which the sacred is eliminated, the language trivialized and the cult turned into a social event. In a word, the real subject of the liturgy is no longer the Christ who through the Spirit worships the Father and sanctifies the people in a symbolic act. The real subject is the human person or the celebrating community.

The exaggerated emphasis from before the 1950s on discipline, obedience, fidelity to the rubrics, the reception and entering of a preexistent entity is replaced by self-will and by the elimination of every sense of mystery in the liturgy. In this case the liturgy is no longer *leitourgia*: the work of the people and for the people with respect to their relationship with God; it becomes a purely human activity.

Fortunately, the trend we have outlined is not universal. Nevertheless, any attempt to evaluate liturgical praxis in our time would be wrong to ignore it.

The Liturgy is beyond Us

There is a liturgical ground rule which runs as follows: The liturgy is first "God's work on us" before being our work on God. Liturgy is datum, a given, in its very essence: It is beyond us and has already existed for a long time, long before we could participate in it. The acting subject of the liturgy is the risen Christ: He is the first and only

High Priest, the only one who is competent to bring worship to God and to sanctify the people.

This is not only an abstract theological truth; it must become evident and visible in the liturgy. The core of the liturgy is already given in the Lord's acts of institution. This does not mean that the individual and the celebrating community are neither capable nor permitted to make a creative contribution. The community is creative, but it is not an "instance of creation." Otherwise the liturgy would no longer be the epiphany of the Christian mysteries through the service of the church, the continuation of Christ's incarnation, crucifixion and resurrection, the "incarnation" of a divine project in history and in the world of human persons via sacred symbols. In such a situation the liturgy would become nothing more than the community celebrating itself.

The liturgy "pre-exists": The celebrating community enters into it as into a pre-established divine and spiritual architecture. To a certain degree this is also determined by the historical location of Christ and his sacred mysteries. The eucharist as such is not a "religious meal" but rather the making present of a particular meal: that of Christ with his disciples on the night before he suffered. In this sense, the liturgy can never be a self-fashioned concoction of the celebrating community: We are not creators; we are servants and guardians of the mysteries. We do not own them nor did we author them.

The Fundamental Attitude of *Homo liturgicus*

This entails that the fundamental attitude of the *homo liturgicus*—both individually and collectively—is one of receptivity, readiness to listen, self-giving and self-relativizing. It is the attitude of faith and of faithful obedience. It is not because a particular caricature of this attitude of obedience led at one time to slavish and nonsensical dressage and rubricism that the sense of "entering in to what transcends us" has been so diminished.

The *homo liturgicus* does not manipulate, nor is his or her action restricted to self-expression or auto-realization. It is an attitude of orientation toward God, a readiness to listen, obedience, grateful reception, wonder, adoration and praise. It is an attitude of listening and seeing, of what Guardini called "contemplating," an attitude which is so alien to the *homo faber* in many of us.

In short, the fundamental attitude of the *homo liturgicus* is none other than an attitude of prayer, of handing ourselves over and letting God's will be done in us.

It should not surprise us, then, that in a period of history like our own, with its active intervention in everyday reality and its submission of that reality to our scientific thinking and our technological expertise, it will be particularly difficult to be genuinely liturgically-minded. The contemplative dimension of the human person is no longer evident these days. This being the case, the core of the liturgy is even less evident.

Active participation, therefore, has to be situated within this contemplative attitude, in which case it must also bear the particular characteristics of such an attitude.

The Incomprehensibility of the Liturgy

One of the primary concerns of Vatican II and of the church is and remains that the liturgy be understood by the celebrating community. Every reform proposed by the Constitution is rooted in that concern. "Understand what you do" is a basic demand of everything we do, including what we do in the liturgy.

The incomprehensibility of the liturgy was blamed, in the first place, on language. Immediately after the introduction of the vernacular, however, it became apparent that it had to do with more than just language usage: The content of the liturgy itself was equally unfamiliar.

The liturgy, of course, is almost entirely structured on the Bible. It is said that the Hebrew Bible or Old Testament is particularly unfamiliar to us. Everything in it takes place in an agrarian context which barely applies nowadays in many parts of the world. At the same time, the biblical texts are rooted in a rural culture, and a peculiarly Mediterranean one at that. Many images, such as shepherds, flocks or water wells are no longer part of the day-to-day vista of the modern city dweller. In other words, the Bible uses a language from a bygone era.

The non-biblical texts in the liturgy are also a little strange. The Latin collects with their succinct and metrical structure are simply untranslatable, not so much because the words cannot be transposed into a modern language, but because the mentality and culture from which they stem has disappeared. A great many texts, when detached from their musical setting, end up seeming extremely archaic; think, for example, of the *Salve Regina* and the *Dies Irae* or even the ordinary sung Gregorian introits and communion antiphons, leaving aside the archaic images of God which such texts maintain (the God who sleeps, the God of wrath, and so on).

Certain symbols, although secondary, no longer seem to function: the drop of water in the chalice, mixing a particle of the host with the wine, the lavabo, the washing of feet. One frequently hears reproaches such as "old-fashioned," "passé," "medieval" and "monastic."

Abbreviate or Eliminate?

People often opt for a short-term solution which barely touches on the real problem. In the case of the liturgy certain terms were replaced with other more understandable terms. There are biblical terms, however, which cannot be replaced. What do we do, for example, with words like "resurrection," "Easter," "eucharist," "metanoia," "sin"? They are part of a sort of biblical and liturgical mother tongue that simply cannot be replaced. These words have to be learned. It is hard to imagine a Jew using a different term for *shabbat* or *pesach*.

Certain biblical images are, indeed, barely perceptible in our modern urban culture. The sight of shepherds and flocks is no longer an everyday occurrence. Does this mean, however, that such images are no longer comprehensible in themselves? Is it because no one has ever met a seraph that the metaphorical power of this angelic messenger no longer speaks to us? Half of the poetry ever written makes use of images and terms that are not part of the daily life and environment of the reader. A great many symbols from medieval German culture were taken up in the Roman Pontifical.

People sometimes opt for alternative poetic texts, especially for weddings and baptisms. Leaving aside the fact that there is a profound theological distinction to be made between an aesthetically valuable text and a biblical text, it is also true that many such texts belong to an even more limited culture than the Bible, which, it would appear, possesses a much greater universality.

The remedy employed in most cases often does not help. Most of the time it is limited to questions such as: "What can we drop?" "How can we abbreviate?" "What would function better to express what is going on in our lives as individuals and as a community?" Is the last question justified, however? What precisely do we have to say in the first instance? What is going on in our lives? Or what God is saying to us? In a manner, of course, which we can understand.

There appears to be only one solution: If the liturgy is not simply a structuring of common human religiosity, but rather the epiphany of God in human history (from Abraham to Christ), then we cannot avoid the need for catechesis and initiation. Liturgy demands schooling because it is both proclamation and celebration of mysteries, mysteries which have occurred in the history of Judaism and Christianity.

What is Understanding?

What exactly is understanding? It is evident that if the liturgy is the epiphany of God's dealings with the church then the deepest core or heart of the liturgy will never be open to our grasp. There is indeed a hard core in the liturgy, the mystery, which is ungraspable. One can only enter into it in faith.

There is more to say about understanding, however. Our contemporaries often conceive understanding as the ability to grasp at first hearing. Something is understandable if we can grasp it immediately. Such an approach is valid for the ordinary objects of our knowledge, which can only be grasped at a purely cognitive level, but this is more a question of registering than understanding. Where the depths of human and divine reality are concerned, this approach does not work. Love, death, joy, solidarity, knowledge of God, can never be grasped at once and on first inspection. In these cases, understanding is more a question of the biblical notion of "knowing-penetrating."

It is a lengthy and progressive process of becoming familiar with a particular reality.

The same is true for the liturgy. It is not an object of knowledge in the commonplace sense of the word. It is not an object of knowledge at all; rather it is a source of knowledge, a source of understanding. This is why analysis is out of place here; only a prolonged listening and familiarization is appropriate. This implies that the liturgy will be open to understanding only from a perspective of empathy. The liturgy lets itself be understood only by those who have faith in it and love it. For this reason it remains inaccessible and incomprehensible outside of the faith.

In addition, the liturgy is only understandable with a certain repetitiveness. Profound realities only gradually yield their full significance. This is why we have the phenomenon of "ritual" in the liturgy; and whoever speaks of ritual speaks of repetition.

Many changes which were introduced into the liturgy in order to make it understandable have been inefficient because they focused on the immediate, cognitive, informative aspect of understanding. They wanted to explain everything, to provide commentary, to analyze. They never lead to familiarity with the liturgy. They are surgical and medical interventions (abbreviating, replacing, scrapping, describing) on a dying reality, a sort of palliative care that can never heal the sick individual. The only approach is the "dialogical" approach: allowing the liturgy time to say what it has to say; listening attentively to its harmonics and allowing its deeper meaning to unfold; not looking for an alternative but letting the liturgy speak for itself and expose its own virtualities.

Our Disrupted Relationship with the Liturgy

The incomprehensibility of the liturgy is not so much due to the unintelligibility of its major symbols. Indeed, all of us are well able to grasp the deep fascination which flows forth from symbols such as fire, light, water, bread, wine, laying on of hands, anointing. These major (natural) symbols speak to us all in our archetypal imagination. Secondary symbols can, of course, be more problematic. At the same time, however, they are of lesser importance, and Vatican II correctly discarded a number of them.

A more significant contributor to the problem of understanding is the fact that the symbolic universe within which such symbols functioned has been lost. Removed from its proper context, a liturgical symbol is like a fish out of water and is left bereft of much of its vitality. Proof of this can best be found in what one might call contrary situations where the symbolic universe continues to thrive even today.

Why is it so that short Latin phrases and Gregorian refrains continue to function in Taizé but not in the parishes? Because they are in their proper place within the religious community of Taizé and its monastic liturgical life. Why is it that the symbols we have been discussing continue to function in the abbeys, the monastery churches and the charismatic communities? For the same reason!

Why does a Gregorian requiem function well at a funeral? Liturgical comprehensibility also depends on a number of non-liturgical surrounding elements. It is our entire relationship with the liturgy — even outside the cultic celebration — that makes so much possible.

The incomprehensibility of the liturgy is not only due to the liturgy itself but in part to us. Our own attitude needs to be worked on. We need to examine our global relationship with God, our faith, our lifestyle and so on. Does the liturgy give meaning to these dimensions of our life or does it turn them into something outside ourselves, a *corpus extraneum?* We need to be aware that understanding the liturgy is far more than a cognitive exercise; it is a loving "entering in." At the same time, our vision or contemplative gaze is weak. Since the Renaissance we have lost our disinterested contemplative ability; it was pushed aside to make way for analytic observation.

What Should We Do? What Can We Do?

Theme and Variations

It is quite clear that "entering into" the already existing structure of the liturgy does not mean that we must exclude any kind of flexibility in our liturgical style. Far from being ruled out, creativity is actually called for. If the problem does not lie with creativity, then where does it lie?

The problem lies with the boundaries of our intervention. One cannot simply transform and rearrange the whole thing. Changes have to be made with intelligence. The liturgy contains certain given themes which, while they cannot be changed, do remain open to possible variation. Some of those clearly delineated and unchangeable liturgical paths were determined by Christ himself. In classical terms they are referred to as the "substance" of the sacraments, over which even the church itself has no power. The liturgy remains Christ's liturgy.

There are also more historically derived elements of the liturgy which one cannot change. There are certain forms of prayer and certain words and ways of speaking which, like the Bible texts, remain unchangeable. Perhaps even the liturgical order of scripture reading, lyrical response (psalm) and prayer falls into this category. It is more than just a liturgical vagary; it is a deep theological truth: God speaks first, and our response follows.

A thorough liturgical training is indispensable in order to be able to establish the boundaries between theme and variations. Liturgy demands knowledge of tradition and history — in short, documentary knowledge. In order to take one's place in the liturgical enterprise, one has to know one's craft: Liturgy requires instruction and insight together with a good helping of spirituality and pastoral awareness. Perhaps the reason for the evident liturgical poverty in so many places throughout the world can be found here. There is no lack of engagement or dedication or imagination: There is simply a lack of competence. There is no point in setting up liturgical work groups if they are not trained for their job.

The Duration of the Celebration

It might come across as strange in the ears of many, but our liturgical celebrations are for the most part too short. The liturgy needs time to deliver its riches. It has nothing to do with physical time or clock time, but with the spiritual time of the soul. Since liturgy does not belong to the world of information but to the domain of the heart, it does not work with clock time but with *kairos*.

Many of our liturgies do not provide enough time or space to enter into the event. In this regard Eastern liturgy provides a worthy example, taking its time and inviting those who participate to "leave all worldly cares behind" (Hymn of the Cherubim). It is not enough that people have heard the liturgy or that it has been spoken: Has it been "proclaimed" to them? Have they been given the opportunity to integrate it? It is not enough for us to have heard the liturgy, we need to have grasped it as well.

A major factor in all of this is silence and the time to interiorize. The liturgy of Vatican II provides time for silence but in practice it is not given much of a chance. Lack of silence turns the liturgy into an unstoppable succession of words which leaves no time for interiorization. Here too is a reason for the liturgy's incomprehensibility.

The Articulation of Word and Gesture

A major handicap of the liturgy as it is practiced *de facto* in the West is its verbosity. In essence, liturgy has become a matter of language and speaking. The word that was once ignored and neglected has made a comeback. How many celebrants consider the homily to be the climax of the liturgy and the barometer of the celebration? How many have the feeling that the celebration is more or less over after the liturgy of the word? Indeed, there is clearly an imbalance in duration between the liturgy of the word and the liturgy of the eucharist.

At the same time too much attention is given to the intellectual approach to the liturgy. There is not enough room for imagination, affect, emotion and properly understood aesthetics. This leads in turn to the liturgy beginning to function in an extremely intellectual fashion and failing thereby to reach many of those who participate in it because they are either nonintellectual types or because they do not consider such stuff to be nourishing for their lives.

A liturgy which is almost exclusively oriented to the intellect is also not likely to involve the human body in the celebration to any great extent. It is small wonder that people end up sitting down for almost the entire celebration, sitting being the typical attitude of the listener, though this is not usually the case in the United States.

There is a serious imbalance in the articulation of word and gesture. Without introducing rhetorical gesticulations and building in theatricality, one can still argue, nevertheless, that the tongue and the ear are frequently the only human organs in use during the liturgy. Liturgy then ends up lapsing from celebration into mere instruction and address.

The Instrumentalization of the Liturgy

One of the consequences of the verbosity we have been discussing is the danger that the liturgy will be instrumentalized and used for ends which lie outside it. Liturgy, however, is a global symbolic activity which belongs to the order of the playful. The uniqueness of play is that one plays in order to play, one plays for the sake of playing. The death of play is competition and financial interest.

Liturgy will also die if it is subordinated to ends beyond itself. Liturgy is neither the time nor the place for catechesis. Of course, it has excellent catechetical value, but it is not there to replace the various catechetical moments in the life of the Christian woman or man. Such moments require their own time. Nor should liturgy be used as a means for disseminating information, no matter how essential that information might be. It should not be forced to serve as an easy way to notify the participants about this, that and the other unless such things are themselves entirely subordinate to the liturgy itself.

One does not attend the liturgy on Mission Sunday in order to learn something about this or that mission territory: One comes to the liturgy to reflect on and integrate one's mission from Christ to "go out to all nations." The establishment of all sorts of thematic Sundays and thematic celebrations has little or no future, except in the death of the liturgy as such. Liturgy ought certainly not to serve as a sort of warm-up for another activity, even a church activity. It is not a meeting but a celebration. It can indeed follow from the liturgy that one departs from it with a greater sense of engagement, faith and love informing and inspiring one's actions.

Liturgy is a free activity; its end is in itself. Although it is the source and summit of all ecclesial activities, liturgy does not replace them nor does it coincide with them.

The Experience of Liturgy

The uniqueness of the liturgy is that it gives pride of place to experience. Experience comes first, and while reflection, analysis, explanation and systematization might be necessary, they must follow after experience.

"Celebrate first, then understand" might seem a strange proposition to some and perhaps even come across as obscurantistic and anti-intellectual. Does it imply a call for irrationality or an abandonment of the massive catechetical effort the church makes in order to prepare people to receive the sacraments? Think, for example, of the creed and confirmation.

The church Fathers adhered to the principle that mystagogical catechesis—in which the deepest core of the sacred mysteries was laid bare—should come only after the sacraments of initiation. Prior to baptism they limited themselves to moral instruction and teaching on the Christian way of life.

Immediately after baptism, during Easter week, the fathers spoke about the deep meaning of baptism, chrism and eucharist. Their pedagogical approach remained sensorial: Participate first and experience things at an existential level in the heart of the community and only then explain. Their entire method of instruction was structured around a framework of questions and answers such as: "Did you notice that . . . ?" "Well, what this means is. . . ."

Perhaps we do not have to adhere to the letter of such a pedagogical approach—the *disciplina arcani* also had a hand in things—but it certainly provides a hint about the right direction. One can only understand the liturgy if one enters into it with faith and love. In this sense no catechetical method will succeed if it is unable to depend on good, community celebrations of the liturgy. In the same way catechesis as such will be of little use if it is not accompanied by a liturgical praxis during the period of catechesis.

Where the liturgy is concerned, the following rule applies: First experience, first *live* the liturgy, then reflect and explain it. The eyes of the heart must be open before the eyes of the mind, because one can only truly understand the liturgy with the intelligence of the heart.

This has consequences for liturgical work groups: Those who desire to work with the liturgy, and, as we already noted, vary the given theme, will first have to listen attentively to that theme and participate in the celebration of the liturgy as it is. If they do not, then their entire liturgical endeavor will turn out to be nothing more than self-expression and not the shaping of a pre-existent entity which has its roots in the liturgical tradition of both the Old and New Testaments and in the living tradition of the church.

What would we think of a composer who refused to listen to his predecessors or a painter who refused to visit a museum? Every musician listens to music and every poet reads poetry. This is simple human wisdom but it applies in full to the liturgy, which is primarily God's work in the assembly.

The worthy liturgist listens first, meditates, prays and interiorizes. Only then can he or she modulate.

Ritual and Boredom

The very terms "rite" and "ritual" summon up the idea of boredom and monotony. "It's always the same," we hear, "day in, day out." Ritual is synonymous with rigidity and sclerosis.

Yet is that really so? It is true that an exaggerated attachment to particular forms does exist, but that is ritualism, unsound ritual. We have to admit that every good thing has its pathology.

Ritual, however, is something other than ritualism. Ritual is priceless and irreplaceable. It has its place in every human activity. Every human being has a morning and evening ritual just as every society has its regular festivities which are celebrated in the same way each year.

Ritual is an unavoidable anthropological given. Every significant human reality is surrounded and protected by ritual: birth, marriage, love, death. Every transition is adorned and embellished with ritual. Every time we encounter something that transcends the human person, we humanize it with ritual.

The distinguishing characteristic of every ritual is its repetitiveness and stereotypical nature. In order for us to interiorize profound matters, we need stereotypes, the reassuring ceremonial wordings we call ritual. This kind of repetition, however, does not necessarily imply monotony or the stifling of any kind of personal element.

Every marriage rite, for example, is stereotypical: Everyone marries in the same manner and with the same words and gestures. Yet in so doing those involved are not left depersonalized, a mere number in the line. Every marriage remains unique even though it took place in just the same way as any other. As a matter of fact, it is essential to every couple that they are able to take their place in line with every other marriage in and through the fixed marriage rite. In this way the fragility of their personal engagement is socialized and, in their eyes, protected and guaranteed. The same is true for the language of love. It remains endlessly unvarying, yet it is experienced as fresh and new each time it is spoken.

Repetitive ritual provides, in addition, the opportunity for in-depth reflection and interiorization. Serious matters (such as the liturgy) cannot be grasped all at once: They need time, and time means repetition. Only pure information such as an order or a computer language does not require repetition since it can be understood immediately. More profound matters only let their real significance emerge over time.

Ritual, finally, provides a protection against direct, un-mediated religious experience. Only the great religious geniuses—such as Moses at the burning bush—are capable of such experiences; the rest of us need the protective mediation of ritual and the decelerating, delaying role of repetition.

Indeed, there will always be a certain monotony and perhaps boredom associated with ritual. Perhaps we simply have to be aware of it and reconcile ourselves to it, as long as we continue to bear in mind how necessary this "tiresome" aspect of ritual can be.

A few further reflections might also be useful. If we constantly emphasize the tiresome aspect of ritual, we reveal just how individualistic our experience of the liturgy has become. Ritual, however, is necessary in order to bring a community together and allow it to celebrate. If we turn the liturgy into the most individual expression of the most individual emotion, then we wipe out any possibility of communal celebration. If, however, we enter into the eucharistic celebration with its fixed *ratio agendi* it is because we want to make it possible for many to celebrate in the same rhythm. There can be no community without ritual.

We need to bear in mind, furthermore, that we attend the liturgy at God's invitation. The liturgy is not a feast we laid out for ourselves, according to our own personal preferences. It is God's feast. We attend by invitation and not simply to satisfy our own particular needs.

A great deal depends, to be sure, on the person of the presider. He is someone who must lead a community event on God's behalf. He is the living vehicle of something that goes beyond him. He is, therefore, neither robot nor actor; he is a servant.

The Cosmic Grounding of the Liturgy

One important fact about the liturgy is its relatedness to the cosmos. Many of its symbols are borrowed from cosmic realities such as fire, light, water, food, bodily gestures. Times and seasons, the position of sun and moon, night and day, summer and winter are also related to the liturgy. In the liturgical event, all the major human archetypes have their place.

What is important, however, is that the cosmic realities in question are given their chance to appear in their full reality as created things. The liturgy must work with real things. Although everything is to a certain degree transformed by culture, it should never be overshadowed by cultural accretions. Fire needs to be real fire, light real light, linen real linen, wood real wood. Time must also be respected, such as the hour for the Easter Vigil celebration. Thus liturgy often becomes the true repository of the authenticity of the objects around us. To serve God we use only the best things of creation. Expediency and comfort need to make way here for authenticity.

We should be aware, however, that all our Jewish and Christian symbols are no longer purely cosmic or natural. They have all been determined and conditioned by the history of God and the people of God. Although all our Jewish and Christian feasts have an agrarian origin, they have been conditioned by the events of salvation, which are historically situated and no longer natural; they are fact-historical.

The Passover feast is no longer purely agricultural; it is also the celebration of the exodus from Egypt. Shebuoth is no longer a celebration of the first harvest but of the giving of the law on Mount Sinai. With Christian feasts that are entirely determined by the historicity of the Christian mysteries it is even clearer. There are no more purely cosmic, natural feasts. The Christian festal calendar is no longer a purely natural calendar; it consists rather of a series of memorial days which celebrate historical events between God and humanity.

The Liturgy and the Senses

Liturgy is closely related to the body and the senses. As a matter of fact there is only one fundamental symbolism: the human body as an expression of the human soul and thus the primary location of all symbols. All other symbolic gestures can be situated in the extension of the human body.

Eyesight is the most active of the senses. In the liturgy nowadays, however, it tends to be somewhat undervalued. There is a lot to hear but little to see. At one time the situation was reversed. At a time when the verbal dimension was not understood, the visual dimension was pushed to the fore. Certain secondary liturgical gestures, such as the elevation of the bread and wine at the consecration are a consequence of this fact. Even eucharistic worship outside of Mass has its roots here. We can certainly re-evaluate the visual side of our liturgy but that does not always mean that we have to supply additional visual effects.

It is always best to let the great symbols function. How, for example, can baptism symbolize reception into the church if it takes place in an almost empty church building? (Again, this is not always true in the United States.) How can it be understood as a water bath if it turns out to be little more than a sprinkling with water? How can we speak of "hearing the message" if everyone is sitting with their heads bent reading the texts in their missalettes at the moment when they should be listening? The three great focal points of the celebration— the presidential chair, the ambo and the altar—also have strong visual significance.

The congregation has the most important place in the Christian liturgy, and rightly so. Liturgy is a celebration of the faith and the faith comes from the congregation. As a matter of fact, if the Christian mysteries being celebrated are all rooted in historical facts and are thus memorial celebrations, then it is equally true that this should be spoken about. History is impossible with the element of narrative.

Of great importance is that the different text genres should be respected; a reading is not a prayer, a hymn is not a psalm, a song is not a *monitio* nor is a homily a set of announcements. Each of these genres requires its own auditive treatment. Furthermore, it is clear that neither rhetoric nor theatricality nor pathos have a part in the liturgy. Reading is not acting: It is allowing oneself to be the humble instrument of a word that comes from beyond. The exaggerated impact of the personal individuality of the man or woman who reads can kill the liturgy and eliminate its harmonics.

Even the place from which the scriptures are read has some significance. It is better not to read from the middle of the community because the word comes to us from elsewhere. It is proclaimed; it does not simply arise out of the community. It is also best to read from the Book of the Gospels and from an ambo surrounded by symbols suggestive of respect: light, incense, altar servers.

The sense of touch finds its most profound expression in the laying on of hands and in anointing. These are among the most physical gestures of the liturgy and they can have an enormous impact on the human person. The significance of praying in the presence of a sick person takes on quite a different character if one places one's hands on that person or anoints them.

The sense of smell, to conclude, is almost completely unused in the liturgy. It is not to our advantage that the use of incense has been pushed aside into the domain of superfluity and hindrance. The Eastern church is much better off than we are in this regard. One rather absurd case is the scentlessness of the chrism which we use to suggest the "good odor of Christ" to our newly confirmed. Here too the Eastern church is ahead of us (perhaps too generously!) in their use of tens of different scents and spices in the manufacture of their chrism.

Inculturation

The problem of inculturation is a recent phenomenon. It was treated in a remarkable document produced by the Sacred Congregation for the Sacraments and Divine Worship in 1994.

We cannot discuss every aspect of the problem at this juncture. The principle, however, is clear: If the liturgy is an incarnational fact, then there is an inherent requirement that it be inculturated in the various cultures of humanity. Such is evident. Liturgy must be inculturated, or rather, liturgy will inculturate itself if it is lived with faith and love of Christ by people of all cultures.

There are also limits, however. The liturgy is not only a structuring of human religiosity; it gives form to the Christian mysteries. These mysteries took place in history, in a particular place and time and using particular rites and symbols. The last supper is not just a common, human religious meal, it is *the* meal the Lord ate with his disciples the night before he suffered. This implies that all eucharistic celebrations need to be recognizable as such, which includes even formal connections and references. No cultural religious meal is equivalent to the Christ meal. In this sense the eucharist can never be completely inculturated.

The liturgy is not only an incarnational datum, it also belongs to the order of salvation. As such it has a salvific impact on the cultures of humankind. Not every religious practice or popular liturgy can be used as a vehicle for Christian liturgy. There are levels of incompatibility and there are prayers and practices which are not appropriate for use in the Christian liturgy. Discernment here will not always be so simple.

Inculturation does not take place so much on the liturgist's desk as in the praxis of liturgy itself. It is not an act of bureaucratic sophistication but rather a faithful, loyal discernment which takes place in the celebration itself. Only after long and deep immersion in the real liturgy accompanied by a great desire for Christ and the sacred mysteries, for church tradition and for the historicizing of the natural liturgy through the coming of Christ will we see the slow but steady emergence of inculturated liturgy. This is how the Jewish liturgy transformed into the Greek and the Greek liturgy into the Roman and the Roman liturgy was supplemented and augmented by the German and Anglo-Saxon liturgy and so forth. Such work of inculturation has always been the fruit of the thoughts and deeds of a few significant church figures and of the patient sensitivity and faith-filled discernment of the many peoples of the world.

Whether we should consider inclusive language to be a question of inculturation remains an open question. The discussion is still in full swing and would demand a separate and more thorough treatment than is possible here. In fact the question remains about whether we are being faced with a radical cultural change or not, and whether or not this has religious implications. It appears to me to be more of an anthropological problem, which is not only significant for biblical and liturgical texts but for the use of language as such and for the whole dimension of conviviality between men and women.

Liturgy and Life

There has been a great deal of discussion in recent years concerning the exotic character of the liturgy and its distance from the everyday life of Christians. It is true indeed that a liturgy, that has no impact on or consequences for the way Christians live their lives is off the mark. If, according to Pope Leo the Great, the Christian mysteries have crossed over into the liturgy then it is equally true that liturgy must cross over into the moral and spiritual life of Christians. *Imitamini quod tractatis . . .* — "Do in practice what you do in the liturgy," resounds the ancient text from the liturgy of ordination.

Some have endeavored to draw from this axiom the conclusion that the liturgy is not important when compared with our day-to-day lives, or that it is a sort of preparation or warm-up for life itself, an option for those who need it but redundant for those who do not. Others have suggested that liturgy and life coincide and that true service to God takes place outside the church in one's daily life.

Liturgy does not coincide with life; rather it has a dialectic relationship with life. Sunday is not Monday nor vice versa.

Aside from the liturgy's profound and significant content as an indispensable source of grace and power for life, we must also bear in mind that the Sunday ritual interrupts monotony and differentiates and articulates human time. The liturgy is not life and life is not liturgy. Both are irreducible and both are necessary. They do not coincide.

It is sometimes said that the liturgy gives shape to life, that it symbolizes life. This is not entirely incorrect. What we do throughout the week in a varied and diluted way, we also do in the liturgy but in a more concentrated and purified fashion: We live for God and for others. Liturgy, however, is not only a symbolization of human life. Liturgy symbolizes and makes present, firstly, the mysteries of salvation, the words and deeds of Christ, but also our deeds in so far as they are reflected, purified and redeemed in Christ. His mysteries—made present to us in the liturgy—are our archetypes. This Christological determination of our lives in the liturgy is of the essence.

On the other hand, it is a fact that the liturgy finds its field of application in daily life. It flows over it and nourishes it but never coincides with it nor complies with it. Life and liturgy are in a dialectic relationship: The life of the Christian is built on two things— cultus *and* caritas, worship and love.

Kathleen Hughes, RSCJ

The Vocation of a Liturgist: A Response to Cardinal Danneels

I t is an honor to offer a response to Cardinal Danneels' paper. It is an honor just to be in this splendid gathering and have the opportunity to take heart from the presence of so many whose labors have brought us to this day and this hour. We have so much for which to give God thanks and praise.

Mary Collins has been asked to speak on "Issues for the Next Decade." I shall leave to Mary the building of an agenda for the coming years, propelled, as we will be, by the urgency of inculturation in an increasingly world church, the theological significance of inclusion, the role and extent to which all of us are preachers of the word, questions of sacramental access and other issues of liturgy and justice, changing symbolic perceptions and shifting sacramental paradigms. My focus will be more modest.

I was very touched by the Cardinal's address. I was delighted that he called us back to the deepest truths at the heart of the liturgical reform. The church in North America needs his words, and we thank you, Your Eminence.

The climate today in our church is one of shocking incivility. The liturgy today has become the battlefield where every ideological division is played out, where charges of heresy abound. There is a proliferation of special-interest groups, groups that look like

Washington lobbyists, all claiming the liturgical high ground, all professing fidelity to the Second Vatican Council and its *Constitution on the Sacred Liturgy.*

Many among us are losing heart. I think of the image of the disciples on the road to Emmaus and the sadness of their discourse: "But we had hoped . . ." Here we are, thirty years after the close of the council, and there is obvious evidence of Vatican restorationism. Many in this room have committed more than thirty years of labor as pastors, teachers, publishers, translators, poets, architects, musicians, administrators of national and diocesan offices.

Where Is the Renewal?

Many of us ponder this question: After thirty years, where is the renewal that so much labor promised? True, we have accomplished the reform of the books and, in some cases, we have second-generation rites in possession. We have reconfigured sacred space; we have retooled presiders and have trained a whole cadre of lay liturgical ministers to function at their side. But where is the renewal of hearts that the reform had promised?

Cardinal Danneels invites us, at this juncture, to become self-critical. He urges us to get to the core of our calling, to reflect on our vocation as liturgists. Two particular comments of the Cardinal intrigued me and led me to this conclusion. There was a time, the Cardinal stated, when "liturgy was simply a given and a good liturgist was seen for the most part as an observant performer."

Later in his presentation he spoke of the task of the liturgist today: "The worthy liturgist listens first, meditates, prays and interiorizes. Only then can he or she modulate [the liturgy for others]."

The Good Liturgist

Doesn't this prompt a question for all of us? Who is "the good liturgist" today? Who is a "worthy liturgist"? How would you define the demands of your calling? I think there are hints of our vocation in the Cardinal's address. I offer four suggestions for our reflection.

First, a good liturgist takes to heart the words of Preface IV for weekdays:

> All-powerful and ever-living God,
> we do well always and everywhere to give you thanks.
> You have no need of our praise,
> yet our desire to thank you is itself your gift.
> Our prayer of thanksgiving adds nothing to your greatness,
> but makes us grow in your grace,
> through Jesus Christ our Lord.

These words suggest to me an attitude that all is gift of God. All our labors to produce something beautiful for God—our speaking and teaching, our pastoral efforts, our brilliant writing and publication— whatever it is, *all* is gift, *all* is from God, even our very desire to give God thanks and praise. If *all* is gift, we must have a certain modesty about our role in the reform coupled with profound gratitude that God has invited us to be part of this movement in the first place.

Second, we must remember that we are neither subjects nor owners of the liturgy, but we are simply stewards of the mysteries of which Christ is the subject. The liturgy does not belong to us but is simply entrusted to us. Does this not demand that we approach our vocation with an attitude of reverence, of fear of the Lord, or—as that gift of the Spirit has now been translated—of wonder and awe in God's presence?

Third, if we see ourselves and our calling as that of "stewards of the mysteries," that suggests that there are different boundaries for our labors, different givens in the work of reform, different indices of success to the work of our hands. Perhaps it demands more generous efforts at inculturation, more attention to global realities, more conviction about the essential inclusiveness of language and ritual prescriptions and patterns—precisely so that the mysteries we celebrate unfold in ways that invite the participation of all in the mystery at their heart: the death and rising of Christ.

Fourth, as "stewards of the mysteries," we know that a contemplative heart is absolutely fundamental. We need to explore for ourselves, as well as for those among whom we minister, what is the relationship between contemplation and active participation—seemingly contradictory emphases on the surface of things but inextricably bound up with each other at the heart of the liturgical act. Perhaps we could ensure that the reform would lead to genuine renewal if we began to foster attitudes of silence, receptivity, interiorization, purification, immersion, readiness and openness to God.

Romano Guardini's question haunts us still: Are we capable of a genuine liturgical act? Maybe a new way to pose that question is to ask not whether we are capable of the act, but whether we are able so to empty ourselves that it is Christ—*the* one and only high priest, the leader of prayer—who is able to act within us and within our assemblies.

A Contemplative Vocation

The vocation of the liturgist, then, as steward of the mysteries, is a contemplative vocation. Cardinal Danneels spoke about developing a posture of listening. It is foundational for engagement in an action which is, at its core, a listening and a response, a listening and a loving reply. A liturgist is attentive to this double movement as it plays itself out each time we gather for prayer.

Yet part of our vocational calling is not to keep this best-kept secret to ourselves but to lead others—our assemblies, our students, our readers, our dioceses—in mystagogical reflection on what they experience when they gather for prayer.

Liturgy demands a schooling of both head and heart. Who will foster it if we do not? We have bemoaned a lack of liturgical catechesis long enough. Perhaps the second-generation Sacramentary, which we hope will see the light of day before long, could serve as a catalyst for a whole new effort at mystagogical reflection on the mysteries entrusted to us. This would lead us to a pattern of reflection more like poetry than prose, a catechesis taking its point of departure from the experience of worship itself—not history, theology, canonical or pastoral reflection in the first instance, but the experience of prayer we have in common.

Kathleen Hughes, RSCJ

That is a hope and a strategy we may realize together, especially if we take our vocation as liturgist seriously and foster the habits and attitudes that will keep us faithful to our calling. We are stewards, pray-ers, attentive and contemplative participants, open to God's action and God's gift, and — especially on an anniversary such as this — filled with gratitude that we have been entrusted with the mysteries. Let us say in reply:

> We thank you for counting us worthy
> to stand in your presence and serve you.

Richard P. McBrien

Liturgy and Church:

A Response to

Cardinal Danneels

It is a singular honor to have been invited to participate in this twenty-fifth anniversary celebration of the Notre Dame Center for Pastoral Liturgy, and to serve as a respondent to one of the Catholic church's finest pastoral leaders, Cardinal Godfried Danneels.

Toward the very end of his paper, Cardinal Danneels refers to the fundamental connection between liturgy and life, calling attention to the ancient ordination text, *Imitamini quod tractatis* — "Imitate what you do," or "Do in practice what you do in the liturgy." I should like to elaborate upon this connection between liturgy and life in a more deliberately ecclesiological way. I propose to do so by way of reference to another ancient though familiar axiom, attributed to a fifth-century lay theologian, Prosper of Aquitaine: *Lex orandi, lex credendi* — literally, "the law of praying [is] the law of believing."

Prosper, a staunch defender of the theology of Saint Augustine, was writing against certain Pelagian heretics who did not believe in the need for God's grace. Prosper pointed out that the church prayed for the needs of people in the prayers of the faithful. Authentic worship, he argued, is an expression of true doctrine.

Although the axiom needs to be explained more fully than is possible in this limited time, it can perhaps serve a practical purpose in helping us better understand some of the basic changes that have occurred since Vatican II in the church's thinking about itself and its ministries, as reflected in the changes in the church's worship.

The great liturgical scholar who influenced so many of us and so many of our own teachers, Joseph Jungmann, wrote in his commentary on the Council's *Constitution on the Sacred Liturgy:* "From the very beginning the revival of the liturgy went hand in hand with the renewal of the concept of the church." (*Commentary on the Documents of Vatican II,* ed. H. Vorgrimler, vol. 1, p. 9). Jungmann continued:

> If such a picture of the church [as a sacramental rather than as a juridical reality] is engrafted on the hearts of the faithful by rendering accessible to them such a liturgy, they will be much better equipped to act in the world as Christians.

Although the *Constitution on the Sacred Liturgy* was approved by the Council before the *Dogmatic Constitution on the Church* and the *Pastoral Constitution on the Church in the Modern World,* the liturgy constitution nonetheless reflected much of the theological shift embodied in the Council's thinking about the nature and mission of the church. The Council recognized that the liturgy had to change because the church's own self-understanding — its ecclesiology — had changed, thanks to the pioneering work of such great theologians as the French Dominican Yves Congar and Gerard Philips of Louvain.

Just as the old Code of Canon Law did not reflect the newer, less clerical, less juridical, less legalistic idea of the church and, therefore, had to be changed, as it eventually was in 1983, so the preconciliar liturgy had to be changed because it had been so centered, as Cardinal Danneels pointed out, on the performative actions of the priest while the congregation simply attended in the manner of passive observers or as parallel worshipers. *Lex orandi, lex credendi.* The pre–Vatican II liturgy perfectly reflected, alas too perfectly, the pre–Vatican II ecclesiology.

What did the council change in the church's self-understanding? Or, perhaps more precisely, what changes in ecclesiology did the council reflect that brought about such fundamental, pastorally fruitful changes in the liturgy? I shall limit myself to three points.

First, the council taught in the *Dogmatic Constitution on the Church (Lumen Gentium)* that the church is primarily a community, rather than an institution to which we belong. We are the church. We are the People of God—laity, religious and clergy alike. This important ecclesiological change is clearly reflected in the way the eucharist has been celebrated since the Council and because of the Council. Instead of being experienced as something Catholics attend or hear, by way of obligation, the eucharist is celebrated as a communal meal (fundamentally linked always with the Last Supper, to be sure) in which everyone actively participates.

Thus, the prayers, the responses, the hymns and other activities (such as the presentation of the gifts) are no longer recited or performed by the priest-presider and the altar servers alone, with the congregation looking on as passive observers or engaging in a kind of parallel liturgy. The whole worshiping community participates, because the eucharist is the affair of everyone present. And the eucharist is the affair of everyone present because the church itself is the affair of every baptized member. Thus, the *Constitution on the Sacred Liturgy* declared: "Such participation by the Christian people as 'a chosen race, a royal priesthood, a holy nation, a purchased people,' is their right and duty by reason of their baptism" (14).

Second, the council insisted that the laity are as integral a part of the church as the clergy. The church is not the privileged preserve of the priests. It is not always up to the priest to decide who will do what, how they will do it and whether they will be allowed to keep doing it.

At a properly celebrated eucharist, the priest-presider does not determine what everyone else does, nor does he himself do what others should rightly do. There is a structure to the liturgy that operates independently of the personal preferences of the priest, as Cardinal Danneels reminded us. Thus, it is the lector, not the priest, who proclaims the word of God in the first two readings before the gospel. It is the lay ministers of the eucharist, not the priest alone, who assist in the distribution of holy communion. And it is the congregation as a whole that prays aloud, responds to prayer and sings.

Third, according to the Council, the church is a dialogical community. Cardinal Danneels reminded us in his paper that the "only approach [in the liturgy] is the dialogical approach." The people do not simply receive the word of God from on high. They actively assimilate and respond to it. They do not simply listen to the prayers of a chosen few acting on their behalf. The whole church is both a listening and a responding community. "It is not enough," Cardinal Danneels said, "for us to have heard the liturgy, we need to have grasped it as well." In other words, reception is an essential part of the process.

No one could participate in today's eucharist and conclude that it is essentially an affair of the priest, with minor involvement by an altar server or two. For the same reason, no one can regard the church today as if it were exclusively an affair of the hierarchy and the clergy, theirs to govern and theirs to shape and direct, as they alone see fit.

In an older, pre–Vatican II model of church, the so-called lay apostolate was defined as the participation of the laity in the work of the hierarchy and clergy. According to the Council, however, the lay apostolate is "a participation in the saving mission of the church itself." And it is not something exercised at the sufferance of the hierarchy and clergy such that the laity's ministerial responsibilities can be withdrawn just as easily as they can be granted. On the contrary, the lay apostolate is communicated sacramentally, not juridically. Laity are commissioned to it by baptism, confirmation and the eucharist itself (*Lumen Gentium*, 33).

That the church is divided into dioceses and that each diocese is pastorally governed by a single bishop is not something dictated by divine law, that is, by the explicit will of Christ, any more than rules of eligibility for ordination are dictated by the explicit will of Christ. The church's diocesan and monoepiscopal structure is an accommodation to changing historical circumstances and pastoral needs.

That parishes are governed and administered entirely by a priest, subject only to the bishop who appointed him, is similarly a pastoral accommodation to changing circumstances. As those circumstances change, so too can the church's pastoral accommodations change. Such structures remain open to continued change as the church is poised on the threshold not only of a new century but of a new millennium as well.

Vatican II's *Pastoral Constitution on the Church in the Modern World* insisted that historical circumstances have indeed changed, and that the church must respond to those changes—those "signs of the times"—accordingly (4–10).

The changes that we have all experienced in the church's worship are reflective of the changes Vatican II brought about in the way we are to understand the nature and mission of the church and the roles of its various ministries. "From the very beginning," Joseph Jungmann reminded us, "the revival of the liturgy went hand in hand with the renewal of the concept of the church."

Lex orandi, lex credendi.

Mary Collins, OSB

Liturgical Renewal in North America: Issues for the Next Decade

I dentifying the agenda for the next decade of liturgical renewal is no small challenge. First, the "North America" in my designated topic eludes me. It is at once too vast and too small to focus on. Too vast, because I cannot pretend to speak in any informed way about the complex liturgical lives of the peoples of Mexico and Canada, much less of the complexities of our own dioceses. Too small, because what I see as the challenges of the next decade extend beyond the confines of this land mass we call North America.

Next, locating the audience I am addressing is not easy. Am I sending my list of issues to the U.S. Bishops' Committee on the Liturgy, to the Notre Dame Center for Pastoral Liturgy, to academic liturgists, to liturgists with a direct pastoral charge? This symposium has gathered people operating in all of these venues, so my scope is broad.

Third, the general agenda for the next decade of liturgical renewal seems not to have changed much since the first decade of this century, when Lambert Beauduin addressed a congress at Malines in Belgium on liturgical piety.[1] The same three issues face us.

First is *liturgical praxis:* revitalizing the way the church worships and renewing its understanding of what we do when we worship.

The next issue is *liturgical catechesis:* formation for active participation in the public worship of the church.

The third issue is *liturgical theology:* identifying the necessary questions for critical theological reflection within the Catholic tradition.

What is different is the era in which we are formulating the issues. We are in a different time in the church, when it is receiving the teaching of an ecumenical council. The post-conciliar generation mediating the reception has only limited direct memory of the Second Vatican Council, of the ecclesial reality it was convened to address or of the liturgical movement that prepared the council to mandate liturgical reform.

We are also in a different moment in human history and in national history in this last decade of the twentieth century. These differences inevitably affect our formulation of the issues for liturgical praxis, liturgical catechesis and liturgical theology.

What Roman Catholics are doing now in our Sunday assemblies in the United States is the matrix for my discussion of issues for continuing liturgical renewal in the next decade. In introducing that agenda, let me distinguish between the actual liturgical practices in our dioceses and parishes and the more fundamental but less conscious religious sensibilities that underlie our actual practices. Our choices among symbolic practices and our quarrels with one another about practices rise from that often unrecognized ground. I think the central issue we will be dealing with through the next decade and beyond is already emerging from our current liturgical praxis. I will call the issue "Locating the Mystery." I will address the liturgical catechesis appropriate to our current situation under the title "Orienting the Church to the Mystery." Finally I will speak briefly about the prospects for significant theological reflection in the next decade.

Liturgical Praxis: Locating the Mystery

For some time some Catholics in the United States have been saying that the mystery is gone from the liturgy. The reference point is often but not exclusively the eucharistic liturgy. What are pastoral liturgists and researchers to make of this chorus?

One response is to interpret the complaint as a matter of aesthetics. From that standpoint we can critique the aesthetic of modernity that was adopted by liturgists in the generation that made the Vatican II adaptations of the rites. Modern tastes for non-representational art and natural materials seem to have stripped the church of its liturgical adornments and its devotional warmth, leaving Catholics cold and naked, exposed as neo-Protestants. This analysis of our current distress is attractive. If the common experience of a lost sense of mystery is interpreted as an aesthetic error, a matter of aesthetic deprivation, the analysis points to a workable solution. We can correct ourselves.

Though the task of correction is not without its difficulties, pastoral liturgists in the next decade could conspire to recreate a distinctively Catholic ambiance of divine mystery. Redress could go in the direction of the Tridentine and baroque, or it could elaborate on the styles and forms of new or old ethnic sensibilities. Yet ambiance without substance will not be satisfying for long, so some caution is in order. Any sound liturgical aesthetic must point beyond itself to something real, as it carries the Catholic people along. But what is the beyond toward which the church at worship is tending? That is the fundamental question.

At its first posing, the question evokes ready response. Catholics have an abundance of religious language on which to draw. Catholics biblically and liturgically catechized will answer that in its eucharistic action "the church accomplishes the mystery of its salvation," or that "we enter into the paschal mystery of new life in Christ." Catholics formed through the language of systematic theology that found its way into Catholic catechisms might say rather that the church's eucharistic action leads to the real eucharistic presence of Christ. Catholics committed to the church's mission to the world might rather say that the eucharistic liturgy forms the church in "the true Christian spirit" that enables social transformation. Vatican II's *Constitution on the Sacred Liturgy* provides warrants for speaking all these ways. But these are not all the same answer in different words. They are answers reflecting different understandings and expectations. Yet the Catholic faith is irreducibly incarnational. Catholic sensibility carries the expectation that mediating symbols will orient the people to recognize the presence of mystery, however they understand it. Put simply, Catholics at worship expect that material forms will show them the way of salvation.

Since this is so, liturgists must take seriously the complaint that the mystery is gone. The refrain demands reflection and interpretation beyond the aesthetic, although a liturgical aesthetic will be integral to any new growth in understanding. The complaint is more than a charge that the liturgists of the reform were spoilers, that they unwittingly showed the Catholic people there was no mystery after all. Few people of faith would agree that the liturgical reform of Vatican II was a mistake, that revising the rites so people could understand them was wrong. They know that not even liturgists can prevail against their radical confidence in the mystery of Christ as a living reality.

Rather, the refrain must mean that the Catholic people of the United States believe that they indeed live within the mystery of Christ, but that the reformed rites as they participate in them do not seem to orient them adequately. They do not recognize what they are looking for through the liturgical practices at hand. In the memories of the middle-aged, the old liturgical practices were more effective for locating the mystery of Christ. Many of the young, who have no such memories, still feel bereft, cheated out of their rumored Catholic birthright.

Is a quick aesthetic fix enough to deal with the Catholic people's spiritual distress? We know from ritual theory that it is possible to reinstitute, in whole or in part, most of the liturgical and devotional practices that once oriented the Catholic people in the United States to the mystery of Christ in the Blessed Sacrament. Parishes still have many of the accoutrements, as well as the living memory of how it all looked and sounded and felt. We can still do billows of scented smoke, opulent appointments for sanctuary and clergy, deep resonance in the voices, devotional images and postures. The U.S. Catholic church could yet restore the old ambiance for the next generation. But would it be enough? Perhaps for some, and for a time.

This way of locating the mystery liturgically, by ritual and devotional practices orienting the church to the eucharistic elements, might get parishes through the next decade. But such strategies would do so only by suppressing or avoiding the basic question: What is the mystery of Christ we are celebrating in our liturgical assemblies? Our liturgical praxis inevitably raises questions for liturgical catechesis and for liturgical theology. We will return to these after probing further our troubled grasp of the mystery of Christ which our liturgy celebrates.

A recently published study by James C. Russell describes the "Germanization" of early medieval Christianity. This work sheds light on the sociocultural context of the direction medieval Western eucharistic theology and liturgical practice went. It is worth considering this formative moment, for the forms still shape Catholic identity. Let me summarize Russell's thesis: To the extent that Christian notions of sin and salvation were assimilated by the Germanic peoples during the early Middle Ages, the Germanic peoples may be said to have been Christianized; to the extent that Christianity became more religicopolitical and magicoreligious during this period, Christianity may be said to have been Germanized.[2] Russell's thesis is a general one; yet the implications of his investigation seem to shed some light on our contemporary spiritual distress about locating the mystery and should not be overlooked. The Germanized ground on which official eucharistic praxis is still being constructed may be key to comprehending the complaint that "the mystery is gone." Russell's use of the term "magicoreligious" does not have a pejorative intent. He is identifying the cultural form that shaped the authentic religious sensibilities of tribal peoples in northern Europe to whom the Latin church went on mission. Their cultural heritage did not lead backward to the world of the Bible or to neo-Platonic thought. Their sacramental sensibility was not shaped by a Platonic distinction between material objects which are shadows and the unseen forms which are reality. The northern peoples were animists, for whom the material world was charged with power that could be directed to good or to evil.

Historian of theology Gary Macy writes that Western eucharistic theology got its impetus because Saxon monks of the ninth century "had trouble understanding exactly what use the Lord's Supper might have."[3] Their perplexity undoubtedly had to do with their native religious sensibilities about sacral power. The first systematic eucharistic treatises of Western Christendom were written by monks who were familiar with the writings of the Latin Christian world to explain the eucharistic liturgy to their confused brothers in Christ.

Russell speaks of what happened in this Carolingian world generally as a "semantic transformation" of belief systems.[4] But his judgment was formed on the basis of available data that the transformation of worldview was limited, one-directional. Russell found limited evidence that a genuine Christianization of the Germanic worldview and value system ensued. Interestingly, he cites "the Germanization of liturgical practice" as evidence to the contrary.

Russell, unlike Macy, is not a theologian. But the reconceptualization of the eucharistic mystery that took place as northerners read and debated the meaning of Ambrose, Cyril and Augustine finds its intelligibility within the magicoreligious worldview he describes. Animists were attuned to the possibility of sacral power in the material world. Missionaries brought them the news that the true power for salvation is in Christ. Christ comes to the church in the eucharistic species by the power of the priests of the church. Through eating and drinking the eucharistic species, human bodies are joined to Christ's and salvation is come to the world.[5]

The explanation was refined by successive generations of theologians in the medieval West. Though there was disagreement on the details, there was little challenge to this Germanized magicoreligious paradigm for locating the eucharistic mystery. Liturgical and devotional practices for a millennium have celebrated and reinforced this sense of the eucharistic mystery, the power for salvation in the eucharistic species. But now, in the secularized Western world, the cry rises up that the Catholic people are losing the sense of mystery. Is this the case? Or is it rather that this particular religious sensibility is losing its hold? Do we have different religious sensibilities than our magicoreligious ancestors in the faith? Do these sensibilities involve conversion to personal discipleship? Is cultural desacralization a new opportunity for evangelization?

The teaching of the important article seven of the *Constitution on the Sacred Liturgy,* about the real presence of Christ in the liturgy, went beyond the narrow popular Catholic understanding that localized the presence of the mystery of salvation in the eucharistic species, but its affirmations stayed within the Germanized magicoreligious paradigm. Article seven declares: "Christ is always present in His Church, especially in her liturgical celebrations." The priest is the first named locus of this presence.[6] Priestly power transforms the eucharistic species, making the power for salvation in Christ accessible to the whole church.

But the *Constitution on the Sacred Liturgy* says more. Christ's power for salvation is affirmed to be present in the Scripture proclaimed in the church. The discourse is still in the Germanized paradigm. Is it responding belatedly to the voice of the German reformers of the sixteenth century? Less clearly, and in something of a paradigm shift, article seven ends with the declaration that the praying and singing church gathered for liturgy is also a locus of the power of salvation in Christ.

Since 1963, much of the liturgical practice and catechesis in the parishes of the United States has shown developing strategies to celebrate these four sites as the locus of the liturgical mystery of salvation in Christ. Pastoral liturgists have worked with all the central liturgical symbols to manifest the power of Christ present in the priest, in the sacramental elements—bread, wine, water, oil—in the scripture and in the assembly. Liturgical specialists with varying interests have struggled to establish these symbols of power in proper relationship or to limit their effective power in games of liturgical checkmate. And in the Germanized mode of our Saxon forebears in the faith, our magicoreligious understanding of the power for salvation has generated religiopolitical power struggles. Yet the longer and harder we have worked within this neo-Germanized magicoreligious paradigm to understand the sacramental liturgy of the Catholic church, the greater has grown the sense of alienation. Perhaps the rising chorus of voices lamenting the disappearance of mystery is the Spirit speaking in this church. What if these long-useful doctrinal explanations of the church's eucharistic faith and the familiar magicoreligious liturgical practices are no longer enough to engage people who still hope for salvation in Christ?

The truth of the matter is that most Catholics in the United States have magicoreligious sensibilities as our birthright. We moderns are descendants of pre-Christian animists from the continents of Europe, Africa, the Americas and Asia. Our Catholic sacramental sensibilities are magicoreligious at least as much as they are neo-Platonic. (Perhaps this is why most systematic theologians, whose vocation is to elevate our thinking, have so little direct traffic with the people at work doing sacramental liturgy.) We surprise ourselves to discover that we like to chant rhythmic incantations, to strike flames against the dark, douse the earth with blessed water, trace crosses in the air, walk a circle to locate a center of power, reverence a morsel of food—all in the name of salvation in Christ. What makes popular religion popular, and good liturgy good, is our confident expectation as believers that what we do locates the power for salvation present in our world and connects us to it.

Our magicoreligious sensibilities are not themselves at fault. Belief that the material world can mediate the grace of God is at the heart of our Catholic doctrines of creation and incarnation and our sacramental soteriology. If there is fault, it is that our common-sense Catholic grasp of sacramentality is underdeveloped. We are fixated on the *sacramentum*. Despite the efforts of Jesus and the evangelists and theologians from Augustine to Bonaventure to Karl Rahner, we persistently locate God's gift of salvation someplace outside ourselves.

Some of our inability to move from a magicoreligious to an ecclesial soteriology lies in the officially prescribed magicoreligious use of symbolic forms themselves. Yet the mystery revealed in Christ is the mystery of the real presence of the Spirit of the Risen Christ Jesus in the church. To consent in faith to the gift of the Spirit in the church is to consent to the absence of Jesus from our midst.[7] It was evidently incomprehensible to our Christian-animist ancestors in northern Europe to become Christians and then consent to the absence of Jesus. It is no easier for us to grasp that the real eucharistic presence of Christ is the mystery of divine-human mutuality. How can we believe that the community called church is the real locus for the visible mediation of divine grace in history? Is discipleship all this is really about?

Much official liturgical instruction and pastoral practice still tends to view the sacramental symbols of the Catholic liturgy as ends in themselves, as *sacra* for a desacralized world. Such an orientation sustains and is sustained by our magicoreligious sensibilities. Yet confinement of our understanding of liturgy to this trajectory will block the achievement of the more profound liturgical renewal that was the hope of the pre-conciliar liturgical movement. We come then to the issues of liturgical catechesis and liturgical theology.

Liturgical Catechesis: Orienting the Church to the Mystery

Much liturgical catechesis in the past three decades has focused on the assembly. It has been somewhat at cross-purposes with sacramental instruction that focused on the priest and the symbolic *sacra*. But as I indicated earlier, even our understanding of the assembly as a place of real presence was often magicoreligious in its sensibilities. To break the hold of this paradigm on the Catholic community, I propose that liturgical catechesis for the next decade become a catechesis that comes to terms with the church door. What would such a "catechesis of the door" involve?

For every Catholic liturgy, worshipers use the door twice. They come in and they go out. The baptized voluntarily enter through the door, leaving their life-world for a short time to take part in the liturgical action of the church. At the end of their common action, they exit the church. They return to the life-world of family, work, neighborhood, society.

The *Constitution on the Sacred Liturgy* gives a meaning to this movement. It says that the church is "present in the world yet not at home in it." Those who would teach the church the meaning of its liturgy could do worse than contemplate the people's passage in and out the door. People who pass in and out voluntarily are negotiating their ecclesial identity and making manifest the mystery of Christ: in the world yet not at home. The voluntary passage tells of the people's readiness to hear Christ proclaimed. The liturgical action in which they participate invites them to identify more intimately with the mystery. Liturgical participation symbolically commits participants to conversion to the gospel way of life. Liturgy is always about conversion. The paradox of the church, not named in the *Constitution on the Sacred Liturgy,* is that we who are the church are seldom at home here either. This side of the grave, modern Catholic people do not rest comfortably with the Spirit of Christ given to them. We come and go, in and out. The Orthodox theologian Alexander Schmemann spoke often of the Orthodox Divine Liturgy as an eschatological epiphany of the church. I would refine his notion, calling the participatory liturgy of the Vatican II reform an epiphany of the church in process in history. Now this is a frightening realization. Like you, I know churches where so many people's perfunctory efforts the liturgical work given them to do is startling. Perhaps to cover for them, the liturgical ministers do it all, as parents of lazy children take on the science fair project.

Despite the axiom of the *Constitution on the Sacred Liturgy,* many adults and their children seem satisfied to be fully present to this society and proud to be there. They are uncertain what the church wants of them. They are unwarranted Christians, and little in the prescribed liturgical practice orients them to their own mystery. Ah, yes. Recognition comes. There, too, are our ancestor's children, with magicoreligious sensibilities intact, confident that the power for salvation is somewhere in the transactions of the sanctuary and in the ministrations of the ministers.

I would argue nevertheless that the church coming in through the door and going out again, coming and going, is a people seeking an identity and a mission in Christ. Will they find one to their liking? If the liturgical celebration of the gathered church directs the people's attention exclusively to the liturgical *sacra* and fails to orient them to their mission to make Christ visible in this culture, liturgical catechesis will have failed the test of the church door. Thirty years of liturgical reform will have done no more than return American Catholics to our pre-conciliar starting point. Is there another way for the church's liturgical practice to show the church its mission? I have no answer, but only further questions. Have our dioceses and our national conference any aspiration to a common Catholic mission to this society? And can such a Catholic mission find symbolic expression in our liturgical celebrations of the mystery of Christ?

What I am going to suggest for such a Catholic mission to this culture may seem counterintuitive. It negates not only dominant social and cultural trends but also resists the direction many current pastoral programs and much liturgical planning are taking in the name of inculturation. My reference point is the multiple divisions among races and

Mary Collins, OSB

classes that characterize this moment of national history. Our diocesan churches generally replicate these social divisions in our parochial lives. Our parishes show a proclivity to give this divisiveness liturgical legitimacy in the name of pastoral care, as in the extraordinary proposal circulating in my own archdiocese that multilingual parishes plan multiple language-based celebrations of Easter.

In this moment, we are faced with the question of what it means to inculturate either the gospel or the liturgy. Self-expression is guaranteed by the first amendment, but it is not yet the good news. The eschatological hope of the church is that all may be one in Christ. If Catholic liturgical action does not dare to reveal this eschatological hope even in the church for fear that the Catholic people of North America will be offended, how can the church dare to presume it is able to evangelize this culture? And if we cannot come to terms with the call to conversion such a mystery entails, will it be anything more than chauvinism to take pride in our numbers: U.S. Catholics, sixty million strong and growing!

Students of liturgical history know the story of how the city of Rome in its early years was a church comprising ethnic communities gathered in various enclaves. Church cohesion was a challenge, and the liturgical life of the city took shape in response to the pastoral need for a cohesion that did not come naturally to the people. Stational liturgies set in various quarters of the city were one strategy that emerged for shaping and maintaining one eucharistic people in Christ. The *fermentum* sent out from the bishop's eucharist to the parochial churches was another manifestation of the mystery. In our own day, the monastery of Taizé in France has committed itself to liturgical celebrations in which peoples of every nation and tongue, race and class can discover themselves in the mystery of salvation in Christ. The Taizé music in particular calls people to participate actively in bringing a fragmented church and polyglot Christians into symbolic unity through sound. Through music, the church works the eschatological promise into present reality, if only for a short time, and it leaves in the bodies of the worshipers traces of the promise realized.

I recall the old city of Rome and Jacques Berthier's music not to suggest that we simply pirate intriguing liturgical practices. I remember them as invitations to consider what we must do in our liturgical assemblies in the next decade to disclose ourselves to ourselves and to the whole world as a Catholic people alive to the mystery of salvation in Christ. With some pastoral intuition and theological reflection I suspect that we too can work in powerful symbolic ways within the liturgy of the Roman rite to make the Sunday eucharist of our metropolitan areas reveal us to ourselves as truly catholic—as a people whose unity in Christ bridges our growing social divisiveness.

Celebrating such liturgy will require new conviction on the part of the church's pastors. They will need to evangelize in the church to prepare it for its new mission to this culture. But new conviction about the church's mission to the culture will be acquired only by creating new venues for pastoral formation. Mystagogical reflection by the people and their pastors together will need to spread throughout the diocesan churches. For I am not so naive as to think that the whole Catholic people is ready to bring the gospel to this culture—we who are so implicated in culture and its folkways. A move from the magicoreligious to the gospel way of life is substantive. We who like to be with "our own kind," with "family," with "the community," are not likely to be immediately open to the insistent claim of liturgical practice and parish mission that people of every race, tribe, tongue and custom are "our own kind." We who are formed by our culture to think of churchgoing as a leisure-time activity will resist being asked each Sunday to work with strangers to show ourselves and our society the church of Jesus Christ in spirit and in truth.

I recognize that the odds are against our taking up such an agenda for liturgical renewal in the next decade. But if not now, when? Perhaps if one parish or diocese leads, others will follow. Such transformation will require more than a decade. Only slowly does the church make the liturgy; only slowly does the liturgy make the church.

Liturgical Theology: Reflection on the Church's Liturgy

My proposal to locate the mystery and orient the Catholic people liturgically over the next decade is intended to help the church at worship recognize its own mystery. The proposal runs at cross-purposes with efforts on the parts of some officeholders and some charismatic leaders who have other plans for the decade. These would once again focus the Catholic people's understanding of the mystery of Christ's presence to the church on the sacrament of the altar. The differences in interpretation are theologically substantial, but my proposals are fully within the Catholic theological tradition.

Yet our de facto lack of adequate processes for critical reflection among the teachers of the church on the liturgical practices of the Catholic people constitutes a major weakness in our present stage of renewal. There is little hope that sustained theological reflection on the church's liturgy will advance in the next decade. The intense interest of the Congregation for the Doctrine of the Faith in liturgical practice illustrates what is at issue here. Systematic theologians are trained to study a tradition of texts. In some rare cases they show interest in ritual practices that have been turned to texts in liturgical documents. But the liturgical work of the Catholic people either escapes the optic of the systematician or is distorted when it gets reduced to discursive form to fit the measure of the optic.

Systematic theologians have long tended to consider the liturgy marginal at best to the theological enterprise, so liturgical theologians are seldom their conversation partners. Systematicians proceed by making distinctions, by separating at the level of theory what is integrated at the level of practice. But liturgical practice cannot live by theoretical distinctions or within the boundaries set by specializations. The liturgical action of the church engages the whole of the mystery of salvation. Or at least it intends this whole. It means to embody belief. To use the conceptual categories of the systematicians as the sole measure of liturgical soundness is bound to be unsatisfactory. Neither what eludes the censure of systematicians, what earns their commendation nor what meets with their indifference is to be automatically credited as evangelically sound in particular circumstances. Liturgy by the books is not yet the liturgical reform that will effect ecclesial renewal. Accordingly, the liturgical community must develop its own theologically critical voice in this next decade.

For its early agenda, I submit what I have brought to this symposium today: matters related to locating the mystery of Christ's saving presence celebrated in the liturgy, and matters related to orienting the Catholic people liturgically to their common mission as church in this culture.

1. See *Liturgy, Life of the Church* (Collegeville: The Liturgical Press, 1926).

2. James C. Russell, *The Germanization of Early Medieval Christianity: A Socio-historical Approach to Religious Transformation* (New York: Oxford University Press, 1994), 207ff.

3. Macy, *The Banquet's Wisdom* (New York: Paulist Press, 1992), 70.

4. Russell, 205.

5. Macy, op. cit.

6. The "how" of this has been explained by one bishop-theologian as the "psychosomatic pneumatic" identification of the ordained priest with the person of Christ.

7. Louis-Marie Chauvet, *Symbol and Sacrament* (Collegeville: The Liturgical Press, 1995).

Rosa María Icaza, CCVI

Hispanic Liturgy:
A Response to Mary Collins

I am very happy to be here and I feel honored to be part of this celebration. Sister Mary Collins, OSB, has presented us a challenging paper with many points to ponder and many others to put in practice not only as we ourselves participate in liturgical celebrations, but also when discussing liturgical renewal.

I rejoiced when Sister Collins clarified the term North America, which includes Mexico, the United States and Canada, also when she acknowledged the complexities in our own dioceses. Her presentation contained three distinct issues:

- Liturgical praxis: locating the mystery

- Liturgical catechesis: orienting the church to the mystery

- Liturgical theology: encouraging theological reflection.

I would like to reflect with you on some of the ideas that she presented to us and I will do this from the Hispanic perspective. With regard to "locating the mystery," she questions whether the remark people make that "the mystery is gone from the liturgy" is a matter of aesthetics. She suggests that it is more than that. Yet I would like to know what she means by aesthetics; is it only ambiance, that is, art and environment?

She lists liturgical adornments together with devotional warmth. For me devotion comes from the heart, from our inner relationship with God, Mary, the saints. External practices and objects would be devoid of meaning. Perhaps what we need is the building of a closer and more personal relationship with the sacred. Certainly, as Sister Collins states, "Ambiance without substance will not be satisfying for long." But my question would be: Is the purpose of ambiance to satisfy? Who is to be satisfied? Or, is the purpose of ambiance to help the community to elevate mind and heart?

I agree that any sound liturgical aesthetic must point beyond itself to something real. This is the role of all symbols and liturgy is particularly symbolic. I believe we understand symbols as a necessary part of sacramental actions giving grace and strength to lead a Christian life, not simply as material forms that show the way of salvation.

The liturgical renewal of Vatican II has been misunderstood by many Catholics, including some of the clergy. And as Sister Collins expresses it: "Few would agree . . . that revising the rites so people could understand them was wrong." However, we know that in order to participate actively and meaningfully the mystery does not need to be understood; but it must be related to life and affirm or challenge our way of thinking and the way we live our Christian faith.

The mystery of salvation, the presence of Christ among us is not limited to moments of liturgical celebration. As Sister Collins states: "[People] know that not even liturgists can prevail against their radical confidence in the mystery of Christ as a living reality."

Yet the basic question remains: What is the mystery of Christ we are celebrating in our liturgical assemblies? It is the paschal mystery expressed through symbolic actions, words, gestures and objects that speak to us of the life, suffering, death and resurrection of Christ, who is our model, guide and strength.

Simply restoring the old ambiance for the next generation without serious reflection on its meaning is not what liturgical renewal points to or what people are asking for. Hispanic, particularly Mexican American, sensibility is shaped by indigenous religious sensibilities with a vision of the world as sacred. Perhaps Hispanics could resonate with what Russell, according to Sister Collins, identifies for the Germanic people without the background of Bible and neo-Platonism.

We believe Christ comes to the church in the eucharist by the power of the priests of the church. But we believe Christ is near us, as are our ancestors who are now enjoying heaven and much more; the eucharistic presence of Christ is one way, but not the only way, as we all know. As the *Constitution on the Sacred Liturgy* affirms the four ways of Christ's presence, Hispanics have been conscious of Christ's presence in these ways:

- in the priest,
- in the eucharistic species, and also
- in our neighbors. Corporal works of mercy are considered as important as or even more important than prescribed liturgical worship.
- in scripture, although we seem to have discovered this after Vatican II and we rejoice in it and particularly
- in the gathered assembly.

As Hispanics we hold firm to the belief Sister Collins named: "Belief that the material world can mediate the grace of God is at the heart of our Catholic doctrines of creation and incarnation and our sacramental soteriology." For this reason, we gladly use many symbolic actions, gestures and objects to express our faith, uniting many of our popular expressions of faith to liturgical celebrations: Holy Thursday and the visit to the seven churches; Good Friday and Pésame.

Yet, as Sister Collins affirms, all of us need to be reminded that "God's gift of salvation is within ourselves" and not somewhere outside of us. Exterior practices and symbols, even if they are "liturgical" ones, are merely helps, reminders of the workings of God within us so that we can be aware of and cooperate fully with God's grace.

The second part of the presentation dealt with "Orienting the Church to the Mystery." This is done, according to Sister Collins, through liturgical catechesis. Today, this catechesis focuses more on the assembly. Sister Collins suggests a "catechesis of the door," but for our people religion is part of life and vice versa. So we cannot leave our life outside to take part in the liturgical action; on the contrary, we incorporate it in our worship. And as we return to life, we take with us the strength and guidance received in the liturgical action.

Certainly, "liturgical participation symbolically commits participants to conversion to the gospel way of life. Liturgy is always about conversion." Sister Collins suggests, though, that we who are the church are seldom at home in the church or in the world. Hispanics have been conscious for many years of the fact that we are pilgrim people, our true and final home is in heaven. Yet, we are asking that our church be a home not a place. (This is clear in *The National Pastoral Plan for Hispanic Ministry*.)

I consider the following statements by Sister Collins of tremendous importance: "The participatory liturgy of the Vatican II reform [is] an *epiphany* of the church in process in history. . . ." "[People] are uncertain what the church wants of them. . . ." "The church coming in through the door and going out again, coming and going, is a people seeking an identity and a mission in Christ. . . ." "If liturgical celebration of the gathered church directs the people's attention exclusively to the liturgical *sacra* and fails to orient them to their mission to make Christ visible in this culture, liturgical catechesis will have failed the test of the church door."

Sister Collins asks, "Is there another way for the church's liturgical practice to show the church its mission?" I would say yes. This is for me the value of inculturated liturgy when we do not separate life from liturgy but we bring to liturgy the ways we live and to life the ways we celebrate: Hospitality, sharing table, joy and hope, and so on.

Again Sister asks: "Have our dioceses and our national conference any aspiration to a common Catholic mission to this society?"

Hispanics have stated it succinctly in the *The National Pastoral Plan for Hispanic Ministry*:

> To live and promote . . .
> by means of a *Pastoral de Conjunto*
> a mode of Church that is:
> communitarian, evangelizing, and missionary,
> incarnate in the reality of the Hispanic people and
> open to the diversity of cultures,
> a promoter and example of justice . . .
> that develops leadership through integral education . . .
> That is the leaven for the kingdom of God in society. (17)

Her suggestion wants to address the mission of the church to the world of "multiple divisions among races and classes that characterize this moment of national history" and seems to imply that multilingual celebrations are not appropriate, but divisive. I wholeheartedly agree. No multiple Easter celebrations, but could we honor in the same celebration the cultural differences of the community? Unity does not imply uniformity, that is, one language.

Speaking of her experience with Taizé, Sister says that "through music, the church works the eschatological promise into present reality, if only for a short time, and it leaves in the bodies of the worshipers traces of the promise realized."

Once again Sister Collins asks: "What must we do in our liturgical assemblies in the next decade to disclose ourselves to ourselves and to the whole world as a Catholic people alive to the mystery of salvation in Christ?" Hispanics are a group of different cultures and nuances of language; we are struggling with multiculturalism among ourselves. Can we honor the diversity as a mosaic, a tapestry, without each one losing its characteristics? Perhaps we can take turns, but always joining in the celebration, in spirit, as one people of God. God gave us the gift of time and we can never do everything at the same time.

Together with Sister Collins, I hope that "[w]ith some pastoral intuition and theological reflection . . . we too can work in powerful symbolic ways within the liturgy of the Roman rite to make the Sunday eucharist of our metropolitan areas reveal us to ourselves as truly catholic [may I say multicultural] — as a people whose unity in Christ bridges our growing social divisiveness."

One last remark on this topic. Sister Collins states that "[w]e who are formed by our culture to think of churchgoing as a leisure-time activity will resist being asked each Sunday to work with strangers to show ourselves and our society the church of Jesus Christ in spirit and in truth." Hispanics would be countercultural to this way of thinking. We have not implemented our unity fully, but we are conscious that we need to strive toward it.

The third part of the paper speaks of theological reflection on the church's liturgy. Definitely: "The liturgical community must develop its own theologically critical voice in this next decade . . ." in "matters related to locating the mystery of Christ's saving presence celebrated in the liturgy," and in "matters related to orienting the Catholic people liturgically to their common mission as church in this culture."

As Hispanics we are seriously reflecting on our popular expressions of faith, many of which accompany our liturgical celebrations. We know that many of them began as a beautiful and effective way of evangelization and include full participation of adults, youth and children. We explore their biblical foundation and their theological implications. We need to understand more deeply the mystery of salvation and to live it more fully. A truly inculturated liturgy will facilitate our celebrating what we have lived and our living out what we have celebrated.

Part II

Traditions and Transitions: Culture, Church and Worship

R. Scott Appleby

Keeping the Faith
in an Age of Extremes

We have all become fairly familiar in recent years with the institutional transformations afoot in the Catholic population in the United States: As the Catholic population itself increases significantly, the number of priests and women religious declines.

The preconciliar church is remembered as a time when priests staffed every parish, sacramental theology made sense to most lay people and nuns in abundance educated and formed five million parochial school students. Since 1960 the Catholic population has grown dramatically, but the number of priests and women religious has declined as a result of resignations, retirements and thinning ranks of new recruits. In 1996 the number of seminarians has dropped to about 5,500, hardly enough to replace the wave of retirements on the near horizon, much less to keep up with the increasing size of the laity. Communities of women religious — the sisters and nuns who built and sustained the U. S. Catholic infrastructure for decades — are also aging dramatically and face an uncertain future. Catholic hospitals and charities rely increasingly on professionals drawn from the secular world.

We can quickly review the situation by scanning the following table.

R. Scott Appleby

	1960	1995	2005 (est.)
U.S. Catholics	40,000,000	60,000,000	*75,000,000
Priests	*52,689	*45,000	*35,000
Active Diocesan Priests	35,000	26,000	23,000
Women Religious	164,922	90,000	65,000
Seminarians	30,000	5,500	——
Lay Degree Seekers	——	**13,500	——
Non-Ordained Paid Professional Parish Ministers	——	**20,000	——

Sources:

1960 *Official Catholic Directory* (New York: P. J. Kenedy)

1995 *Official Catholic Directory* (New York: P. J. Kenedy)

*Richard Schoenherr and Lawrence A. Young, *Full Pews, Empty Altars*: *Demographics of the Priest Shortage in United States Catholic Dioceses* (Madison: University of Wisconsin Press, 1993)

** Bernard Lee, *The Future Church of 140 BC: A Hidden Revolution* (New York: Crossroad, 1995)

Significant change is occurring already in the 2,000 Catholic parishes without a resident priest; this is 10% of the total, and growing. Hundreds of them are administered by lay and religious women acting in effect as pastors without portfolio. In such settings the liturgy of the word — the proclamation and preaching of the scriptures — replaces the consecration of the eucharist as the primary act of communal prayer, thereby threatening the centrality of the sacramental tradition that has defined American Catholic worship for generations. Although considered a stopgap measure, the introduction of parish administrators also means that Catholics are experiencing gifted and compassionate women acting in a quasi-priestly role. In time the laity may not care to observe the distinction between the new Christ-bearers and ordained priests, despite the Vatican's "infallible" teaching that the former are forever excluded from the ranks of the latter.

The shifting Catholic demographics are documented extensively in *Full Pews, Empty Altars,* a controversial study of the priest shortage by Lawrence A. Young and the late Richard Schoenherr. Whether or not the trend is irreversible, as the book argues, it has begun to transform the relationship among priests, women religious, the new pastoral administrators, permanent deacons and lay ministers. The resulting new configuration of Catholic ministry challenges basic theological and ecclesiological assumptions informing the way Catholics have thought about themselves and articulated their mission in the world. It also raises daunting organizational questions, especially regarding the future of seminary education, the allocation of resources for lay ministry training and certification, and the inadequacy of the financial structures of the church to provide both retirement benefits for a graying clergy and a living wage for full-time lay pastoral associates who have their own families to feed.

In his important new book, *The Future Church of 140 BC: A Hidden Revolution,* Bernard Lee argues that we are at a critical turning point in Catholic Christian history, one in which "lay interpreters" of the Catholic story are emerging to take their places alongside clerical interpreters. At St. John's University in 1977, there were about a hundred seminarians and perhaps a dozen lay and religious students. By 1985 there were about fifty seminarians and over fifty lay students. Today there are about three times as many men and women in graduate programs in religion, theology and ministry who are not on an ordination track as there are seminarians in the four years of theology before ordination. American Catholics constitute 25% of the general population but over 40% of the college population. "No other church in Christian history has been so well educated generally and had so many lay people educated in Scripture, theology, church history, pastoral counseling skills, and so on," Lee writes.

Here are a few key passages from his book:

> What is unique to the U.S. Catholic church at this point in its life is that never before in the entire history of the church has there ever been a Catholic laity as generally well educated as the U.S. Catholic laity; nor has any nation ever had as many lay Catholics with graduate degrees in theology, ministry, and religion — and this number grows; nor has any church ever taken so many lay-women and laymen into active church ministry and active church leadership. All of these educated and committed laywomen and laymen work and live outside of the juridical corridors of power. When the great churchmen meet, laypeople may be invited to observe and for consultation, but never to vote on how Catholic faith will be interpreted. (156)

> Personally, I do not agree with the judgment I often hear, that if we are more faithful and pray better, God will send us the

R. Scott Appleby

vocations we need. Vocations to ministry are, in fact, abundant: They just do not look like what we are used to seeing them look like. They often look like laywomen and laymen. We are neither much worse than we used to be nor much better than we used to be. We are the same old beautiful, grungy souls we always were. My intuition is that God is doing a new thing with us, and that includes declericalizing an overly clericalized *ecclesia*. Knowing how power functions in all human institutions, and knowing that the church is a human as well as a divine institution, it is most unlikely that we clerics would declericalize. "Cleric" will not disappear, and should not, but will look very different on the other side of all this change. "Lay" will also look very different on the other side of the transformations afoot—it already does. (146)

There is something remarkable about the new experience of God's real presence in Word, and that is the integral role of community interpretation in the process. This new and heightened experience of God's real presence in Word is facilitated by a new arrangement in the interpretive pattern of the community. The lay contribution does not replace the clerical interpretation but works in a dialogic relationship with it. Lay hearts, lay minds, lay ears, and lay tongues are effectively and collaboratively contributors to Word's great presence. Marginal Small Christian Communities are the place where this second kind of presence is being felt and named. The lay hermeneutic is a constitutive feature of this second real presence. (153)

Leading us to this point have been traumatic developments unfolding over the last thirty years—developments which, taken together, constitute a watershed for Catholicism as for other American Christian communities. In his apocalyptically titled *The Gathering Storm in the Churches* (1969), sociologist Jeffrey Hadden saw the North American Christian churches in general entangled in a web of compounded crises: a crisis of doubt over the most basic Christian doctrines, a crisis "over the meaning and purpose of the church," and a crisis of religious authority. Together, said Hadden, these three crises amounted to a debilitating crisis of identity. He held out hope, however, that a "new breed" of culturally engaged, theologically articulate clergy could reverse the situation. Within a few years his optimism had vanished. The emergence of the counterculture, he argued in

1971, was evidence of "the failure of traditional religious institutions and belief systems to provide meaning in these terribly complicated times." The extinction of established religious institutions is certain; the only question now is "whether they will experience a rapid and violent death or if the process will be a slow, silent demise reflecting the institutions' irrelevance to the human community."

Like other prophets of doom, Hadden eulogized prematurely. A quarter of a century after he ventured these predictions, Christian institutions remain relevant to American society, even as they experience internal transformation, including downsizing. Yet Hadden's basic concern was neither trivial nor misplaced. Moreover, it stands squarely in a rhetorical tradition reflecting a heightened awareness of Christianity's increasing vulnerability to the diverting enticements of a "post-Christian" American culture.

Although a perennial theme of Christian reformers, the discourse of decline has become particularly acute in the current historical period, described as "late modernity" by the British social philosopher Anthony Giddens. Late modernity is characterized by the rapid acceleration of "disembedding" processes generated by the high-tech revolution of the twentieth century, processes that have led late modern institutions to "differ from all perceived forms of social order in respect of their dynamism, the degree to which they undercut traditional habits and customs, and their global impact." Late modernity fosters the notion that social and personal identities are "constructed" by a selective appropriation of elements—teachings, behaviors and other cultural forms—from complex and once coherent social systems. Through mass markets and mass communications technologies in particular, millions of American viewers and listeners are exposed instantaneously to otherwise remote events and practices, alternate cultural forms and a seemingly endless variety of lifestyles and beliefs. These "disembedded" bits, relocated across time and space, are recontextualized by the media and recombined with heterogeneous elements to form the raw material for new configurations of "modernity" and "tradition."

Late moderns tend to hold external authority in contempt; they replace traditional sources of wisdom with "systems of accumulated expertise which form important disembedding influences, represent

R. Scott Appleby

multiple sources of authority, [and are] frequently internally contested and divergent in their implications." The radical individualism of the age, enhanced by the market economy's surpassing skill at creating "need" and forming consumers, erodes one's sense of personal responsibility to a larger community or tradition. "In the settings of late modernity—our present-day world—the self, like the broader institutional context in which it exists, has to be reflexively made," Giddens writes. "Yet this task has to be accomplished amid a puzzling diversity of options and possibilities."

The sociologist and cultural critic Peter Berger was among the first to analyze the impact of this "puzzling diversity of options and possibilities" on American religion. In his book *The Heretical Imperative* (1979), Berger explored the difficulties of sustaining an orthodox religious community whose members are accustomed to living individualized lives in a culture of choice. A series of important and disheartening sociological studies of the religious individualism of the baby-boomer generation followed Berger's trenchant analysis. Born between 1946 and 1964 and numbering approximately 75 million, the boomers transformed the most intimate realms of life, extending to gender roles, personal lifestyle and family structures, "the very same operative principles that have long characterized the public spheres." As the upwardly mobile boomers came of age, the 1970s saw the rise of *The Culture of Narcissism* and the "me generation"; the 1980s were "the decade of greed," punctuated by the mid-decade warning of Robert Bellah and his associates that unbridled individualism was eroding the communitarian *Habits of the Heart*—the capacity for making and honoring commitments to causes larger than one's own interests. In 1996 Bellah reported that he had actually *under*estimated the pervasiveness of individualism and its corrosive effects on American institutions.

A generation ago, Christians were able to take for granted a degree of moral and religious symmetry among home, school and church: Messages conveyed and values taught in one setting were reinforced, or at least not consistently undermined, in the other two. Pluralism did not necessarily inspire relativism, diversity did not extend to the core affirmations of right and wrong, individualism had not yet deteriorated into rising divorce rates and falling church membership.

Inevitably, however, secularizing trends took deep root as Americans experienced postwar prosperity and upward social mobility.

Today Americans are deeply committed to the principle of religious choice. Gallup pollsters report that 81% of respondents agree that "one should arrive at his or her religious beliefs independent of a church or synagogue," and 78% agree that "one can be a good Christian or Jew without attending a church or synagogue." Many people have privatized views on religion. In religious as well as moral values and practices, young Catholics are moved less and less by exhortations couched as obligations from the church, more and more by their own consciences.

The personally expressive mode of religion is a contemporary American cultural form. Sheila Larson, a nurse whose interview with Robert Bellah is recorded in *Habits of the Heart* (1985), described her faith ("my own little voice") as "Sheilaism." Writing about analogous changes in the religious patterns of the family, Wade Clark Roof and Lynn Gesch reported that a 1988–89 survey of baby boomers, who made up approximately one-third of the nation's population, found them split evenly between "family attenders" (of church or synagogue services) and "religious individualists." Of the religious individualists, 41% said that children should be allowed to make their own decisions about attending church or synagogue; 73% of the religious individualists and 54% of the family attenders agreed with the statement: "Church is something freely chosen by each person rather than passed on from generation to generation."

By 1995 the link between family and religion was alive and well "only for a specific segment of the population with traditional views about family participation and traditional family structures to match." Several studies showed that traditional family structures, while still in the numerical majority, were increasingly seen as but one viable arrangement among many acceptable options.

Equally troubling, however, are the implications of a new awareness taught in universities and colleges of "the social construction of reality." We are socially configured and predetermined, the new critics say, leading us to a "false consciousness" — our inability to perceive the socially limited structures and assumptions that narrow our horizons and prevent us from breaking free of the moral constraints of church and tradition. In linguistics and cultural anthropology, at the same time, there has developed a radical doubt that symbol-systems refer to objective reality, much less to identifiable structures of meaning or to an objective moral order. Indeed, these concepts are seen as instruments of oppression in various forms. (See, for example, the cultural criticisms of colonialism and post-colonialism.) Here again, the emphasis is on self-construction, on "discourse constituting the self" without reference to a reliable plan or structure. In this view the world is chaotic, as at the subatomic level, but also, somehow, susceptible to human agency.

The social effects of this cultural turn can be called "de-centering." Can religion help but be influenced, even transformed by this awareness? Decentering and multiculturalism and tribalization are not far apart; but on the positive side, they create space for religion apart from its captivity within systems radically compromised by hegemonic cultural or political forces. As a result of these trends, we are experiencing a time not of celebrated establishments but of reformulations and grassroots ferment. We observe declining institutions yet continuing religious vitality, a weak public religious presence yet strong personal spiritual energies, and the dissolution of older culture and support structures yet rediscoveries of mythical unities. The personal, private and autonomous is celebrated at the expense of the communal, the public and the derivative; emphasis is placed on meaning rather than on inherited patterns of belonging; attention is given to the local rather than the cosmopolitan; concern is for the practical and affective life instead of the devotional and intellectual, the feminist as opposed to the male-dominated; and commitment to separate causes rather than to larger, encompassing purposes.

The Situation of American Catholicism

Let us imagine the labors of a historian of the future chronicling the fortunes of the American Catholic community in the 1990s, a full generation after the close of the Second Vatican Council. Her thesis: It was a time of crisis for the church, in the sense of a time of both danger and of opportunity, a potential turning point for the church.

The church had weathered countless crises, but this one had a particular character: It was a protracted, phased crisis, and thus was not always perceived to a crisis to the historical actors.

The shortage of priests and women religious became acute, our historian will conclude, at a time when Catholics needed unified and vigorous pastoral leadership more than ever. Consider the scope of the challenges and opportunities that present themselves in the 1990s. Although 63% of the twenty million Hispanic Catholics in the United States are native-born, neither that majority nor the immigrant populations from Mexico, the Caribbean or Latin America have been fully integrated into the mainstream of American Catholic life. Individual pastoral success stories abound, but the goal of forging a common Hispanic American identity remains largely unfulfilled. The greatest obstacles to unity may exist within the multicultural Hispanic community itself.

The Mexican American population, for example, exhibits a strong popular religiosity but lacks clergy in sufficient numbers. And ministry to second- and third-generation Hispanics requires a specialized approach, in that the younger generations tend to speak English but want to express their faith in Latino cultural forms. Ethnic and racial diversity is nothing new to the Catholic community in the United States, of course, but the legacy of pastoral care is being put to the test not only by Mexicans, Cubans and Puerto Ricans, but by a generation of Filipino, Korean and other Asian immigrants as well.

In the official documents, where the historian looks first, she finds compelling evidence of an impressive network of Catholic agencies and institutions engaged in the service of the common good and the pursuit of social justice. Perusing the index of *Origins*, the weekly publication of representative documents and speeches compiled by the Catholic News Service, our imaginary historian will note the following initiatives taken at the national, diocesan and parish levels in 1995: Providing alternatives to abortion; staffing adoption agencies; conducting adult education courses; affirmative action; development aid to Africa; addressing African American Catholics' pastoral needs; funding programs to prevent alcohol abuse; lobbying for arms control; eliminating asbestos in public housing; addressing Asian American Catholics' pastoral needs; supporting the activities of the Association of Catholic Colleges and Universities (227 strong); challenging atheism in American society; establishing base communities (small faith communities); providing aid to war victims in the Balkans; conducting Catholic research in bioethics; Canadian Catholic Bishops and the referendum on Quebec; publicizing the *Catheticism of the Catholic Church*; battling child abuse; strengthening the relationship between church and labor unions; deepening the structures and expressions of collegiality in the local and diocesan church; opposition to the Contract with America. Catholic Charities' extensive network of 1,400 charitable agencies serving 18 million people; the Catholic Health Association's 600 hospitals and 300 long-term care facilities serving 20 million people; Campaign for Human Development's efforts to organize and empower the poor, with 200 local anti-poverty groups working to improve policies, practices and laws affecting low-income individuals.

While this type of data is impressive, it tells only part of the story, masking concerns about the gradual depletion of the resources and personnel needed to maintain these programs, not to mention their Catholic identity. No doubt our sharp-eyed historian will also note that a relatively small percentage of the Catholic population actually participates in or contributes to the range of services and pastoral initiatives celebrated in the documents of the official church. The data will also demonstrate, in other words, that there are enormous untapped financial and personal resources in the broader Catholic community.

In 1995, as in every other year for more than a decade, giving as a percentage of income to all mainline churches, Protestant as well as Catholic, declined. Yet Catholics fared much worse than all of the Protestant congregations studied, including those supporting private schools. A 1992 study of 330,000 Catholic households from 280 Catholic parishes, for example, found that whereas the average annual family income was $41,000, the average annual contribution to the parish—not including school tuition—was $276.51, less than 1% of income.

By other markers as well, increasing numbers of lay Catholics seem detached from the central beliefs, religious practices and everyday ministries of their church. Less than one-third of the U.S. Catholic population regularly attends weekly Mass. A 1993 Gallup poll found that, of those who do, only 30% believe they are actually receiving the body and blood of Christ in the eucharist; and only 21% under the age of fifty so believe. Meanwhile approximately one-fourth of Catholics agreed that Christ becomes present in the bread and wine only if the recipient believes this to be so.

One need not be a stickler for orthodoxy to find such attitudes toward the doctrine of the real presence of Christ in the eucharist—a, if not *the,* central affirmation of the worshiping Catholic community—to be cause for alarm. Our historian will find additional evidence of a catechetical crisis in postconciliar American Catholicism—evidence that suggests a parallel to the experience of some mainline Protestant Christian denominations whose "lay liberal" members, recent studies show, are somewhat fuzzy on the basic theological ideas and doctrinal convictions that defined their denominational identity until very recently.

In short, one can wonder if younger generations of Catholics are even absorbing the stories and wrestling with the symbols and Catholic narratives they have inherited. The comments of Sister Janet Baxindale, who lectures around the country on the spiritual potential of Catholic traditions like the Liturgy of the Hours, reflects the experience of most Catholic educators today: "Among the adults I teach, more often than not, a simple presentation of the theology of the liturgy and the role of all the baptized in the liturgical prayer of the church is greeted with 'I never knew that.'"

What shall we conclude, then, about American Catholicism in the 1990s?

On one hand, a broad range of ministries and social action programs involve informed, dedicated and faithful Catholics in almost every aspect of local, regional and national society. The impressive public witness of American Catholicism, disputes notwithstanding, reflects a clearly defined set of principles by which to pursue the common good. These principles, set forth in an accessible style by a striking series of postconciliar pastoral letters, have been critically received and generally acclaimed not only by the vigorous and able company of Catholic intellectuals working in universities and the media, but also by influential segments of the non-Catholic elite in the United States.

R. Scott Appleby

In its pastoral life the U.S. church, by and large, embodies compassion, sustains a gentle sense of irony and offers a remarkable witness to the possibilities of holiness in everyday life. Priests, sisters and lay ministers continue to baptize, confirm, educate and be educated by a bewildering variety of American Catholics drawn from dozens of racial and ethnic backgrounds. Most remarkable, perhaps, they balance loyalty to a universal church and its pontiff, who is not daily ministering to the North American cultural environment, with the demands of a lay population often unrealistic in its expectations of the clergy, or merely indifferent, distracted by a culture of self-absorption.

On the other hand, one finds a thin layer of dedicated professionals at the pinnacle of the Catholic organizational pyramid, a sizeable gap between the professional elites and the people in the pews and thus an increasingly unstable base of operations. The church is relatively ineffective in mobilizing resources not only politically and socially, but pastorally and ecclesially.

Despite the efforts of individual bishops, the church may also be criticized for ultimately turning a deaf ear to the expressions of pain and frustration voiced by faithful women, many of whom have no desire to be ordained, working as diocesan social action directors, parish-based directors of religious education, parish administrators, and in a host of other critical capacities. Many of these women suffer isolation by virtue of their status, or lack thereof, within the institutional church. In most dioceses parish administrators, for example, are not regularly included in presbyteral conferences and pastoral planning meetings.

Is the poor record of resource mobilization attributable to a lack of generosity on the part of the great mass of baptized Catholics? Given the historical record, this seems a difficult case to make. Have catechetical programs in the postconciliar era failed to inculcate a sense of institutional loyalty? Do lay Catholics demand greater participation in the financial decisions of the local church? Do policies on ordination lend credibility to feminists' charges of inherent sexism in the church? Do pastoral leaders possess the self-confidence necessary to welcome a diversity of gifts from the laity — including intellectual leadership at the parish and diocesan levels? Do significant morale problems exist among segments of the presbyterate who feel closed off from the decision-making process?

The liturgy, as always, is the contested site of Catholic identity. In some circles there is an attempt to retreat to an era that has passed. Bishop Donald Trautman, chairman of the U.S. Bishops' Committee on Liturgy, has said that "those who seek a return to liturgical life as it was prior to Vatican II offend the teaching of that very council, which calls us to a full, conscious and active participation." Trautman encourages liturgists "to avoid one-sided simplistic approaches such as traditionalism with its emphasis on the Latin Mass, clericalism with its non-collaborative ministry, congregationalism with its forced isolations from the broader church, radical feminism with its blurring of distinctions for sacramental ministry, biblicism and the like."

How, then, can we summarize the challenges before us? As today's Catholic lay and clerical revolutionaries, we are faced with the goal of widening significant personal involvement of the laity in the church and its impressive range of social services, liturgical celebrations and community building. This requires Catholic leaders honestly to confront the alienation of the laity from the ongoing life of the church—precisely the opposite effect intended by Vatican II—and develop new strategies of engaging them in the life of the believing community.

As membership in religious orders declines, for example, many orders are developing profound collaboration between laypeople imbued with the order's charism. They will continue together making a gift of that charism to the world. Laypeople must come to realize that the charisms of religious orders are susceptible to lay appropriation and leadership.

The church has found itself in similar situations in the past. Colonial-era Catholicism on the East Coast adjusted to a potentially hostile cultural environment and overcame centrifugal tendencies by relocating the sacred from church building and public square to home, extended family and a domesticized piety. Priestless parishes thrived in republican-era Maryland, Pennsylvania and New York when independent laymen of means stepped forward with the resources and talent needed to sustain Catholic identity during a time of organizational immaturity. And the late twentieth century is hardly the first time that ethnic diversity, competing claims to Catholic ortho-doxy and overwhelming numbers threatened to eclipse the best pas-toral efforts of the relatively few professional Catholics.

Today's challenges call for different specific adjustments, of course, but the basic solution remains the same: Catholics, in the words of Sister Mary Collins, OSB, "must be able to name where and how the mystery is at work among us." Naming the mystery, in turn, entails the work of identifying and empowering the people and ideas capable of generating creative Christian responses to the perennial problem of human suffering. If Catholics are thus to rediscover the source of their strength in God's hidden presence, two concrete reforms must be enacted by the always reforming church.

Bernard Lee proposes "dialogic community" as a model for ecclesiological reflection on a suddenly evolving praxis of lay women and men, learned in the tradition, effectively leading and ministering in Catholic community. To tell the Catholic story in a new way will mean that lay Catholics will be called upon to interpret the commu-nity's ritual life, ways of holiness, personal relationships, gifts of sex-ual love and children and effective public witness to God's mercy and justice through reform of U.S. social systems; it will also mean that lay Catholics enter more fully into an animated, mutually respectful and critical dialogue between faith and culture.

In this vision the ordained priest pastor may serve in a role sim-ilar to that recently filled by the bishop: supervising the creative and faithful apostolic ministries, representing by his ordination the link between the local and universal church stretching across time and space, standing as a symbol of divinely graced unity amid Catholic diversity. You see, I am not suggesting that our priests have no role in the new revolution: I have just promoted them, in fact! But they will also continue to join in partnership with a new generation of women and men in faith who continue the traditional work of retrieving from the inheritance of Christ empowering and liberating treasures, ever ancient, ever new.

Edward Foley, OFM CAP

Liturgical Factions and Violent Reactions: Evolution or Revolution?

O ver the past three decades our common worship has changed, and changed radically. Lest we forget just how extreme that change has been, I offer you this brief litany of remembrance.

First, the conspicuous: The language of our rites has changed — from Latin to the vernacular; from Ciceronian construction to American cadence; from court rhetoric to familial images.

Changed too are the settings of our rites: from proscenium-style churches to movement in the round, from imposing reredos and tabernacles imbedded in altars to freestanding tables, chapels of reservation and an environment that gives higher priority to our faces than the backs of peoples' heads.

Of course, the music has changed also, from polyphony to folk rock, from sacred chants to ritual song, from organ to synthesizer, and from choir-centered Masses to eucharist in which the assembly is respected as the primary musician.

Finally the rites themselves have changed, from convert classes and private baptism to the Rite of Christian Initiation of Adults, from extreme unction to the sacrament of the sick and from the Requiem Mass to the Order of Christian Funerals.

Edward Foley, OFM Cap

In the liturgical arena we have experienced such a fundamental alteration in so many names, terms and definitions one almost needs an ecclesiastical equivalent to Webster's unabridged dictionary just to figure out who is where and what's being done to what in today's worship. The associate used to say Mass, but now this redefined parochial vicar and member of the parish ministry staff presides at the eucharist at which the assembly is the principal celebrant. The laity used to go to confession, but now this recently re-envisioned people of God experience reconciliation in a variety of sacramental modes — some of which require presbyteral presidency, and some which do not.

And then there is the pastor: He used to run the parish, but now he, if it is a he, is the primary facilitator for ministries and coordinator of charisms — liturgical and otherwise — in the local faith community.

These linguistic and ecclesiastical developments are so pervasive that it is sometimes difficult to know just how to address each other in the post-conciliar church. Priests are no longer priests: They are members of the order of the presbyterate — or presbyters, for short. Converts have become inquirers, catechumens, elect or neophytes depending on their progress in the journey toward full initiation. The organist and choir director are no longer simply amateur volunteers but unionized pastoral musicians. And in some places even the housekeeper has become a parochial consultant for hospitality.

These changes are not simply surface-level alterations — not merely a fresh veneer of *cognomina* or a rearrangement of the liturgical furniture — but they are symbolic of fundamental theological and ecclesiological shifts that have emerged — or, sometimes, exploded — within the Roman Catholic church during the past half-century.

A few brief examples will have to suffice to make this point. The 1969 Order of Mass is not simply a refinement or adaptation of the 1570 Tridentine rite. Rather, the 1969 ritual embodies a very different theology reflected in sometimes subtle but nonetheless important liturgical revisions.

In the Tridentine rite, for example, an "offertory" preceded the canon of the Mass, and in that "offertory," the priest alone offered the "spotless host" and the "chalice of salvation." In the 1969 rite, however, there is no offering during the preparation of the gifts, but only a communal blessing prayer, a *berakah,* that anticipates the offering that will occur later during the eucharistic prayer. This is not simply a surface modification. Rather, this is a significant textual and structural change that shifts the action of offering from priest to people and balances sacrificial and intercessory elements with the action of blessing.

The Judeo-Christian instinct to begin all prayer with blessing and thanksgiving—an instinct reflected in the experience of Jesus—is foundational for a much more subtle change in the eucharistic prayers of Pope Paul VI, a change which yet eludes presiders. In the Tridentine rite, the words and gestures of the consecration made it clear that the priest blessed the bread. The text read: "The day before he suffered, he [Jesus] took bread into his holy and venerable hands, and with his eyes lifted up to heaven, to you God, his almighty Father, giving thanks to you, he blessed + it, broke it and gave it to his disciples saying, 'Take and eat all of this, for this is my body.'"

In the 1969 rite, however, the bread is not blessed—similar to what we find in the New Testament, which clearly indicates that Jesus never blessed bread, an act that would have been inconceivable for a Jew. Rather, Jesus, like other Jews of the time, spoke a blessing to God over bread—thus making God, not the bread, the recipient of the blessing.

Consequently, the institution narrative of the current rite reads, "On the night he was betrayed, he [Jesus] took bread and gave you thanks and praise. He broke the bread, gave it to his disciples and said, 'Take this, all of you, and eat it. This is my body which will be given up for you.'" In the text of the current rite, therefore, the bread is not blessed; rather thanks and praise are rendered to God over bread.

But is this a significant change? Is it not simply another surface modification, like the removal of the offertory from the preparation of the gifts? My response is, again, an unequivocal no. Rather, this change in the institution narrative is a significant textual nuance that restrains the Tridentine instinct to focus on objects rather than people. The change recalls that the Christian model of prayer, founded on the Jesus experience, gives pride of place to blessing and thanksgiving, not intercession.

Edward Foley, OFM CAP

Things have changed, and changed profoundly. The current rites of the Roman Catholic church are not simply new translations or slight modifications of the Tridentine rite. Rather, they are authentic developments that offer us very different images of God, Christ, the Spirit, the church and our own salvation. Thus, the reintroduction and integration of a catechumenal process into the church's initiatory procedures was not, to my way of thinking, simply a gesture toward twentieth-century sensibilities or a recruitment ploy for an embattled religion. Rather, the reintroduction of the catechumenate is an affront to sacramental theologies that value abstraction over relationship and instantaneous ontological change over a process of conversion and a journey in faith.

The offering during the eucharistic liturgy was transposed from an intercession-laden offertory — with its expansive sacrificial gestures, declarations of sinfulness and prayer that we be spared from eternal damnation — to a place just after the institution narrative and therefore inextricably linked to anamnesis:

> . . . calling to mind the death your Son endured for our
> salvation, his glorious resurrection and ascension into heaven,
> and ready to greet him when he comes again, we offer you in
> thanksgiving this holy and living sacrifice.

This euchological transposition and reconstructive surgery was not essentially a gesture toward literary finesse nor a blow for new structural niceties. It served, rather, as an ineludible challenge to a prayer style that often appeared more concerned with divine manipulation than with praise and thanksgiving.

These were, and still are, incredible changes, radical shifts, phenomenal developments. But if you think that these changes, shifts and developments have all been moving in the same direction the past three decades, then you have not recently been talking with many of the young men who populate our diocesan seminaries, you have not been reading the Snowbird statement on church music, nor have you been watching the Eternal Word Television Network. These sources indicate that radical change is yet afoot, liturgical, ecclesiological and theological changes as well. But these changes are moving in a very different direction.

Liturgically, for example, we have not only viewed the virtual elimination of communion in the hand and the withdrawal of the cup from the laity during certain regularly televised Masses, but also the fabrication and interpolation of elaborate gestures of adoration by communicants before communion, which in some places are being transposed, thanks to the omnipresence of television, from sanctuaries in Alabama to the local parish.

On another liturgical front, benediction and holy hours are on the rise. But the televised models of this come-back devotion are not the parochial rituals that some might remember from their childhood—with parish priest, pre-adolescent servers and hordes of engaged believers belting out "Holy God, We Praise Thy Name" and "Tantum Ergo." No, the epitome of benediction as symbolized in the unrelenting rebroadcast of one such service situates benediction in a long monastic choir, presided over by a relatively stern-looking mendicant, with the preamble of a long camera shot of the procession of the ministry into the choir, all the while accompanied not by "Tantum Ergo" or "Holy God" but a recording of selections from Mozart's *Requiem*. It is an unusual twist on this once-standard devotion.

Not only are such high-church variations of benediction on the rise, but a growing penchant for perpetual adoration as well. The sanctuary design for Mother Angelica's community epitomizes this trend. There, over the choir screen separating the community of sisters from the assembly, a free-standing monstrance graced by two adoring golden angels towers over the ritual. Contrary to the current law of the church, the exposed host is not removed from the monstrance during the eucharistic celebrations in the place, but simply covered. The impact of this televised symbol is clear, for in increasing numbers ordinary parish communities are now requesting permission for perpetual adoration in their churches.

The introduction of elaborate rituals of adoration before communion, the regal celebrations of benediction and the new esteem for perpetual adoration are not, however, simply surface-level alterations in the liturgical landscape, nor are they minor variations in some shared ritual imagination. Rather, these are symbolic of fundamental theological and ecclesiological perspectives that are direct challenges,

Edward Foley, OFM Cap

if not to the spirit of the Second Vatican Council, then at least to the spirit of the official liturgical reform that flowed from that council.

Some argue that the renewed liturgy in the vernacular and the subsequent permission to receive communion in the hand and to drink from the cup bring God too close. The reintroduction of Latin, the return to communion on the tongue, the withdrawal of the cup from the laity and the introduction of elaborate gestures of adoration before communion re-emphasize the transcendence of God. Yet they point to a divinity who is more powerful than familial, more righteous than forgiving and less the fount of mystical delight than the seat of judgment, commanding respect and not just a little fear. The resurgent interest in benediction and the new developments around perpetual adoration are clear challenges to developments in sacramental theology that explain the various modes of the real presence of Christ more in symbol-sacramental terms, rather than in metaphysical, substantial and corporeal ones. And the real clericalization in these liturgical counterdevelopments is unquestionably a theological reassertion of the primacy of a male hierarchical priesthood in the Roman Catholic church and a reassertion of the perceived male and hierarchical character of the God of Jesus Christ.

Things have changed and changed radically over the past three decades, but not all in the same direction. The almost bi-polar developments in liturgy, ecclesiology and theology remind me of the supposedly true story of the captain of a frigate who was standing on the bridge, watching the ship steam through the dark night. Suddenly the first officer yelled out, "Captain, a light off the starboard bow." The captain answered, "Is it turning or steady on its course?" The junior officer yelled, "Steady on its course." The captain had the communications officer signal, "Turn 20 degrees to port." A message came back, "You turn 20 degrees to port." The captain sent another message: "I am a captain in the United States Navy and I order you to turn 20 degrees to port." Another message came back, "I am a seaman 1st class and I respectfully instruct you to turn 20 degrees to port." Finally, his temperature rising, the captain had the communications officer relay, "This is a United States naval frigate! You turn 20 degrees to port and do so smartly." The reply came back, "This is a lighthouse. You turn 20 degrees to port and do so smartly."

In the current debate—mixed, as it is, of parts liturgical, ecclesiological, theological—within the Roman Catholic church in English-speaking North America, we might be moved analogously to ask, "Who is the lighthouse, and who is the frigate?" Are the vernacular reforms, ICEL, the Bishops' Committee on the Liturgy and those who are demanding inclusive language in our worship the lighthouse? Or are the Latin counter-reforms, the EWTN network, Ignatius Press and Mother Angelica the lighthouse? Are those who advocate highly participatory worship, an equal role for women and men in liturgical leadership, a richness of cultural expression in our public prayer and contemporary sounds in our ritual music the frigate? Or are those who favor a quiet devotionalism at public worship, the unchallenged primacy of male liturgical leadership, the ritual and cultural normativity of the Roman liturgy and the unchallenged priority of a forever closed treasury of sacred music the frigate?

Any attempt to answer questions of lighthouses and frigates, of course, could devolve into an exercise in announcing who is right and who is wrong in the current debate, who is the beacon of light and who must yield right of way. Perhaps, therefore, the quest to discern lighthouses from frigates is the wrong move here, the inappropriate question and ultimately an act of theological self-indulgence.

Maybe more to the point is theological reflection on the question of whether the God of Jesus Christ, who is the source and summit of all worship, is more appropriately conceived of as lighthouse or frigate. Is the God of Jesus Christ a beacon of constancy and unwavering light, stolid as a lighthouse, the coastal unmoved mover? Or is the source and summit of our worship more like a ship at sea, heading out into deep water and threatening to leave behind those who steadfastly cling to the security of a safe and certain harbor?

This presentation is about evolution and revolution, and it asks whether the tension and acrimony that mark the current debate are a natural evolution for the postconciliar church or signs of a real revolution within the church. But turning to that question prematurely could also be problematic or at least unproductive, for it could lead us to wonder which "party" in the postconciliar church is the party of evolution and which is the party of revolution, which is the movement which naturally flows out of the spirit and documents of the

Second Vatican Council, and which is the movement that revolts against the spirit and direction of the Council. Is it sharper first to consider whether the God of Jesus Christ, in whose name all things conciliar are done, is a God of evolution or of revolution? Is the God of Jesus Christ an evolutionary deity who follows the rules of genetics, charts out divine revelation in line with the principles of natural selection and raises up prophets according to explanations of the inheritance of variability in individuals of the same species? Or is the God of Jesus Christ a divine revolutionary who will not be controlled, predicted or contained by the rules of the very creatures that the Divinity called into being?

In more biblical language, to consider whether the God of Jesus Christ is frigate or lighthouse, a God of evolution or a God of revolution, is to discern whether the Holy One is a God of myth or a God of parable, a God of mediation or a God who shatters the reconciliation and sure path we creatures so easily construct? Maybe if we ponder the God of Jesus Christ, the God Jesus illumines in the gospels, the God lurking before, beside and behind the liturgies we so vociferously promulgate, postulate and defend, then maybe we might take a step toward wisdom and discover not who is right or who is wrong in the current liturgical upheaval, not decide whether to subscribe to *Adoremus* or the *WE BELIEVE!* newsletter but, instead, we might discover where the God of Jesus Christ is being revealed and, in that revelation, we may hear anew where the Holy One is beckoning us.

A Consideration of Myth and Parable[1]

In his early study of parables, *The Dark Interval,* John Dominic Crossan suggested that of all the language forms that human beings employ for storytelling, the limits of a story's possibilities are best defined through the categories of myth and parable.[2] Myth for Crossan does not mean a pleasant story that is untrue, or what he calls sophisticated lying. Nor is it some type of legend populated with gods and goddesses. Rather, in the technical sense in which he employs it, myth is mostly about mediation and reconciliation.

Crossan draws upon the work of the French philosopher Claude Lévi-Strauss and accepts his basic thesis that "myth performs the specific task of mediating irreducible opposites" (Crossan, 51). Myth in this sense bridges the gap between apparently irreconcilable stances, individuals or situations, and demonstrates that mediation is possible.

Consider, for example, the classic fairy tale "Beauty and the Beast," resurrected over the years as a television series, a full-length animated film and a piece of musical theater. In its simplest form, the story is about Beauty, the youngest and most beautiful daughter of a once wealthy merchant. She is dedicated to her father, even though he has lost his fortune and has been abandoned by his other children. When the father becomes lost in a forest and accidentally wanders into the den of a fearsome Beast, he becomes the Beast's captive. Eventually the father is ransomed by his daughter Beauty who exchanges places with him. Ultimately the Beast falls in love with Beauty. When the Beast finally wins her over and she consents to marry him, he is released from the spell that had possessed him, and revealed to be a handsome and wealthy prince.

This fairy tale is a myth in the technical sense that Crossan employs. It is a tale of many opposites: beauty/beast, poor/rich, commoner/royalty, woman/man, captive/free and so forth. In the conclusion of the story, however, all of these apparently opposing forces are reconciled. In the process, this and other true myths reveal their core meaning: that mediation is possible. Crossan concludes, "What myth does is not just to attempt the mediation in story of what is sensed as irreconcilable, but in, by, and through this attempt it establishes the possibility of reconciliation" (53). Thus myth's double function is both the resolution of a particular contradiction or set of contradictions and, more importantly, the creation of a belief in the permanent possibility of reconciliation.

Parable, on the other hand, is not about mediation, but about contradiction. In Crossan's language, parable "does not create reconciliation for irreconcilables, but . . . creates irreconciliation where before there was reconciliation" (55). An example of such a parable is a story I recently heard concerning a woman psychologist who was asked to visit one of the many refugee camps of Rwandans in Tanzania in the aftermath of the massacres that took place in Rwanda in the early 1990s. It seems that the women of this particular camp, though safe from the slaughter, were not sleeping. During her visit to the refugees, the psychologist learned that the women, who had witnessed the murders of family and friends, had been told not to speak of such atrocities in the camp. The women followed this instruction, but the memories of the carnage haunted them, and they could not sleep.

The psychologist decided that in response to this situation she would set up a story tree: a safe place for the women to speak of their experiences. Every morning she went out to the edge of the camp and waited under the canopy of a huge shade tree. The first day no one came. On the second day one woman appeared, told her story and left. Another showed up the following day, then another and another. Within the span of a few days, hundreds of women were gathering under the tree each morning to listen and to share their tales of loss, fear and death. Finally, after weeks of listening, the psychologist knew that the story tree was working. Reports confirmed that the women in the camp were now sleeping. The only difficulty was that the psychologist wasn't.

Parable creates irreconciliation where before there was reconciliation, here poignantly reflected in a true story of the healing of shattered lives and the shattering of at least one life or life-perspective through such healing. Yes, it is true that in the narrative process around the story tree, the healing of memories began, some equilibrium was reclaimed and restorative sleep was reintroduced into the lives of many refugee women. This narrative is no myth in the Crossan sense, however, for it does not announce that everyone and all things have been made right, that the massacre has been wiped from human memory, that its perpetrators have repented and been absolved and that the specter of this nightmare will never rise again. To the contrary, the sleeplessness of the psychologist announces that reconciliation is not attained, that mediation is not achieved and that the shade of genocide looms large—not only in her imagination, but now in the minds and hearts of all who hear her story. Before she arrived at the camp, there was some modicum of peace in her life and in her world. She could sleep. Her encounter with the women refugees, however, shattered her well-ordered universe, and pulled the rug out from under her own secure place in that universe. As we leave her, sitting alone underneath the story tree, stunned and fresh in her vulnerability, it is unclear how well she will respond to this new image of the human condition. What is clear, however, is that no matter how she proceeds, her story-frame is forever altered. The story tree worked, but not in the way the psychologist planned.

Mythic narrations comfort and assure us that everything is going to be all right; parables challenge and dispute the reconciliation that our myths have created. Myths allow us to dream and to believe in a future better than the present; parables disallow us from living in a dream world, call us to confront the present and deter us from trusting in any hope that does not face the hard reality of the present. The irony, of course, is that myth and parable are complementary narrative forms and human beings need both of them. We need a tale that stretches us across the bipolar opposition of myth and parable, so that we might live in the precarious yet salvific tension of the in-between.

If our story-telling and story-living are out of touch with the parabolic, for example, there is the real danger that we will be trapped by a dishonest dream. Yet life devoid of mythic narration is a life devoid of the possibility of reconciliation and ultimate peace. It is true that parables challenge the myths and the reconciliations we have created. Yet, in doing so, parables always give rise to a new reconciliation, and therefore to a new myth. Thus parables are not about eliminating reconciliation; rather, they are about challenging the reconciliation with which we are comfortably living. The elimination of all myth, therefore, is not the goal of the parable; for without myth, without the ultimate possibility of harmonizing all of those discordant strands in our lives, we are left awash in meaninglessness or on the brink of despair.

While both mythic and parabolic narrations, therefore, are important for healthy story-tellers and ritual-makers, it is the parabolic which is more difficult to master. Human beings are much more inclined to revel in the world of the mythic than drink in the parabolic. There are obvious reasons for this. The underlying message of mythic narration is that things are going to be all right. Or, in terms of our previously recited fairy tale, "If things could work out for Beauty — who was separated from her poor and ailing father, and was the captive of a Beast—then they certainly could work out for me." Myth engages the natural optimism of the human spirit, and the physiological instinct of the human organism. Our bodies struggle to live, and, with every ounce of strength, reject the ultimate parable of our own death. Thus, as a norm, it does not appear that many—especially in our own culture—suffer from the threat of parabolic overdose.

Myth and Parable, Lighthouse and Frigate, Evolution and Revolution

I have embarked upon this excursus into parables and myths because I believe that these bi-polar categories can aid us significantly in understanding something of the current liturgical and ecclesiological upheaval in the Roman Catholic church. Religions, like the human spirits that shape them, have a penchant for the mythic in Crossan's sense; that is, religions often display an overriding concern with mediation and reconciliation. While Karl Marx's comment that religion is the opium of the people is so overstated as to be erroneous, there is a kernel of truth in his aphorism, which admits that inherent in most religions is the instinct to mollify, calm and assure people that everything is going to be all right. In the process, of course, religions can also sedate believers.

While myths have a certain capacity for tolerating, explaining and even embracing change, their real strength is contributing toward stability, constancy, reconciliation and peace. Myth serves more the evolutionary than the revolutionary instincts of religion. It has a capacity to admit incremental modification; but such modification always needs to be folded into and validated by some overriding mythic structure. When the change appears too radical, the challenge too threatening to the fabric of the central myth, the evolution so rapid that it cannot adequately be assimilated into the myth, then such change is rejected, posited outside the mythic structure and in some situations even demonized.

I contend therefore that, within this frame, the assertion of the religious right in general and its insistent reassertion in the post-conciliar Roman Catholic church in English-speaking North America in particular is a move toward the mythic. It is an announcement on the part of some that the capacity for change and assimilation has—at least for the time being—been met, that the evolution has become revolution and that new directions, ideas or beliefs can no longer be accepted without shattering the myth. Thus there is a return to what we might call lighthouse thinking and lighthouse rhetoric.

Phrases like "pillars of the faith," "infallibility," "discussion of the topic closed" and even "excommunication" suggest a mythic retreat into the lighthouse, accompanied by strong, intimidating, even threatening broadcasts announcing that everyone else should turn 20 degrees to port, and do so smartly. Magisterium, tradition and infallibility are all invoked to shore up, protect and defend the underlying religious myth about God, church and salvation. And these authoritative sources in turn declare the mythic foundations of the faith not only to be well, but are so through divine intent.

If the religious right in the current moment in our ecclesial history can be identified with the assertion of the mythic, then what is "left" is appropriately aligned with the announcement of the parabolic. In other words, if the mythic can be considered to be that which serves the more evolutionary side of religion, then the parable fuels religion's revolutionary instincts.

Consider the key ritual issues, for example, championed by one organization that advocates the so-called liberal agenda, *WE BELIEVE!* From my perspective as president of that organization's board, I would include among our main issues concerns about inclusive language, the appropriate adaptation of worship forms to varying peoples and cultures, the centrality of the symbolic in ritual forms and language and advances in liturgical leadership that would acknowledge and respect the gifts of all the baptized.

Each of these could be perceived as a challenge to the mythic reconciliation which the Roman Catholic church has constructed in its worship and theology, and to this point has been considered adequate for mediating the natural tensions between insiders/outsiders, universal/local, literal/symbolic and women/men. To advocate inclusive language, for example, questions not only the way we have subsumed all feminine categories into the masculine, but it resists a

dominant strand in our collective religious imagination that postu-
lates one gender as constitutive of all three persons in the Trinity. To
champion continued and more dramatic cultural adaptation of the
liturgy is to question the mythic presumption that the language, rituals and cultural symbols of an imperial, medieval, European-based
liturgy can be effectively translated for and celebrated by all peoples
of every ethnic and cultural stripe around the world. To advocate in
speech and action the symbolic rather than the literal, the metaphoric
rather than the didactic, the poetic rather than the pedestrian is to
question any mythic mediation that intimates that God, salvation or
even church can be reduced to formulaic explanations or foolproof
recipes. And, maybe most frightening of all, to even consider the possibility of women and men sharing equally in the leadership of worship and the leadership of the church, not as competitors for power
but collaborators in Christ, is to take exception to the cultural, now
become ecclesial, myth that all men are equal but women are not; or
that men are created in the image of God but women are created in
the image of men. Or, maybe even more frightening is the possibility
that advocating a balance of feminine and masculine in our worship
is a challenge to our mythic perception of the God who is the source
and summit of that worship.

Eric is deaf. Sunday school was a particularly difficult experience for him, because his Sunday school teachers could not sign.
Thus, while he could read their lips and understand what they were
communicating to him, the only way that he could communicate
back was through writing. One Sunday morning, his Sunday school
teacher said to him, "Eric, isn't it wonderful that when you go to
heaven, you will be able to hear?" "No," he wrote back, "I am deaf.
When I go to heaven, God will be able to sign."[3]

Dominic Crossan suggests that parables are not about mediation, but about contradiction. In his language, parable "does not create reconciliation for irreconcilables, but . . . creates irreconciliation
where before there was reconciliation" (55). Challenging what for
many are comforting images of God, acceptable definitions of church
and hopeful formulae for salvation is a dangerous and unsettling task.
Some call it prophetic; others oppose it as demonic. This is, I believe,
the crucible in which we now find ourselves.

Jesus the Christ: Myth or Parable?

Having charted the current liturgical-ecclesiological seas as counter-vailing tides of myth and parable, evolution and revolution—or, in our earlier analogy, as an encounter between frigates and lighthouses—it remains to be discovered whether there is any way to steer an accept-able passage between these two admittedly caricatured extremes. Or are we left to communication misfires and liturgical-theological broadsides at each other? In an effort to steer such a course it could be useful to consider, for a moment, the central incarnation of our faith in Jesus the Christ, and there discover to what extent these mythic and parabolic assertions find a foundation in the central reve-lation of our faith.

It needs to be acknowledged, on the one hand, that Jesus Christ is the ultimate articulation of the mythic: the incarnation of mediation and reconciliation. In Jesus the Christ humanity and divinity are rec-onciled. He is the pre-existent logos who lives forever, and yet he lived and died in a particular moment in human history. He was himself without sin, yet proclaimed a kingdom that not only tolerated but welcomed sinners. He healed the sick, comforted the broken-hearted, proclaimed the poor to be rich and taught the rich to be poor. And in the ultimate paschal mediation he obliterated the power of death by dying and resurrected life through his rising. Anyone who finds it dif-ficult to assert the mythic core of Jesus the Christ has neither broken open the gospels nor broken a loaf of bread in his name. For both ren-der him present in all the power of his mediation and reconciliation.

And yet, this divine mediation we name Jesus the Christ achieves all mythic reconciliation in parabolic mode. Yes, Jesus proclaims, eter-nal life is possible, forgiveness of sins is possible, peace with enemies is possible, union with God is possible, but none of it through magic, easy rituals or special knowledge. Rather, each of these is achieved by abandoning the comfortable reconciliation we have constructed for ourselves. Eternal life is achieved only through dying; forgiveness of sins is conceivable only by embracing our own sinfulness; peace with enemies is accessible, but only by embracing those we would rather hate; and union with God is possible as well, but only if we allow God to be God, calling us to a kind of union we never expected, with a deity we never imagined.

Edward Foley, OFM CAP

To my way of thinking, and even to my way of believing, Jesus points to a God who is more revolutionary than evolutionary, a God who is truly other, who does not fit our categories, who is not simply a more evolved human being, but is the Holy One of unfathomable difference, who is accessible to us not because of some genetic likeness or neurological compatibility, but because of an inexplicable and unrelenting love that stalks us in Jesus Christ. The God of Jesus Christ is not, therefore, appropriately imagined as a placid, smiling grandfather cushioned on a bejeweled throne surrounded by perfectly coiffed cumulus clouds, but more like Jack Shea's image of a wide-eyed divine insomniac, pacing the corridors of heaven, scheming and plotting to get us back.

While our preference or the preference of those to whom we minister might be the domestication of God, the embrace of the mythic and the assertion of divine reconciliation at any cost, such an instinct must be at least balanced if not challenged by the assertion of the parabolic. This must be especially true in our worship. True, most Roman Catholics do not want worship to be a disturbing event. Rather, it is to be a tranquil, contained, graceful, controlled event. Worship from this perspective is often imagined as a pleasant, almost cultural experience, in which dappled sunlight plays on stained-glass windows in a high-ceilinged building with a Gothic spire, where a smiling, grandfatherly figure leads a well-mannered congregation in mellifluous tones through agreeable prayers and congenial hymns. It is a very pleasant image of worship. Unfortunately it has little to do with authentic Christian worship.

Christian worship is a disturbing event: God is present among us; God calls us to recognize sin, to embrace our enemies, to transform our lives and to announce the kingdom in the world. It is a dangerous, precarious, explosive undertaking. Thus it must be approached with care—yes, with attention to form, structure and even rubrics. But with the parabolic awareness that God is not contained by rubrics, that the sacramental action of Jesus Christ in the Holy Spirit is not in a book, but in people's faces. When the fundamental assessment of our worship devolves into counting genuflections, checking pronouns and scrutinizing one's conformity to printed rubrics, then know yourself to be in the land of the mythic, where God's good action has given way to canonical query and rubrical scrutinization.

Conclusion

Karl Rahner is purported to have once commented that all people living at the same time are not necessarily contemporaries. Few situations in the Roman Catholic church this day demonstrate that more than the polarities that have developed around our common worship. Each side protests the other's authority, asserts their own basis in tradition and argues that their vision is the true vision for the church of the 21st century. Increasingly, however, I am convinced that these various polarities are not necessarily mortal enemies. Nor must one necessarily be right while the other is proven totally wrong. Rather, I believe their existence appropriately reflects the human tension of experiencing the God of Jesus Christ, a God of myth and parable, who promises ultimate reconciliation and mediation of all apparent contradictions in our lives and in our world, but does so if only we will give up the reconciliations and mediations we have ourselves constructed. Thus I believe the so-called progressive and so-called conservative agenda around public worship can together serve the proclamation of the gospel and the building of the kingdom.

In order for that to happen, however, there is need for charity at every turn. There is need for justice for the outsider as well as the insider. There is need to respect the struggle for faith, wherever it occurs. And, maybe most important of all, there is need for humility and the recognition that God's ways are not our ways, are not my ways.

Quite frankly, I wouldn't mind being a lighthouse or a frigate, but in struggling for a new mediation, a new myth through the parabolic, I feel more like a rowboat. In her poem, "An awful rowing toward God," Anne Sexton so imagines her journey toward God when she writes,

> God was there like an island I had not rowed to. . . .
> I am rowing, I am rowing
> though the oarlocks stick and are rusty

Edward Foley, OFM CAP

and the sea blinks and rolls
like a worried eyeball,
but I am rowing, I am rowing
though the wind pushes me back
and I know that the island will not be perfect
It will have the flaws of life
the absurdities of the dinner table
but there will be a door
and I will open it
and I will get rid of the rat inside of me
the gnawing pestilential rat
God will take it with two hands
and embrace it.[4]

Like the poem, this moment ends with us still rowing toward God. Yes, we long for the harbor that once seemed very near. But those heady days of high-flying liturgical reform were no harbor; they were a mythic haven we created while still at sea. So now the parable has returned, as has frustration, disappointment, disillusionment. But I urge you to stay the course, to keep on rowing, that awful rowing toward God, in the sure hope that Jesus Christ, who could calm every sea, will surely be our haven.

1. Much of what follows is reliant upon material from my *Mighty Story—Dangerous Ritual,* coauthored with Herbert Anderson (San Francisco: Jossey Bass, 1997).

2. John Dominic Crossan, *The Dark Interval* (Niles: Argus Press, 1975), 47–62.

3. I am grateful to Valerie Stiteler whose unpublished manuscript was the source for this story.

4. Anne Sexton, *The Awful Rowing Toward God* (Boston: Houghton Mifflin, 1975), 83.

John Hibbard

Sunday Worship in the Absence of Eucharist

Examining Sunday celebrations of the word is much like discussing the role of food banks in attacking the problem of poverty. From a theoretical and detached point of view it is possible to argue that they are a temporary solution that keep people dependent upon them without attacking the real problem. However, when people are hungry they cannot afford the luxury of questioning where the food comes from or what long-term affect it will have on them. All they know is that they are starving.

Such is the situation for the church as we discuss the theological, ecclesiological and liturgical ramifications of celebrating Sunday liturgies of the word without the eucharist. Some might say: "We have done wrong," but to do nothing is to stand idly by while communities are starving. Yet we are in a no-win situation. Anyone who has given even a cursory thought to the growth of Sunday celebrations of the word in Canada and the United States should, at the least, have mixed feelings about it; others are reacting more strongly on one side or other of the debate.

As one who has contributed to the Canadian edition of the *Ritual for Sunday Celebration of the Word and Hours,* I am not sure what we have created or how it will develop or what will result from it in the long term. I do know the reaction of many communities who are proud to be able to celebrate their faith and are puzzled by the negative reactions of many theologians and the reluctance of many liturgists to give wholehearted approval to liturgies of the word celebrated on Sunday in place of the eucharist.

James Dallen says that Sunday celebrations of the word are a liturgical solution to an ecclesiological problem. We need to heed seriously the voice of theologians such as James Dallen and Kathleen Hughes as they unpack for us the theological and ecclesiological implications of Sunday celebrations of the word. Yet we must also be mindful of those communities that cannot celebrate the eucharist. We cannot overlook the people affected by the shortage of priests and focus exclusively on the theological issues. In the final analysis, theology must to applied to the pastoral situation. For this reason my presentation will deal both with some of the theological and ecclesiological implications of Sunday celebrations of the word and with ecclesial and liturgical issues surrounding the format and content of the celebration.

Name of the Celebration

The first issue is what to call this form of celebration. Kathleen Hughes reports that there are twelve names for the phenomenon we are discussing today. The most common name in many places is "Sunday worship in the absence of a priest"; others that I have heard are "Sunday worship in the absence of the eucharist" or "non-eucharistic liturgies." A name that is predominant in the western provinces of Canada (where these celebrations are common) describes the service in terms of the minster who leads the celebration; thus they speak of "lay-led liturgies" or "lay-led Sunday worship." In French-speaking areas of Canada it is the custom to talk of "Sunday celebrations in anticipation (or expectation) of the eucharist." This title seems to be inherited from Europe, specifically from France. Another term that is frequently heard is "priestless Masses." In his foreword to James Dallen's recent work, *The Dilemma of Priestless Sundays* (Chicago: Liturgy Training Publications, 1994), Bishop William E. McManus makes the point that calling these celebrations priestless insinuates that no priest, not even Jesus Christ, is essential for Sunday worship pleasing to God.

The problem is that most of the names describe this form of worship in negative terms, that is, these names define the celebration or gathering in terms of who is not present or what is not celebrated or who does or does not lead it. This is not part of our Catholic tradition, yet it seems to be a hard habit to break. A number of years ago I was reporting to a group of liturgists about the problem of naming this form of Sunday celebration. Everyone agreed with the point made previously, but in the informal conversations of the conference, terms like "in the absence of a priest" or "lay-led liturgies" or "lay presider's book" were the order of the conversations.

If we take seriously the *Constitution on the Sacred Liturgy* when it says that the assembly is the celebrant of the liturgy, then it seems more appropriate that we use terms and names that describe what we are doing and who is gathering. Sunday liturgy of the word or Sunday celebration of the word is what we are doing, no matter who leads it. As I wrote elsewhere,

> Some importance should be attached to whatever name is used to designate the Sunday worship of a community without its normal leader. For names have a power to form or convey a basic truth. The basic element in Sunday celebrations of the word is the people of God who have gathered to celebrate their faith and to give praise to God.

The popular title "Sunday celebration in the absence of a priest" says a lot. This is no doubt derived from the Roman Directory for Sunday celebrations in the absence of a priest. However, this title does not respect the nature of an established community or the liturgical assembly. It does say a lot about how we define the church in terms of the priest who leads the community or the community that gathers around its leader. For this reason the bishops of Canada, at least those of the Episcopal Commission for Liturgy, have decided on a different approach. Thus the title of the ritual for Canada makes a statement: Sunday Celebration of the Word and Hours.

John Hibbard

The Eucharistic Tradition

A second theological issue centers around the tradition of celebrating the eucharist on the Lord's Day. I don't have to say much about how the celebration of the word or hours alone is a break with this Catholic tradition. The importance of the Lord's Day and of celebrating the eucharist in memory of Jesus Christ as the summit and source of Christian life is well known to all of us. Others have written eloquently on this topic.

The ramifications of Sunday Celebrations of the Word or Hours are profound. It is possible that many Catholics will be living a non-eucharistic life. In many northern communities in the Canadian Arctic, the eucharist might be celebrated two or three times in a year. The issue is larger than even the eucharist; the result is a basically non-sacramental form of Christianity. The same communities that are without the eucharist are also without most of the other sacraments, except for baptism and marriage, which can be celebrated by the community without an ordained minister.

When members of the community are sick, they cannot be anointed; there is no access to the sacrament of reconciliation. The sacraments of initiation cannot be celebrated in their integrity, or, in the case of children, in the proper liturgical seasons, but only when the priest visits the community. Reformation theology acknowledges two sacraments of baptism and the Lord's supper and their primacy in the life of the church. In Catholic communities without a priest, the only two sacraments accessible to the community are baptism and marriage.

If Sunday celebrations of the word continue to grow in number and become the normal Sunday experience and worship of many communities, then we have some serious questions to ask. Can we continue to define ourselves as a sacramental church? Will our worship be sacramental? Can we claim that the eucharist is the summit and source of our life as Christians?

Form of the Celebration

One of the major differences between the U.S. and Canadian editions of the ritual is the recommendation for the preferred form of the celebration. The U.S. bishops recommend that Morning or Evening Prayer be the first option for celebration. In Canada we have gone a different route. In dioceses where Sunday celebrations of the word are a common phenomenon, a liturgy of the word is by far the most common form of celebration. It seems logical that they would stick with a form of worship that would be familiar to the members of community. In Canada, the celebration of the Liturgy of the Hours is not a common phenomenon, except in larger parishes and then only during Advent or Lent. Thus Morning and Evening Prayer are forms of worship totally unfamiliar to most assemblies.

Since the Roman Directory strongly encourages the proclamation of the three Sunday scripture readings of the eucharist, a problem arises with Morning or Evening Prayer. The addition of three Sunday readings to Morning or Evening Prayer results in a bewildering format. In most communities, a Sunday celebration of the word or hours is celebrated once or twice a month. Without the continuous celebration of the Liturgy of the Hours, the community will have difficulty learning and appropriating the complex format of Morning or Evening Prayer with the incorporation of the three Sunday readings and their responses and acclamations. In the end it must be said that we are left with neither a celebration of the word nor Morning or Evening Prayer. Add to this a communion service, and the result is an even more complex rite.

The liturgy of the word and the Liturgy of the Hours have different dynamics. The liturgy of the word is a dialogue between God and the assembly. God speaks to the assembly through the word and the community responds to that word. The Liturgy of the Hours is not primarily a dialogue, but the ascending praise of the assembly to God. The purpose of the psalms and the reading of Morning and Evening Prayer is not for the mediation of the community but as a vehicle for singing the praise of God. Mixing these two dynamics does justice to neither and results in a complex form of texts that will burden and confuse the assembly.

Another concern is the fact that the Liturgy of the Hours is essentially a monastic office. How can a parish community pray this monastic office in a meaningful way? Most communities do not have the facility to chant the psalms, so how can this be anything but an office that is read? Even then, most communities are not used to reciting psalms in two alternating choirs. It would appear that there has been little thought given as to how to help a community pray this office. The Canadian ritual does include Morning and Evening Prayer as possible forms of worship to be used in place of the eucharist by a community. However, these are for communities that have a tradition of using this format. In this case, only the first or second reading from the Sunday lectionary is proclaimed, and the rite of distribution of communion outside the eucharist is positively discouraged for the Liturgy of the Hours. In addition, the Canadian ritual includes some elements from the cathedral style of Morning or Evening Prayer. In this format the psalms are sung responsorially (verses sung by a cantor and the refrain by the assembly) from the Catholic Book of Worship II or III. The gospel canticles are in the style of hymns to be sung by the whole community. Suggestions for a sung response to the intercessions are also provided.

It is for these reasons that the National Liturgical Office and the Episcopal Commission for Liturgy decided that the liturgy of the word should be the recommended form of Sunday worship when the eucharist cannot be celebrated. The proclamation of the Sunday readings also provides an important continuity to a community cut off from the celebration of the eucharist.

I suspect that a decision to recommend Morning or Evening Prayer and avoid the celebration of the word on a Sunday is an attempt to introduce a form of celebration that would avoid the danger of confusing this celebration with that of the eucharist. Later in this article I will discuss the possibility of making minor adjustments to the liturgy of the word in order to give it a character distinct from the eucharist.

Ritual Elements

If it is true that word and sacrament complement and balance each other, what happens when one celebrates only the word for a prolonged period of time? The danger of celebrating word in isolation from sacrament is that there will be little ritual element in it. Word without ritual leads to an overly rational form of worship and to literalism and fundamentalism; ritual without word leads to superstition or rubricism. What ritual elements can and need to be part of celebrations of the word or hours? This is not an idle question. To my mind it has not yet been addressed. If Catholic worship is to be reduced to celebrations of the word, what will this do to our understanding of sacramental theology? From the point of view of the local community, what will happen to our worship?

In my research for the Canadian bishops I discovered that in some places, lay leaders of prayer were forbidden to use incense, assume the orans position of prayer, extend the hands in greeting, use candles in procession, wear an alb or make the sign of the cross at the gospel or blessing. These, lay ministers were told, were reserved for the priest. A major initiative in the Canadian ritual and in the pastoral notes that accompany it was to include precisely those ritual elements that belong to the church as a whole. The ritual encourages the community to have a procession and enthronement of the word, complete with the use of candles and incense. The procession and enthronement take place not at the entrance rite, but at the beginning of the liturgy of the word, after the opening prayer and before the first reading. As an acclamation is sung, the lector carrying the lectionary, preceded by ministers carrying candles and incense, enters the assembly and proceeds to the ambo. The lectionary is placed on the ambo and incensed. Then the leader of prayer speaks these words from the rite of dedication of a church:

> May the Word of God always be heard in this place,
> as it unfolds the mystery of Christ before us
> and achieves our salvation within the Church.

Then all are seated and the readings are proclaimed.

A brief look at the journey to Emmaus in Luke 24 reveals that while the disciples' hearts burned as their Lord opened for them the scriptures, it was in the breaking of bread that they actually recognized Jesus. The opening of scripture within the community was then and is still an important element, but it needs to be partnered with the ritual action of celebrating the eucharist. In this way the church of today is also able to recognize the presence of Jesus Christ in its midst.

Distribution of Communion outside the Eucharist

While liturgies of the word may restore an emphasis on the word that had been weak in the Roman Catholic tradition, it will also weaken an equally feeble notion of the role of ritual in the eucharist. In light of this, can one then argue that the distribution of communion be attached to the Sunday celebration of the word? This question cannot be easily settled. Despite a recommendation to the contrary, most communities will add the distribution of communion to their Sunday liturgy of the word. Communion is, after all, the Catholic thing to do, and in the minds of most people it is a natural thing to do. Nevertheless, the distribution of communion can never be a substitute for the celebration of the eucharist.

The eucharist is an action of Christ and the community, the dynamic activity of God in Christ within the assembly, transforming the assembly and forging the many members of the community into one assembly, one body of Christ. This understanding of the eucharist is not yet in the consciousness of the average assembly. It remains the ongoing task of the liturgical renewal. This problem will be compounded if the celebration of the eucharist is not part of the community's Sunday worship and experience. The fourfold action of the eucharist stands at the center of the community's involvement in the celebration of the eucharist.

The absence of the fourfold action of the eucharist impoverishes the ritual action of the community. There is no collection and procession of our offerings and gifts of bread and wine to give focus and meaning to our giving. There is no breaking of bread to symbolize our unity in the one bread. There is no receiving from what we brought forth to emphasize the transforming power of God within the assembly. There is no communion under both kinds to symbolize the unity of the body of Christ and the renewal of the covenant in the Lord's blood.

This affects our perception of the eucharist as a sacrificial banquet. In the distribution of communion outside the eucharist, the community is receiving that which it did not offer, receiving that over which it did not give thanks and receiving that which it did not break. The connection to the community and Lord's Day that is present in communion to the sick and shut-ins is not present for the whole community. Communion from the tabernacle and not from the eucharistic banquet at the Sunday eucharist deadens our perception of this problem.

This leads to another consequence of separating communion from the eucharist: the loss of the assembly as the body of Christ. Often the eucharist is seen only as the real presence of Christ, a static presence. While that may be adequate for Catholics who experience the eucharist as a devotional union between Christ and the individual, the eucharist is indeed much more. The union of the whole church to its head, Jesus Christ in the living body of Christ, is another goal and challenge for liturgical renewal: It is in the celebration of the eucharist that the community is actualized as the body of Christ, the church, a visible sign to the world. The community can be a visible sign in the celebration of the word or the hours (because these are the official liturgies of the church), but it is not actualized as a eucharistic community, the body of Christ.

One of the beneficial side effects of Sunday celebrations of the word is to challenge all communities to understand what they are celebrating in the eucharist and to celebrate it well. This includes helping the community to see itself as the body of Christ, its role in offering a sacrifice of praise that includes the lives of all members of the assembly in union with our high priest, Jesus Christ, the connection between the sacrificial banquet and meal by receiving communion from the table and under both kinds.

In summary it is clear that the distribution of communion outside the eucharist presumes and will perpetuate the notion that the laity's participation is limited to receiving communion and that the only difference between the eucharist and a Sunday celebration of the word is the absence of the priest. In reality what is really absent is the celebration of the eucharist.

John Hibbard

Relationship of the Ordained Minister to the Community

Sunday celebrations of the word also have repercussions for ordained ministry in the church. In a consumer society that sees and judges by the standard of effectiveness and success, we may judge ministers of the church by what and how they do. This functionalism fits very well into the uncritical attitude of accepting Sunday celebrations of the word. Ordained ministers, bishops, presbyters and deacons will become functionaries and not leaders who pray and walk with the community. Thus the traditional link between presiding and leading the community will disappear. Priests will become circuit riders, not pastors who share the pain and joy of the community. The priest will not be a pastoral agent, but a sacrament dispenser.

Sociologists will be able to list for us the consequences of this both for the community and for the individual. If we thought we had clergy problems in the past, imagine what will happen in the future to those who will live their lives divorced from Christian community and from meaningful human encounters.

The implications of Sunday celebrations of the word apply not just to the ministers themselves, but also to the parishes and communities of the church. What happens to our communities if there are no permanent ministers? Can only ordained ministers exercise pastoral ministry? Which is primary: that the community celebrates the eucharist or that an ordained minister celebrates the eucharist? Does the eucharist flow from community or only from ordination? If the eucharist, as well as all liturgy, is the celebration of the church, then there is a contradiction. Our present practice suggests that eucharist is tied only to ordination: It really is a celebration by the priest.

Sunday celebrations of the word imply that there can never be any permanent leadership in a community other than that of an ordained minister. Many communities have permanent lay leadership; it is part of the reality of many areas of North America. Yet these leaders cannot truly lead their communities in prayer. I do not mean only that they cannot be ordained. I mean that there is hesitance about allowing them to preside fully, even at liturgies of the word or hours. Are new forms of ministry arising in the church?

From a ritual point of view, the full expression of the presence of Christ in the ordained minister is absent, just as the fullness of ministry and service is diminished within the community.

The Place of the Lay Presider in the Liturgical Assembly

The hesitance about accepting lay leadership is seen in little things concerning the celebration of the word. The role and place of the lay leader of prayer in the liturgical assembly is one example. The directory for Sunday celebrations in the absence of a priest states that a lay person should not use the chair of the pastor and should not use the same formula of greeting or blessing as the ordained. Some people deplore the use of separate formulas for ordained and lay presiders. Even the language that we might use for the lay leader must be different from that for the ordained leader.

In the consultation that took place in Canada, we found divergent practices concerning the role of lay leaders. In some places the lay leaders sat in the presidential chair and used the same liturgical formulas as the ordained. In other places another chair was placed next to the presidential chair or in another part of the sanctuary, and in still others the leader sat in a pew of the church and came to the front whenever he or she had to address the community. In the last case, the reasons among different communities for doing the identical thing might be very different. In one diocese the bishop forbade lay leaders to sit in the sanctuary because they were not ordained. In other dioceses and communities, it was a deliberate decision on the part of the local community who wanted to emphasize that the leader came from the assembly and "was one of them." However, it seemed to the consulting committee that presiding is more than addressing the assembly or saying a prayer in front of others.

Presiding is leading the community in the spirit and attitude of prayer, and that is larger than leading the community in an actual prayer. Presiding is about presence. A true presider also leads the community in listening to the word of God. A true presider also leads the community in singing, in ritual action and in being silent and reflective. Thus the presider must be always visible to the assembly, and the assembly visible to the presider. The presider, ordained or lay, is the first member of the assembly and leads the assembly in what it does. Every presider, lay or ordained, is a member of the assembly. Not to understand this is not to understand what liturgical presidency is all about. The conclusion reached was nearly unanimous: Lay presiders need to preside from a place where they can model to the assembly what it is and does. This is more than a functional approach to presidency.

In terms of the liturgical greetings, we made the best of a difficult situation. In the end it was decided that lay presiders would use a different formula of greeting and blessing. However rather than change a single word, such as "The Lord be with you" to "May the Lord be with you" or "May the Lord be with us," we devised new formulas. In fact some of them are so beautiful I am a little envious.

> The minister may say:
> Blessed be God in the Church
> and in Christ Jesus for all generations
> who has strengthened us with power in the Spirit.
> Bless the Father and the Son and the Holy Spirit.
>
> A seasonal greeting for Advent may be:
> Blessed be Jesus Christ
> who was, who is, and who is to come.
> Bless the Father and the Son and the Holy Spirit.

The response on the part of the assembly is "Blessed be God for ever." We chose "Bless the Father and the Son and the Holy Spirit" as the lead-in to the community's response because we wanted to avoid making the assembly parrot the presider. It is not a perfect solution, but we were strongly against repetition.

The Permanent Short-Term Solution

Nothing lasts longer than a short-term solution. Despite what is said and despite all the cautions that this is not a permanent solution, most of us know otherwise. The many complex issues that have led the Catholic church in North America to its present situation will not be resolved quickly. The situation of a persecuted or missionary church, or a church suddenly in the midst of a power hostile to Christianity, holds more hope of being temporary than what we now face. We are describing our environment, our society, our culture, our church. We are products of a mixture of good and evil, elements conducive and non-conducive to faith. This is our heritage, and we cannot change our environment quickly or easily. In discussing Sunday worship without the eucharist, we are examining the whole range of ecclesial, theological and disciplinary issues of the Catholic church at the end of the twentieth century in North America.

Format of the Liturgy of the Word

In the process of developing the ritual for Canada there were several concerns about the structure and content of the celebration. In our consultation many recommended that the format of the celebration should be distinct from that of the eucharist. This was a challenge. Make the format too different and the assembly would find it difficult to own the celebration. Make it too similar and many would not see the difference between the eucharist and the liturgy of the word, especially with the distribution of communion. The committee responsible for the development of the ritual first issued a pilot project. The proposed rite had several distinctive elements:

1. The rite contained no penitential rite. The introductory rite included the opening song, the sign of the cross and the greeting, followed by the opening prayer.

2. There was a procession and enthronement of the word of God after the opening prayer, before the first reading.

3. The proclamation of praise was placed immediately after the homily, followed by the general intercessions and the creed. The position of the proclamation of praise (prayer of thanksgiving) was an important consideration. Our reasons for moving it were threefold:

    a. The committee pondered the theological purpose of the prayer. In many models in use throughout Canada, this prayer was almost an eucharistic prayer without an institution narrative. In other places it was an extended thanksgiving for communion. Believe it or not, some were a thanksgiving for the eucharist, which was not celebrated. Since the celebration was a liturgy of the word, it was felt that the prayer should be a thanksgiving for the word as proclaimed and lived by the community. Thus the prayer should be positioned fairly close to the proclamation of the word.

    b. In many rituals there was a succession of three prayers which did not seem to be related to each other or flow naturally from one to the other. These were the creed, the general intercessions complete with a closing prayer and the prayer of thanksgiving or praise. The positioning of the prayer of praise after the intercessions seemed to give it the place of the eucharistic prayer and made it the important element. We felt that by switching the prayer of praise and the creed, the creed would be the final element and climax of the liturgy of the word, and a fitting conclusion to the liturgy of the word.

4. Most prayers in the liturgical tradition move from praise and memorial to intercession. In most diocesan rituals the prayer of praise followed the intercessions so that the prayer of the community moved from intercession to praise.

The results of the pilot were mixed. This new order was not well received. Most wanted some form of the penitential rite and the traditional order of the creed followed by the intercessions.

The compromise was that the proclamation of praise would be the closing prayer of the intercessions.

Other issues centered on the content and structure of the prayers of praise and thanksgiving that had evolved in many communities:

1. The name of the prayer of thanksgiving was problematic. Its name and often its content were too close to the eucharistic prayer, the great prayer of thanksgiving. It was decided that since this act could take the form of a prayer or sung hymn or litany, it

would be better called the proclamation of praise. When it takes the form of a prayer, it should be called the prayer of praise.

2. Many prayers seemed to have little internal structure or development. Since most prayers contained acclamations, it looked as if four paragraphs were present in order to provide four or five acclamations by the assembly. In some prayers the same themes or ideas were repeated without any development of thought. It was felt that these prayers would not stand the test of time and repetition. Since these prayers have no structure, as opposed to eucharistic prayers with their elements of thanksgivng, invocation, narrative, memorial, oblation and intercession, it was decided to base most prayers on the scriptures.

3. Whatever form the proclamation of praise would take, it should contain some participation by the assembly. This might be a hymn or psalm of praise, sung entirely by the assembly or with a refrain, or a litany or prayer of praise with a suitable acclamation.

Positive Elements

As I draw to a close I feel it necessary to make a few positive comments about Sunday celebrations of the word:

1. The celebration of the paschal mystery is not restricted to the eucharist. The transformation and conversion of the community, the building up of the body of Christ, the strengthening of the faith of the assembly, and the affirming of the identity of the community can still be ongoing within the life and worship of the community. When all else fails, the assembly is still the prime symbol of the presence and activity of God.

2. The laity can take ownership of their parish, including its worship. They can still gather in response to God's call. They can still celebrate the paschal mystery. They can still minister to one another and be strengthened in service.

3. The awareness of baptism as incorporation into the body of Christ and sharing the priestly mission of Jesus Christ is empowering the baptized.

4. The importance and centrality of prayer and scripture is being restored in the life of people.

5. The importance of assembly on the Lord's Day is emphasized. People are assembling on Sunday; they are opening the scriptures so that Christ may speak to them as their hearts burn. The directory itself points out that there are three elements to the observation of the Lord's Day:
   a. gathering of the faithful in response to God's call;
   b. recalling the paschal mystery in the proclamation of the scriptures; and
   c. celebrating the eucharist. If the community is the prime symbol of worship, then each community should do as much as it can.

6. In most places there is a renewed desire and appreciation for the eucharist and ordained ministry within the community. In some cases it is helping to restore a proper balance between the ministry of the ordained and the laity.

Whatever confusion exists in the church between the eucharist and Sunday celebrations of the word existed before Sunday celebrations of the word began.

Canadian Ritual

By invitation and design, my presentation addresses the question of why the Canadian ritual is so different from the ritual in the United States. This is a difficult question because I do not know the process involved in the development of the U.S. ritual book. Therefore, rather than make any assumptions about what might have happened in the Liturgy Secretariat of the United States Catholic Conference, let me explain the process involved in the development of the Canadian ritual.

There is a tradition in our Conference that calls us to shape all our rituals to meet the pastoral needs of the churches in our country. In addition Canada has a very small population in comparison to the United States. This allows a process of consultation among the bishops and liturgists of Canada. The Episcopal Commission for Liturgy also has a tradition of a more hands-on approach to pastoral liturgy than other conferences. The directors of our liturgical office also have pastoral experience in addition to their academic training.

In relationship to the ritual itself, there was a five-year period of consultation, evaluation, reflection and testing. The committee established by the Episcopal Commission for Liturgy to develop the ritual was national in scope, with a representative from each of the three English-speaking regions of Canada. The committee began its work by examining the diocesan rituals in use throughout the country and consulting the regional liturgical conferences. The insight and experience of those who had been involved with Sunday celebrations of the word was invaluable. In addition, the committee did a lot of thinking and reflection on this experience. Lastly, the revision of the sacramentary provided some possibilities for the ritual. It was decided early on that we would use the revised translations of the collects and the scripture-based opening prayers prepared by ICEL. These, plus the ICEL proposal for the simplification of the introductory rites, helped the project.

As the committee talked to liturgists, pastors, diocesan directors, local leaders and bishops, it became obvious that extensive pastoral notes were needed to help in the selection and training of leaders of prayer. One experience in western Canada made this evidently clear to me. At a liturgical conference on Sunday celebrations of the word, parish teams were invited to lead abbreviated liturgies of the word in place of Morning or Evening Prayer. It became obvious that the lay leaders had picked up the bad habits of their pastors and priests, who, of course, had trained them. It was not only training by the clergy that had ingrained some bad presiding skills in these lay leaders, it was also the repeated patterns of worship that were not consistent with liturgical renewal. A lack of reflection on the role of the presider in relationship to the community was evident. At one point, the notes were almost a complete course on liturgy. Their length was prohibitive. However, in conjunction with the pastoral notes that would accompany the revised translation of the sacramentary, it was felt that these would provide a vehicle for education. It was a teachable moment.

The final word needs to be about the assembly, the true body of Christ. Any ritual cannot be concerned only with the presider. The chief concern has to be what is going to help the assembly to worship. This fashioned the pastoral notes of the ritual as well as the content, structure and layout of the ritual.

Conclusion

In the fall of 1990, at the Western Liturgical Conference in Edmonton, Alberta, Mark Searle addressed the issue of Sunday celebrations of the word. He reminded us that we are a catholic (universal) church. We enter the church through a particular church; therefore what we do in the local church affects the whole body of Christ. We can narrow people's vision of what the church is or we can enlarge their vision of church. I believe that this point is applicable to Sunday celebrations of the word. When it is not possible to celebrate the eucharist, the church still exists and lives. We are still in need of transformation and conversion. We are still God's people, redeemed through Jesus Christ, living in the Spirit. We still must proclaim the mighty deeds of God for God is still acting in our midst. Despite whatever problems we face in the church, let us still work to enlarge people's vision of the church. Let us believe that God is at work in our midst.

James Schellman

A Look at the
New Sacramentary

As Roman Catholics, we have had nearly thirty years, the equivalent of a generation, experiencing Mass in its postconciliar form and in our own language. This is not a great deal of time if measured against the several hundred years of the Tridentine Mass and hundreds of years more of celebration in a language most would not have fully understood. But together we have learned and can take justifiable pride in how far we have journeyed in so short a time.

Thirty years ago we began to experience the first major change in our liturgical books and rites in nearly four hundred years. Steadily, day by day and Sunday by Sunday, these resources for our assemblies at prayer before the living God have helped to remake the church, to shape it in the form of a living body, Christ's body, in dialogue together and in worship before the triune God.

Wisely, the Second Vatican Council and its postconciliar directives saw the need for periodic revision of the liturgical resources mandated by the Council. This seemed necessary because our corporate prayer texts were now cast in living and, therefore, evolving languages. In addition, the territorial Catholic bodies known as conferences of bishops were to continue to look to the needs of their worshiping assemblies and to make cultural and other adaptations of the books in response to the needs of worship assemblies in their areas.

It is this second round of change and consolidation in which the church in the English-speaking countries is now immersed. The liturgical books produced in the first years after the Council are now being carefully considered and improved. This is an incremental process of learning from the experience of our celebrating communities over the last few decades.

Results of Consultation

When ICEL, the International Commission on English in the Liturgy, started to envision what a changed edition of the Sacramentary would look like, it carried out two consultations (in 1982 and 1986) with the Catholic church throughout the English-speaking world. Bishops, national and diocesan liturgical commissions, liturgists, pastors and other interested persons were invited to reflect on the first or 1973 English edition of the Mass texts and to indicate where improvement was needed. This in summary form is what they told ICEL.

Propers

Prayers assigned to the various days, the opening prayers, prayers over the gifts and prayers after communion, needed substantial revision. These are prayers heard in general once a year, for example, the prayers assigned for the Third Sunday of Easter. Many of these translations were thought to have over-simplified the content of the Latin originals. Since they are proclaimed and heard so infrequently and so would not have entered the memories of most presiders and other worshipers, significant revision seemed both possible and advisable.

Order of Mass

A very different reaction was offered in the consultation on the texts of the Order of Mass, that is, the eucharistic prayers and other texts heard repeatedly throughout the year. Proclaimed, heard or responded to during Mass as we have known it for the past few decades, these prayers have entered the memories of presiders and the rest of the

Catholic people. They were judged by most who took part in the 1986 consultation as having generally worn well in liturgical use. Where revision seemed necessary it should be discreet and cause as little pastoral disruption as possible.

Original Texts

The texts we currently use at Mass include a small number of so-called new or original texts, that is, texts not translated from Latin originals. Such texts were created by ICEL in the early 1970s to supplement the Latin translations. The 1973 edition of the Sacramentary which is used at present offers about ninety original texts. Examples of these are the memorial acclamation "Christ has died, Christ is risen, Christ will come again," the invitation to the Lord's Prayer, "Let us pray for the coming of the kingdom as Jesus taught us," and, of course, the alternative opening prayer offered for each Sunday celebration.

Respondents to the Sacramentary consultations desired a greater number of new or original texts. In particular, interest was expressed in new opening prayers, like those in the 1983 edition of the Italian Sacramentary, which were inspired by the scripture readings assigned and heard on the day that the prayers would be proclaimed.

Pastoral Issues

A number of pastoral issues were raised in the consultations. The several most significant and consistently mentioned issues were:

- a need to clarify and, in a few instances, slightly adapt some rubrical or ritual elements of the Mass;
- a need for simplification of the introductory rites of the Mass; these rites were considered by many to be too cluttered and, as a result, often inadequately celebrated.
- a need for the use of inclusive language.

This is an unavoidably very distilled view of the results of the consultations on the Sacramentary. What follows now are a few examples (out of more than 2,000 texts!) of how the directions indicated in the two consultations have taken flesh in the new Sacramentary.

James Schellman

Revised Translations

The vast majority of texts and prayers in the Sacramentary are trans-lations from the Latin prayers for Mass. As reported, prayers assigned to particular days have been substantially revised, so much so that in many cases these new English-language prayers are completely different from what we have been accustomed to. For the opening prayers, prayers over the gifts and prayers after communion, the prin-ciples of revision included:

- an effort to achieve a wider prayer vocabulary,
- closer attention to the sequence of thought in the Latin original
- and the creation of an evocative and more memorable prayer through care for rhythm and cadence.

A few examples of how these principles shaped the revision of these prayers follow.

From the 1973 edition of the Sacramentary:

Opening Prayer, 18 December

All-powerful God,
renew us by the coming feast of your Son
and free us from our slavery to sin.

Grant this through our Lord Jesus Christ, your Son,
who lives and reigns with you and the Holy Spirit,
one God, for ever and ever.

This 1973 translation took the essence of the Latin prayer and con-veyed its meaning in a straightforward English composition. In the revised version of 1996, ICEL has rendered the Latin in strong imagery and with attention to cadence to create a coherent and evocative prayer.

All-powerful God,
we are oppressed and weighed down
by the ancient yoke of sin.
Grant that the birth of your only Son,
so long awaited, yet always new,
may deliver us and set us free.

We ask this through our Lord Jesus Christ, your Son,
who lives and reigns with you in the unity of the Holy Spirit,
God for ever and ever.

The compelling image of "the ancient yoke of sin," a translation of *vetusta servitute,* anchors the opening section. The expansive rendering of exspectata *Unigeniti tui nova nativitate liberemur* creates a memorable English petition.

From the 1973 edition of the Sacramentary

Opening Prayer, Fourth Sunday of Lent

Father of peace,
we are joyful in your Word,
your Son Jesus Christ,
who reconciles us to you.

Let us hasten toward Easter
with the eagerness of faith and love.
We ask this through our Lord Jesus Christ, your Son,
who lives and reigns with you and the Holy Spirit,
one God, for ever and ever.

This is the 1996 revision of the prayer.

In a wonderful manner, Lord God,
you reconcile humankind to yourself
through your only Son, the eternal Word.
Grant that your Christian people
may press on toward the Easter sacraments
with lively faith and ready hearts.

We ask this through our Lord Jesus Christ, your Son,
who lives and reigns with you in the unity of the Holy Spirit,
God for ever and ever.

In this revision, the strong address calls attention to the reconciliation theme of the prayer. "Toward the Easter sacraments" replaces "toward Easter" and renders *ventura solemnia* strikingly. This image serves to capture the essence of the season of Lent, the culmination of the experience of the risen Christ in the sacraments of initiation at Easter.

James Schellman

The texts of the Order of Mass, by contrast, have been revised with great restraint. Because these are now well-known, the general principle was to revise them only where there was compelling need. Revisions were to be done in a discreet fashion to avoid pastoral disruption as much as possible.

Most of us in the United States are familiar with the recent change in the words accompanying the scripture readings: "The word of the Lord" after the first and second readings, and "The gospel of the Lord" following the proclamation of the gospel reading. Small though they are, these slight changes in translation attempt to overcome a sometimes narrow perception of the word in celebration, as though the word of God is the book itself rather than its living proclamation in the assembly of believers.

A parallel change has been made in the invitation to communion. The text now reflects the scriptural allusion in the Latin more closely:

> Behold the Lamb of God,
> who takes away the sin of the world.
> Blessed are those called to the banquet of the Lamb.

Careful changes have been made in the eucharistic prayers, mostly to bring out more clearly the flow and meaning of the original Latin text. There were some requests for a substantial recasting and more literal rendering of Eucharistic Prayer I in particular. But, as with the translations of the other eucharistic prayers, most of those who took part in the 1986 consultation on these texts felt that the translation of Eucharistic Prayer I had worn well over time as a rhythmically strong, supple, contemporary English rendering of the Latin original.

The limited changes in the eucharistic prayers include "connective" expressions intended to carry better the flow of thought in the Latin *(unde, igitur)* from one section of the prayer to another. This is evident, for example, at the beginning of the anamnesis section of Eucharistic Prayer I. Following immediately upon the recitation of the institution narrative and the proclamation of the memorial acclamation, the anamnesis now begins with the connective "and so":

> And so, Lord God,
> we celebrate the memory . . .

Similarly, the revised opening to the anamnesis section of Eucharistic Prayer II carries this sense of connection with the narrative and acclamation that come before:

> Remembering therefore his death and resurrection,
> we offer you, Lord God . . .

And, in the same section of Eucharistic Prayer IV:

> And so, Lord God,
> we celebrate the memorial of our redemption . . .

One of the more striking revisions in these prayers is in the first few lines of Eucharistic Prayer III. There was strong feeling that the scriptural allusion to Malachi 1:11 in the Latin should be brought out more clearly. As a result:

> From age to age you gather a people to yourself,
> so that from east to west
> a perfect offering may be made
> to the glory of your name . . .

has been replaced by

> From age to age you gather a people to yourself,
> so that from the rising of the sun to its setting
> a pure offering may be made
> to the glory of your name.

An interesting debate occurred over the phrase in the anamnesis section of Eucharistic Prayer II.

> We thank you for counting us worthy
> to stand in your presence and serve you.

Some of those who responded to the ICEL consultation thought this should be changed since at this point in most of our assemblies in the United States and some other parts of the world, only the priest and perhaps one or two others in the sanctuary are actually standing. The decision, after brief discussion, was to maintain this rendering of the Latin which presumes the universal norm of the church that the whole assembly stands during the eucharistic prayer.

James Schellman

Many more examples of revised translations could be given, particularly of the vastly improved collects. But this is beyond the scope of this article.

Original Texts

The 1973 edition of the Sacramentary has a limited number of original texts, about 90. The new Sacramentary will have nearly 300. These are an intimate part of the historic effort of the church over the last few decades and in all the major language groups (English, German, Italian, French and so on) to graft onto the received tradition of prayer a small branch reflecting our own contemporary experience of Christ using the idiom and genius of our own languages. Below are several major groupings of these 300 texts.

Scripture-Related Opening Prayers

At present in the Sacramentary we have a single alternative opening prayer for the Sundays and major feasts of the year. These prayers were conceived as a kind of expansive paraphrase in English of the ideas in the Latin prayer of the day. In the consultation they were criticized as perhaps being too lush, having a diversity of images and using concepts and language now seen as a little dated.

One of the ways forward with the alternative opening prayer in the new Sacramentary was to take advantage of the postconciliar biblical revolution among Roman Catholics and to look closely at the three-year cycle of readings used in the Lectionary for Mass. A quarter-century of exposure to these cycles of readings has helped to imbue Catholics as a people with biblical concepts, language and imagery. Inspired by a new set of opening prayers in the 1983 edition of the Italian sacramentary that are related to the Scriptures of the day, ICEL has created three alternative opening prayers for each Sunday and major feast. These take their inspiration from the scriptures assigned to the day, the gospel reading in particular. The choice in any celebration will be between the translated opening prayer and the alternative opening prayer that corresponds to the readings of the day.

This part of the Sacramentary project comprises about 200 of the approximately 300 original prayers. These took nearly ten years to develop. As with the revised translations, these original prayers went through many stages of preparation.

An example of the new opening prayers follows:

Second Sunday of Advent, Year B

With tender comfort and transforming power
you come into our midst,
O God of mercy and might.

Make ready a way in the wilderness,
clear a straight path in our hearts,
and form us into a repentant people,
that the advent of your Son
may find us watchful and eager for the glory he reveals.

We ask this through him whose coming is certain,
whose day draws near:
your Son, our Lord Jesus Christ,
who lives and reigns with you in the unity of the Holy Spirit,
God for ever and ever.

John the Baptist makes his appearance in the gospel readings assigned to this Sunday in all three years. His message permeates the language of this prayer. The gospel reading puts in the mouth of John the moving words from Isaiah chapter 40, the first reading. And so the prayer begins by evoking the very image of God in Isaiah, a God of tenderness and power, of mercy and might. In the petition of the prayer, the wilderness that God transforms and the paths made straight become something inherent in us that God is asked to transform. And the end of this transformation is the repentance John preached, a repentance that will make of us a people on eager watch for the coming of Christ.

The focus of the Advent season on the coming "day of the Lord," so compellingly expressed in the second reading from 2 Peter, is brought out in the unusual doxology that concludes the prayer. This is a seasonal doxology created for the new prayers for Advent. Repeated over these several Sundays, it can become a ritual cue and an evocation at the beginning of the eucharistic celebration of all that we are to be about this season and throughout our lives: watching for the one who is to come, the Christ in whom all the unfinished

James Schellman

business of our lives and of creation as a whole will be consummated. Shorter seasonal doxologies are also features of the new prayers for the other seasons: Christmas, Lent and Easter.

Fifth Sunday of Lent, Year A

Merciful God,
you showed your glory to our fallen race
by sending your Son
to confound the powers of death.

Call us forth from sin's dark tomb.
Break the bonds which hold us,
that we may believe and proclaim Christ,
the cause of our freedom
and the source of life,
who lives and reigns with you in the unity of the Holy Spirit,
holy and mighty God for ever and ever.

The dual themes of the fall of our first parents and of restoration in Christ are proclaimed at the beginning of Lent in Year A and underlie the season. This theme comes through strongly in the opening section of the prayer and is applied directly to Christ's vanquishing "the powers of death." The body of the prayer subtly evokes the gospel story of the raising of Lazarus on this Sunday of the third scrutiny. And so, "Call us forth from sin's dark tomb. Break the bonds which hold us. . . ." In this, the prayer lays claim to the power of the resurrection in our lives now, that "we may believe and proclaim Christ." The doxology uses part of the seasonal conclusion developed for the Sundays of Lent, "holy and mighty God." The other part of the seasonal conclusions in Lent uses one of two phrases in apposition to Christ: "our liberator from sin" or "our deliverance and hope" (for instance, "Grant this through Christ, our deliverance and hope. . . .").

Easter Vigil

O God,
your saving plan has brought us
to the glory of this night.
Slaves, we become your sons and daughters,
poor, your mercy makes us rich,
sinners, you count us among your saints.

> Bring us to know the place that is ours
> in the unfolding story of your purpose,
> and instill in our hearts
> the wonder of your salvation.
>
> Grant this through Jesus Christ, our passover and our peace,
> who lives with you now and always
>   in the unity of the Holy Spirit,
>
> God for ever and ever.

This is the single alternative prayer for the Easter Vigil. Within the structure of the Vigil, this is less an opening prayer than a collect that serves as the ritual transition from the Vigil readings, prayers and Gloria to the proclamation of the great passage from Romans 6 and the gospel account of the resurrection. The prayer serves to bring together the many themes that have preceded it in the readings and the experience of the singing of the Gloria after the community's lenten fast from this great hymn. The prayer acknowledges God's saving plan that has "brought us to the glory of this night." In a brief series of contrasts, it proclaims what God has done through the mystery being celebrated: Slaves become sons and daughters, poor become rich, sinners are made saints. The petition, placing the assembly firmly within the story already proclaimed in the Vigil readings, asks that we may know our own place "in the unfolding story of your purpose," a story still being told in us. Above all, we ask for wonder in the face of God's mighty saving acts on behalf of our fallen race. The first line of the doxology is new and is original to the Easter Vigil: "Grant this through Jesus Christ, our passover and our peace . . . ." This offers a striking allusion to the whole paschal context of the Easter Triduum.

Order of Mass

A number of new original texts have been added to those already used within the Order of Mass. Some examples follow.

Greetings

Several new scripture-based greetings have been prepared. Here is an example:

James Schellman

The grace of our Lord Jesus Christ,
whose table we share,
be with you all.

Litany of Praise

What we know at present as Form C of the Penitential Rite has been given the new title "Litany of Praise." It has been retitled as part of a change in the introductory rites which will be explained below. Three new invitations have been composed for this Litany of Praise that are more suited to the content of these litanies than the present invitations to the penitential rite. Here is an example:

Before listening to the word
and celebrating the eucharist,
let us praise the Lord Jesus Christ.

Kyrie and Gloria

Both the Kyrie and Gloria have several invitations that may now be used. These were felt to be helpful in light of the slight change in the introductory rites. The new invitations to the Kyrie each have the same cue for the assembly, "Acclaim Christ . . ." Here is an example:

God is making all things new.
Acclaim Christ, the first fruits of the new creation.

The new invitations to the Gloria each conclude with a reference to God's glory, for example,

Let us sing the praises of the Lord,
the God who made us,
whose glory is from age to age.

Memorial Acclamations

There are now four alternative invitations to the memorial acclamations, each assigned to go with one of the acclamations. These will help to cue the assembly to which acclamation follows and to help avoid some of the regrettable practices that have taken place at this moment in the celebration. The acclamations remain unchanged.

Great is the mystery of faith: Christ has died . . .
Praise to you, Lord Jesus: Dying you destroyed our death . . .
Christ is the bread of life: When we eat this bread and drink
   this cup . . .
Jesus Christ is Lord: Lord, by your cross and resurrection . . .

Other Acclamations

Three additional congregational acclamations for the eucharistic prayers have been provided in the musical settings of the eucharistic prayers.

Invitation to the Lord's Prayer

The three current invitations to the Lord's Prayer have been retained. Two of these are original texts. To these have been added three others, for example:

In Christ we have received the Spirit of adoption.
Now, as sons and daughters of God,
we dare to say.

Invitation to the Sign of Peace

There will be two further invitations to the Sign of Peace, for a total of three. Here is one of the new texts.

As children of the God of peace,
let us offer one another
a sign of reconciliation and peace.

Invitation to Communion

There will be two new invitations to communion. Here is an example of these:

This is the bread come down from heaven:
whoever eats of it will never die.
This is the cup of eternal life:
whoever drinks of it will live for ever.

Prefaces

Six new prefaces are offered by ICEL: Sundays in Ordinary Time, Weekdays in Ordinary Time, Initiation, Chrism Mass, Ascension, Ministry.

The new preface for Christian initiation should fill a real need on occasions apart from the Easter Vigil when the sacraments of initiation are celebrated:

It is truly right and just,
our duty and our salvation,
always and everywhere to give you thanks,
holy Father, almighty and eternal God.

Through the preaching of the gospel
you form a community of faith
which you bring to life-giving waters,
seal with the gift of your Spirit,
and welcome to the table of the Lord.
By these mysteries you fashion us
in the likeness of Christ
and make us one in him:
one in the faith we profess
and one in our witness to the world.

With joyful hearts we echo on earth
the song of the angels in heaven
as they praise your glory without end:

Other New Texts for Various Needs and Occasions

A significant new offering among the original texts is an alternative to the *Exsultet,* the Easter proclamation. This new text has a recurring refrain for the assembly throughout.

At the back of the Sacramentary there is a collection of prayers for particular needs: for unity of Christians, for those who serve in public office, after the harvest, for rain, and so on. This collection has been filled out by ICEL with about thirty new prayers to address some further needs of contemporary society. Individual countries will no doubt add to these offerings with other prayers for their specific needs.

Among the thirty prayers added to this section by ICEL, several examples follow:

On the Reverent Use of Creation

By your word,
Lord God,
we and all creatures
are formed, sustained, and fed.

Teach us to live in peace
with the world your hands have made,
that, as faithful stewards of your good earth,
we may reverence you in the works of your creation.

We make our prayer through our Lord Jesus Christ, your Son,
who lives and reigns with you in the unity of the Holy Spirit,
God for ever and ever.

In Time of Industrial Conflict

God of justice and peace,
we are drawn together to hear your word
as we seek an end to conflict.
Since all resources come from you,

hear the prayer of your Church:
provide for the needs of both workers and employers
and guide us to solutions fair to all,
that we may once more work together
in harmony and peace.

We ask this through our Lord Jesus Christ, your Son,
who lives and reigns with you in the unity of the Holy Spirit,
God for ever and ever.

For Victims of Abuse

O God, in whose enduring love we trust,
bind up the wounds of those betrayed
by abuse at the hands of others.

James Schellman

Heal them and make them whole,
that they may once more receive and give love
with confidence in their dignity as your sons and daughters.

We ask this through our Lord Jesus Christ, your Son,
who lives and reigns with you in the unity of the Holy Spirit,
God for ever and ever.

For the Addicted

O God,
whose will is health and wholeness
for all your children,
look with compassion on those bound by addiction.
Remove the fears that beset them
and guide their steps toward recovery,
that, encouraged by the support of (family and) friends,
they may know your love
and find rest and new life in your strength.

We make our prayer through our Lord Jesus Christ, your Son,
who lives and reigns with you in the unity of the Holy Spirit,
God for ever and ever.

Pastoral Issues

Various pastoral issues in the celebration of the Mass needed to be addressed for an edition of the Sacramentary meant to carry English-speaking Catholics into the new century.

Rubrical and Ritual Clarification

At the level of ritual and rubrical clarification, much has been done that would be of little interest except to those who did the work (and even for them, not all was of equal interest!). But some of this work, narrow and limited as it seems, has weighty potential for eucharistic celebration in many of our parishes. Such clarification in part means taking material from the official introduction to the celebration of Mass that is really rubrical and putting it in place with the rubrics where it belongs for the sake of the ministers who need this direction. I offer here a small selection in hopes that it will illustrate the significance of this part of the work for the future form of celebration in the average parish.

Word

Because of the importance of the word of God in our postconciliar liturgical celebrations, the first example is taken from the liturgy of the word.

At the beginning of the liturgy of the word, the minister (and pastoral planners) will now find in place the rubric about possible times for silence found in the General Instruction of the Roman Missal (23) and in the 1981 introduction to the Lectionary for Mass (28). These times are at the beginning, after the first and second readings and after the homily. The most significant of these silences, of course, is the one following the homily. The direction concerning this is now inserted in place within the Order of Mass:

> Following the homily, the priest returns to the chair. A period of silence may be observed.

How many of our parishes even come close to observing one or two of these possible silences? At stake here, I believe, is the full, renewed weight of the liturgy of the word within the Mass. As the General Instruction and the introduction to the Lectionary claim, the liturgy of the word and the liturgy of the eucharist are so closely connected that they form but one single act of worship. For in the Mass the table of God's word and of Christ's Body is laid for the people of God to receive from it instruction and food (GIRM, 8).

Both, then, are a form of communion in the one Lord—one in his word, the other in his body and blood. What could bring this home more clearly or invitingly than parallel silences following the homily, the breaking open of the word, and following the assembly's reception of communion? For those parishes that have not experienced this, perhaps this little clarification will help.

Ministry

There are small ways in which the postconciliar principle of a variety of liturgical ministries is underlined now by material brought into the rubrics from other official documents.

Under the liturgy of the word, for example, the rubric indicates that if there is a second reading (on Sundays, for example), "it is read . . . if possible by a second reader." With regard to the gospel, the full direction from the General Instruction has now become part of the rubrics:

> If, however, there is no deacon, another priest . . . or, in his absence, the presiding priest himself (proclaims the gospel).

This helps to clarify that the presider proclaims the gospel only as a last resort. Together, he and the rest of the assembly are to listen attentively to the proclamation of the word.

In the rubrics of the eucharistic prayer, provision is now made for the priest or deacon to say the invitation to the memorial acclamation.

Communion Rite

The possibility of communion under both kinds is at long last addressed directly in the rubrics of the communion rite. At the breaking of the bread:

> . . . the priest takes the consecrated bread and breaks it over the plate into several parts for the communion of the faithful and, as necessary, prepares any additional cups with the consecrated wine, so that in sharing in the one bread of life and the cup of salvation, the many are made one body in Christ.

Another clarification concerns the communion song. In order to invite better celebrational practice in many places, a sub-heading, "Communion Song," has now been introduced right after "Lord, I am not worthy," and is accompanied by the rubric

> While the priest is receiving the body of Christ, the communion song is begun.

I do not believe this is a small matter. With the necessary increase in communion ministers over the last couple of decades, it is not unusual to find an extended communion rite for the priest and other ministers in the sanctuary, with the communion of the rest awk-wardly delayed. Possibilities for overcoming this are brought up in the pastoral introduction. But the situation is made altogether worse, and the sense of two communion rites intensified, if the communion song does not begin until after the priest and some or perhaps all of the ministers have received.

Pastoral Introduction

The greatest contribution to good pastoral practice will be found in the sixty-page pastoral introduction now supplied with the Sacramentary. This is to be read in conjunction with the General Instruction and as a kind of pastoral commentary on the celebration. It is suggestive and reflective, bringing together in one place material from various official sources bearing on the celebration of Mass but also reflecting insights learned in the English-speaking world over the past thirty years as our communities of faith have embraced and been embraced by the renewal of liturgy. A brief but illustrative excerpt from the pastoral introduction appears at the end of this article.

Introductory Rites

A need to simplify the introductory rites was strongly expressed in the 1986 consultation. The proposal calls for the sequence of

> Entrance Procession
> Greeting
> Opening Rite (Blessing and Sprinkling or Penitential Rite or
>   Litany of Praise or Kyrie or Gloria)
> Opening Prayer

The newly titled "opening rite" is to consist of one of the several ele-ments that at present may be combined: blessing and sprinkling of water, or Kyrie, or Gloria, or penitential rite, or litany of praise (the present Form C of the penitential rite).

Another change occurs at the prayer over the gifts. The celebrant may say the usual "Pray, brothers and sisters . . ." before the prayer over the gifts or may say simply "Let us pray," after which would fol-low a pause for silent prayer and then the prayer over the gifts.

James Schellman

Relocation of the sign of peace was not part of the ICEL proposal but has been taken up by the U.S. bishops. This proposal allows for the sign of peace to take place either at the end of the liturgy of the word, just before the preparation of the gifts, or in its present place within the communion rite.

Inclusive Language

The need for inclusive language in our liturgical texts has long been accepted in the ICEL process. The principle goes back twenty years to 1975. All texts since then have used inclusive language as it is understood in reference to people. These texts have been approved by the conferences of bishops throughout the world and confirmed by the Apostolic See.

A limited number of significant texts used at Mass required attention for inclusive language. Notable among these was the section of Eucharistic Prayer IV immediately following the Sanctus:

> Father most holy, we proclaim your greatness:
> all your works show forth your wisdom and love.
> You formed man and woman in your own likeness
> and entrusted the whole world to their care,
> so that in serving you alone, their Creator,
> they might be stewards of all creation.
>
> Even when they disobeyed you and turned away
>   from your friendship,
> you did not abandon them to the power of death,
> but extended your hand in mercy,
> that all who search for you might find you.
>
> Again and again you offered the human race a covenant
> and through the prophets nurtured the hope of salvation.

With the Sacramentary project, ICEL for the first time decided upon a moderate principle with regard to language referring to God. In the 1973 texts currently in use, "Father" appears many more times than it does in the Latin originals. This had to do with contemporary biblical scholarship in the 1960s and the desire to make the abstract titles of the Latin prayers more concrete. The revision has avoided using "Father" where it does not appear in the Latin. The principle of doing something with the bare Latin titles remains. And so phrases in apposition to "God" or "Lord God" are now used (often scripture-based) that express qualities of God mentioned in the rest of the prayer, for example, "God of mercy," "God of loving kindness." This is also true of the new scripture-related opening prayers. Because of the number of times that Father is used in the fixed texts of the Order of Mass (for example, the sign of the cross, creed, eucharistic prayer, Lord's Prayer), it was felt possible to avoid male pronouns for the First Person of the Trinity in some other texts that did not require them. This in fact affects very few prayers in the Sacramentary since most of them directly address God rather than speak about God. They are therefore largely cast in the second person ("you").

Conclusion

The revised Sacramentary represents the fruit of our experience in the celebration of Mass over the past thirty years. Its preparation has been a labor of love that has spanned the past decade and a half and has drawn on the talents and commitment of bishops, scholars, pastors, other ministers and many other members of the church throughout the English-speaking world. Pastoral ministers and leaders will find the new Sacramentary a resource which, though not perfect, should help serve our communities of faith at worship before the living God as we move into the new century.

Excerpt from Pastoral Introduction to the Order of Mass

Distribution of Communion

I. Faithful to the Lord's command to his disciples to "Take and eat," "Take and drink," the assembly completes the eucharistic action by eating and drinking together the elements consecrated during the celebration. It is for this reason that the faithful should not ordinarily be given communion from the tabernacle. Also for this reason, it is most desirable that the faithful share the cup. Drinking at the eucharist is a sharing in the sign of the new covenant (see Luke 22:20), a foretaste of the heavenly banquet (see Matthew 26:29), a sign of participation in the suffering Christ (see Mark 10:38–39). Provision should be made for this fullest form of participation in accord with the conditions laid down by the conference of bishops.

II. Although a communion procession is not obligatory or always possible, it should be the normal arrangement for both practical and symbolic reasons. It expresses the humble patience of the poor moving forward to be fed, the alert expectancy of God's people sharing the paschal meal in readiness for their journey, the joyful confidence of God's people on the march toward the promised land.

III. All signs of discrimination or distinctions among persons at the Lord's table are to be avoided.

There should be a sufficient number of ministers to assist in the distribution of communion. This will normally mean two ministers of the cup to each minister of the bread.

It is desirable that all who minister the eucharist take full part in the entire liturgy and thus experience the proclamation of the word, the eucharistic prayer, and the consummation of the celebration in eucharistic communion.

When communion is administered under both kinds, the deacon who ministers the cup is to receive from it after the assembly. This expression of eucharistic hospitality and service may also be followed by all other communion ministers in order to facilitate the distribution of communion in a timely and orderly manner. If there are many concelebrating priests, the communion of the assembly should not be delayed but should be begun after the presiding celebrant has communicated. There is no need for all the concelebrating priests to finish receiving communion before distribution to the assembly can commence.

When the conference of bishops allows the reception of the consecrated bread in the hand, the choice whether to do so is the prerogative of the communicant.

When the conference of bishops and the local bishop have determined that communion under both kinds may be given, the pastor or priest celebrant should see to its full and proper implementation. Even when communion is given under both kinds, however, the communicant may refrain from drinking from the cup.

Should communion under both kinds sometimes be given in the form of intinction, the communicant may choose to receive under the form of bread only. When communion in the form of intinction is given, the following formula is said, "The body and blood of Christ," and the communicant responds, "Amen."

Communion may be received standing or kneeling, in accord with the decision of the conference of bishops. The manner of reception customary in the community is followed so that communion may truly be a sign of familial union between all who share in the same table of the Lord.

By tradition the deacon ministers the cup. Beyond this, no distinctions are made in the assignment of the consecrated elements to particular ministers for distribution. Therefore when a concelebrating priest or priests and other ministers share in the distribution, the elements are not assigned on the basis of any distinction between the ministers, cleric or lay, male or female. All may minister either element. This avoids any seeming depreciation of one or other of the consecrated elements or of a particular ministry.

1. See GIRM, 48:3, 56:8, 240, 241, 242.

2. See GIRM, 137.

3. See GIRM, 246.

4. See *Eucharisticum Mysterium*, 34, a: AAS 59 (1967), 560.

5. See GIRM, 61, 244.

John Allyn Melloh, SM

Preaching:
Pondering, Ordering,
Creating

Introduction

"Fulfilled in Your Hearing: The Homily in the Sunday Assembly"[1] (henceforth FIYH), published in 1982, is the Roman Catholic preacher's *vade mecum*. Though less than fifty pages long, the document is chock-full of useful insights into the restored homily of post–Vatican II times and presents its material in four main sections: the assembly, the preacher, the homily and homiletic method. The chapters are preceded by an introduction and concluded with an epilogue on the power of God's word.

FIYH presents a model for homily preparation, discussing the major components of this process. While this generalized model is helpful in giving an overview of the necessary steps in homily preparation, students of preaching sometimes need more assistance when it comes to the actual drafting of the initial homiletic manuscript.[2]

I often describe the entire process of homily preparation as three movements: pondering, ordering and creating. Pondering involves prayerful reading and meditation on the scriptural texts, followed later by careful study and exegesis; it is what FIYH speaks of as reading, listening, praying, study and further reflection. Pondering requires time; it is a period of incubation, when the subconscious can work silently; FIYH names this "letting go."

Ordering is the second movement and aims at determining a homiletic focus.[3] This process involves an "ordering of the ponderings," and will, of necessity, involve a choice of a single focal notion and letting other insights go.

Creating is the shaping of a homiletic text. The movement seeks to give the focus a shape, a form. It is often here that preachers run into a stumbling block.[4]

In this article I will present a variety of homiletic forms or general structures for preaching, fully aware that this list is not a comprehensive catalog. Regarding form, Tom Long notes that the scriptures themselves employ diverse literary forms and points out that "[n]o one form is adequate to display the fullness of the gospel"; each form expresses some aspect of the gospel on a particular occasion.[5] His counsel regarding preaching is wise: "Every sermon form, then, must be custom-tailored to match the particular preaching occasion." How to speak the homiletic word — God's good news — is the result of an interplay of the word spoken and the ones to whom it is said.[6] What follows is a listing of various homiletic forms with comments.

Models

Opposition Model

One strategy for a homiletic form is to allow the opposing forces in a biblical text to be the opposing forces in the sermon. Tom Long puts it this way: "Some biblical texts pit opposing forces, ways of living, or visions of the world against each other, thereby calling upon the reader to make a choice. The sermon can regenerate this conflict and its accompanying call for decision."[7]

Here is one example. Psalm 1 is an uncomplicated presentation of two ways of life, that of the righteous and that of the wicked.[8] The just person is imaged as a fruitful tree, planted by running streams, while the wicked are like chaff, blown away by the wind, "trackless, directionless, doomed."[9] The frenetic non-productive motion of the wicked contrasts with the calm solidity of the just, those who have an inner understanding of God's way.

The effective sermon will not only describe the contrasts, but will recreate the visual and emotional impact of the psalm itself.[10] Which are contemporary images of frenzied ungodly activity? How do they contrast with images of the righteous?

The well-known story of Zaccheus[11] provides another clear example. Toward the end of the narrative the reader is given two starkly contrasting pictures: the annoyed crowd murmuring against Jesus who has gone to "a sinner's house" and the welcoming joyful Zaccheus who is willingly parting with his wealth. Long suggests that these scenes occur simultaneously, rather than sequentially; thus, a successful sermon could engage the congregation in wondering, "Where would I rather be, outside with the crowd or inside with Zaccheus and Jesus?" The sermon would present contemporary examples of the murmuring of the crowd and the changed attitude and action of Zaccheus, leading to the question of with whom the hearers would choose to be.[12]

The presentation of fundamental oppositions, radical antinomies can be an effective sermon strategy, following the basic form of "on the one hand, and on the other." In the case of the Zaccheus narrative, the wise preacher, however, will allow the congregation to feel the tension generated by the recognition that at times we all mimic the behavior of the murmuring crowd as well as of the transformed Zaccheus. In other words, the preacher should not present the murmuring crowd in so woeful a manner that the congregation is let off the hook, as it were, and finds no point of identification with the "bad guys," but identifies completely with a renewed Zaccheus. Realistic preaching takes as a starting point that we are—all of us—both sinful and graced; we are *in via* and in need of on-going conversion.

Antithesis/Paradox Model

Perhaps this second form is actually a subdivision of the first. It is a homiletic form shaped through antitheses or paradoxes. In his "On Catechizing," a brief treatise written in reponse to a request from Deogtatias, a Carthaginian deacon asking advice on the "catechizing of inquirers," Augustine reveals his homiletic flair. Within the discussion of the coming of Christ and the church, "the sixth age," Augustine summarizes his understanding of the good news of Christ, not so much the "facts" of the gospel, but its underlying "meaning," mapped out in a long series of paradoxes.

> [Christ] hungered, he who feeds all.
> He thirsted, he who created all we drink,
> He who spiritually is both the bread of the hungering and the
>   wellspring of the thirsting.
> He became as one dumb and deaf in the presence of revilers,
> He through whom the dumb spoke and the deaf heard.
> He was bound, he who freed us from infirmities' bonds.
> He was scourged, he who drove out every scourge of pain
>   from peoples' bodies.
> He was crucified, he who put an end to all our crosses.
> He died, he who raised the dead to life.[13]

A second example comes from the pen of Augustine; in Sermon 214 he juxtaposed Christ's two births, from the Father and from Mary, stressing the marvel of each.

> This one is from the Father without a mother;
> that one is from a mother without a father;
> this one is outside time,
> that one, in an acceptable time;
> this one is eternal,
> that one, timely;
> this one, in the heart of the Father without a body;
> that one, with a body without violating the virginity
>   of the mother;
> this one [happens] without sex;
> that one [happened] without a man's embrace.[14]

One may question whether the latter example is sufficiently rooted in or tied to a biblical text to be considered biblical preaching. In my opinion it is clearly a development of the "mystery" of Christ's births which is founded on scriptural texts. FIYH offers convincing advice: "The preacher then has a formidable task: to speak from the Scriptures . . . to a gathered congregation in such a way that those assembled will be able to worship God in spirit and truth, and then go forth to love and serve the Lord. . . . The homily is not so much on the Sciptures as from and through them."[15]

This Augustinian excerpt is surely "from and through" the scriptures. Likewise, the *Constitution on the Sacred Liturgy* declares: "The primary source of the sermon, moreover, should be scripture and liturgy, for in them is found the proclamation of God's wonderful works in the history of salvation, the mystery of Christ ever made present and active in us, especially in the celebration of the liturgy."[16] Thus, Augustine is truly proclaiming the *magnalia Dei,* the mystery of Christ celebrated in the liturgies of Christmas.

Augustine, a skilled rhetor tutored in classic rhetoric, may not provide for us immediately "transportable" examples of style. Yet, these illustrations are helpful for considering how one may employ paradox or antithesis in preaching.

Movement Model

Especially useful with narrative texts, the form of the movement model fashions the sermon so that its movements mirror the unfolding of the scriptural narrative.[17] The scriptural path is the homily's route.

David Buttrick gives a full illustration of his handling of the story of the Ten Lepers (Luke 17:11–19) in his masterful work *Homiletic: Moves and Structures.*[18] He outlines the Lukan story as follows:

1. Lepers: "Have pity on us!"

2. Jesus' command: "Go! Show yourselves to the priests."

3. They go and, "it so happened," are healed.

4. One of them returns, glorifying and thanking.

5. Jesus: "Where are the nine?"

6. "Your faith has made you whole."

After a homiletic analysis, Buttrick presents a possible structure for a narrative sermon:

1. The lepers cried "Have pity!" and we can understand.

2. How does Jesus answer? With a commandment, "Go!" Isn't that just like God?

3. Well, they went: Faith is doing the word of Jesus Christ.

4. But if faith is only obedience, it can turn into dead law.

5. One came back to worship: Christian worship gives thanks.

6. So the Christian life is both obedient faith and worship.

Notice that the narrative movement of the scriptural text is replicated in the homiletic structure. This structure is then enfleshed using analogs of congregational experience.

While this parallelism of scriptural text movement and homiletic movement is especially "user-friendly" for narrative texts, it can also be used for non-narrative texts. Every text has its own inner logic and thus has a "movement." Sometimes the preacher will need to rearrange the elements in the reading for the sake of clarity or for effectiveness. Consider the brief text: "For God so loved the world that he gave his only Son, so that everyone who believes in him may not perish but may have eternal life" (John 3:16, NRSV). The text may be arranged in different fashions:

1. God loved the world.

2. As a result, God gave his only Son.

3. Whoever believes in the Son will have eternal life, not perdition.

1. Because God loved the world,

2. God gave an only Son

3. who gives eternal life to believers.

What is important in this outlining process is to make the connections seen in the grammatical conjunctions clear, so that the preacher can see the inner logic of the non-narrative text.

Consider the second reading for the feast of Pentecost:

> [3][N]o one can say "Jesus is Lord" except by the Holy Spirit.
> [4] Now there are varieties of gifts, but the same Spirit; [5]and
> there are varieties of services, but the same Lord; [6]and there are
> varieties of activities, but it is the same God who activates
> all of them in everyone. [7]To each is given the manifestation of
> the Spirit for the common good. [12]For just as the body is one

John Allyn Melloh, SM

and has many members, and all the members of the body, though many, are one body, so it is with Christ. [13]For in the one Spirit we were all baptized into one body—Jews or Greeks, slaves or free—and we were all made to drink of one Spirit. (1 Corinthians 12:3b–7, 12–13 NRSV).

The movement of the text is as follows:

1. No one can say "Jesus is Lord" except by the Holy Spirit, that is, as a result of the Spirit's power.

2. There are varieties of gifts/services/activities, but the same Spirit/Lord/God. God activates gifts/services/activities in each. [Varieties vs. same/unity; God is active in each]

3. Manifestations of the Spirit are given to each for common good. [Different manifestations in each, but given for common good.]

4. Physical body has many members, but is one; Body of Christ has many members, but is one. [An analogy: Variety vs. unity]

5. Different people are baptized into the one same Body, by the one same Spirit; drink the same Spirit drink. (v. 13) [An argument: Differences transcended by Spirit's action]

The above may be organized in various ways to provide a narrative outline, that is, an outline of key theological statements drawn from the scripture and arranged sequentially. Here is one possibility:

God is active in each person, bestowing a variety of gifts,
  (v. 4–6)
which are given for the common good, (v. 7)
which is preserved by the Spirit's action (v. 12–13)
manifested in baptism into the Body of Christ (v. 13)
and manifested in the proclamation "Jesus is Lord" (v. 3).

Thus, the movement model, which takes the scriptural logic as homiletic outline, can be used with both narrative and non-narrative texts.

Transformation Model

What makes a story (or any text, for that matter) interesting is change or transformation. What has made folktales or Grimm's fairy tales so captivating are the transformations (often conflict, followed by resolution) that take place in each story—Cinderella is married to the prince; Hansel and Gretel return safely to their father; Snow White is befriended by the dwarfs and becomes queen, and so on.

Similarly, biblical texts often center around a significant change or transformation. The preacher can shape the homily by exploring the dynamics of transformation within the text. This model zeroes in on the central transformation, while the previous model takes the entirety of the movement of a text.

The Geresene demoniac (Mark 5:1–20) provides an illustrative example. The initial verses set the scene—a demon-possessed man living among the tombs, no longer able to be restrained with shackles, spends night and day howling and bruising himself. Seeing Jesus from a distance, he runs to meet him and bows down. Jesus commands the unclean spirit to depart and the demoniac addresses Jesus as the "Son of the Most High God." After the unclean spirits depart, the cured man begs to go with Jesus, but Jesus commands him to go to his family and proclaim how much the Lord has done for him. This he does in the Decapolis.

Quite simply the story begins with a possessed man and ends with a rescued individual. If one considers, for example, the topographical dimensions of the text, the man's movement is from the tombs, to an encounter with Jesus, to the Decapolis. This topographical movement could itself provide an outline for considering the dynamics of transformation. The preacher may consider titling this sermon "From the tombs to the Decapolis."[19] The first consideration would be the "tombs": What are the tombs in which we live? What makes our own existence like that of the demoniac? What are the "dead bones" in our lives?

The second consideration is the encounter with Jesus: Where do we encounter Jesus? How do we "bow down" before him? How do we address him? What are our types of encounters with Jesus?

The third consideration is the result of our transformation: Where are we sent? How do we proclaim how much the Lord has done for us?

The questions listed above are not meant to be a "quiz for the preacher," but are offered to stimulate reflection on the transformation dynamics of the biblical text. The resulting homily would have a tri-partite structure: from tombs, to Jesus, to the Ten Cities (Decapolis).

The Plot Model

Eugene Lowry strongly adheres to the notion that the sermon is an "event-in-time."[20] Unfortunately older sermonic models presumed a spatial metaphor: that the sermon is an assemblage of parts, logically connected. Thus sermon writing is a work of "construction." Lowry attends more to the temporal dimension and sees the process of sermon preparation as "development"; thus the sermon is a narrative art form:

> [A] sermon is a plot (premeditated by the preacher) which has as its key ingredient a sensed discrepancy, a homiletical bind. Something is "up in the air" — an issue not resolved. Like any good storyteller, the preacher's task is to "bring the folks home" — that is, resolve matters in the light of the gospel and in the presence of the people.[21]

For Lowry there is a basic shape to the "plotted sermon." It consists of five elements which he has playfully termed: oops!, ugh!, aha!, whee!, yeah!. The first, "oops," is an upsetting of the equilibrium; it is analogous to the introduction or tension or conflict in the opening scenes of a play. Its purpose is to "trigger ambiguity in the listeners' minds."

The second, "ugh," is analyzing the discrepancy; it is a diagnostic wrestling with the problem:

> The actual process of diagnosis/analysis in the preparation stage of a sermon is relatively easy to state and difficult to effect. Simply, it is to ask why and not be content with your asnwers. As you continue to reject each answer with another why you will find increasing depth in your analysis. . . . [22]

Disclosing the clue to resolution, "aha," is the third stage. During the analysis stage, "often there comes a revelatory sense of receipt — and you know you 'have it.' When that moment occurs you will have advanced to stage three in the sermonic plot. . . ."[23] Often the revelatory insight is not what was expected, comes from where one wasn't looking and turns things upside down. Like the parables of Jesus, the "aha" is often a reversal of the presumed.

Stage four, "whee," is the experiencing of the gospel, allowing the efficacious Word of God to do its work. If the preacher has attended carefully to the previous two stages, then the gospel will be experienced.

The last stage, "yeah," is anticipating the consequences. The preacher now asks, "What — in light of this intersection of human condition with gospel — can be expected, should be done or is now possible?"[24] Lowry is not suggesting that the preacher offer prescriptions, but that, in light of the gospel proclamation which has indeed created a new situation in the lives of hearers,[25] the preacher can reflect on choices that could never have been made before.

Eugene Lowry's sermon "Swept Upstream"[26] is based on the anointing of Jesus in the house of Simon the leper (Mark 14: 1–10). The manuscript reveals the "plot" structure of the sermon.

1. Upset the equilibrium: Not an ordinary dinner party, but a "pre-execution dinner of somber farewell."

2. Analyze the discrepancy: Why was the alabaster jar's ointment wasted? It could have been given to the poor. The woman is reproached. Yet Jesus shocks the guests even more — no rebuke.

3. Disclose a clue to resolution: "Leave her alone! She has anointed my body beforehand for burial."

4. Experience the gospel: Jesus' logic was not understood, nor was the woman's gracious act. While the guests didn't see grace at work, the woman had "done what she could."

5. Anticipate the consequences: What she did will be told in memory of her, a "woman — swept upstream with gratitude."

While this model has an affinity for narrative texts, non-narrative texts can also be arranged using the plotted structure.

Narrative and Story

A second-grader was asked what a story is. She said, "It just begins, it moves right along, something happens and then it ends."[27] Actually her definition is a fine description of what effective preaching is — it begins immediately, moves along, something happens and then it ends. Thus, to a certain extent, preaching can be described as story-telling according to our second-grader's definition.

Unfortunately today the notion that preaching is story-telling often gets translated into "Good preaching always includes a story," a very questionable position. Sometimes a good story can be illustrative of God's word proclaimed, and it is true that good stories are engaging. Yet effective preaching does not demand that a story be part of the sermon development. In fact, laboring under the illusion that contemporary preaching is story-centered can militate against good preaching. First, it would be extremely difficult — well-nigh impossible — to find a story each week that captures effectively the message of God's word. As a result, stories that don't quite fit are inserted to hold the congregation's attention; they may hold attention but don't contribute to the proclamation of God's word. Second, lengthy stories tend to take on a life of their own. Consequently rather than helping to exegete God's word, they become the focus of the preaching and are themselves exegeted.

In his *How to Preach a Parable*, Eugene Lowry identifies four narrative sermon designs which he calls running the story, delaying the story, suspending the story and alternating the story.[28] Lowry, however, is speaking of the biblical story and not stories imported into the sermon.[29]

Generally speaking, a story-like sermon can be quite effective without the importation of stories into the sermon. Shorter anecdotes or illustrations can serve the proclamation of God's Word better than a lengthy or ill-fitting story.

Central Image Model[30]

FIYH notes that "[t]he more we turn to the picture language of the poet and the storyteller, the more we will be able to preach in a way that invites people to respond from the heart as well as from the mind."[31] In a similar vein, Elizabeth Achtemeier writes that "if we want to change someone's life from non-Christian to Christian, from dying to living, from despairing to hoping, from anxious to certain, from corrupted to whole, we must change the images, the imaginations of the heart."[32]

Advertisers have long known the power of the image to shape people's lives—for better or for worse. Today's preacher would do well to attend to the power of the image. Images within the sermon are not ancillary or merely decorative; they are bearers of theological freight, since images contain within them the conceptual. No less a homiletician than David Buttrick notes that "[h]omiletic thinking is always a thinking of theology toward images."[33] In fact an entire sermon can be an exploration of a central scriptural image.

"Imaginal preaching takes seriously Jung's statement that concepts are coined and negotiable, but images are life. If we wish to sustain life in the world, one way is to cultivate the images that will give life."[34] James Wallace provides some general rules for exploring the image.

First of all, stick to the image. Don't seek to reduce the image to allegory or view it as a symbol pointing to something else. Often preachers will read a text hastily because it's familiar—and so the parable of the prodigal son is about forgiveness or the Zaccheus story is about saving the lost. But to attend to the image in its precise formulation is to try to see, hear, feel and even smell it so that new awareness will burst forth.

Wallace relates that in trying to attend to the text of the good Samaritan (Luke 10:25–37), he became aware of that pivotal moment in the parable which hinges on a slight movement of body:

> The priest and Levite looked and passed by on the other side; the Samaritan looked and *approached* him. It all hinged on that simple movement, a pivotal turn toward the other. This kind of detail is what makes the talk memorable. It awakens and invites play. How did he approach? Did he go by, then hesitate before moving toward, or move immediately toward the body lying on the road, or . . . ? That simple act of approaching the other became the simple image that fired my imagination and drew me into the story in a fresh way.[35]

Second, twist the image.[36] Twisting is another way of speaking of playing with the image. It is not being unfaithful to the image, just as in retelling any story there are variations in the details. In a workshop on storytelling, participants were asked to tell a story from the point of view of one of the objects. Wallace had chosen to tell the story of David's receiving word of the death of his son Absolom:

> In the retelling I imagined the scene of David pacing up and down in the courtyard of the palace, awaiting word of what had happened to Absolom. This time I imagined myself as a set of steps that led up to his private quarters. I became these steps with a view of the pacing king, but also gifted with its own memories. I recalled how it used to feel to have the feet of the king's children—Absolom, Tamar, and Amnon—fall upon me as they raced up to greet their father, and of the weight of the king himself at different times of his life, times of success and failure . . . [37]

The exercise took the story and twisted it, but it made the story of David and his grief more real; that would not have occurred without the seeing, hearing and feeling of the event, Wallace asserts.

Third, craft the image.[38] Crafting is an act of making, a *poesis*. One enters into active engagement with the image and eventually crafts it in words.[39] An image well-crafted can draw others into its world with astonishing results—the soul can be awakened, cultivated and engaged, because images are truly living presences that mediate mystery.

A student working on a master's of divinity degree who had been working as director of religious education for primary school children prepared a sermon for the occasion of First Communion for second- and third-graders. The text to be proclaimed was the Pauline institution narrative (1 Corinthians 11:23–26). During the previous week, the children had baked bread and this experience became the foundation for the preaching, with the image of the mixing bowl being central.

I shall reconstruct the main outline of the preaching, in no way doing justice to what I consider one of the best homilies for children I have ever heard. The following is not a transcription; also during the preaching there were interactions with the hearers, such as responses to some of the questions.

> This week we all baked bread. What was your favorite part? Mine was always mixing. Some of you told me you liked to measure or add the water. . . . But everyone liked baking bread together. Have you ever been to the Great Harvest bakery? They

always have samples of bread for you and they say they don't care if you buy their bread, they just want to share some with you. They have a big sign on the wall: "There's nothing a baker likes better than to share bread with others."

I know you have done a lot of thinking and studying and praying about this Holy Bread, this communion bread. . . . Let's for a moment imagine that God decides to make bread and turns this church into a giant mixing bowl. Now I know you can imagine this, but you may have to help your parents and friends here to imagine. So we're all in this mixing bowl together and it doesn't matter how many are here because two or three would even be enough for God to make bread out of us. And God pours water on us — oh, God doesn't have to measure it, because, well, God is God. And that water is just like the water poured on us at baptism. Imagine! God knew even then — at our baptism — that God was going to make bread out of us. And we're getting stuck together; it doesn't matter if we're boys or girls, thin or fat, black or brown or red or white or yellow; it just matters that we're together. And God mixes and stirs and stretches the dough and we feel the gentle tugs as God turns us into bread. And then we're ready for the oven. Oh, don't be afraid — it won't hurt. It's like the fire of the Holy Spirit, the fire of God's love for us. And God waits and waits . . . and then we come out of the oven, all golden brown and warm and toasty and smelling wonderful!

And then what does God do? Well, remember what the baker likes to do best? Yes, that's right — share the bread. God wants to share us — this bread — with others. What does that mean? Well, it means that we have to be nice to one another, even if somebody is mean to us, we have to listen to the older people, we have to take care of people who are hungry or need clothes. And that would be very hard, if we were alone. But remember, we're all together in this mixing bowl; we're all together to be shared together.

And do you know what God does then? God takes this wonderful loaf of bread, and hands it to Jesus. And Jesus takes this bread and raises it up and says: "This is my Body."

What this gifted student had done — even if not consciously — was to follow the three rules above: stick with the image, twist the image, craft the image. The central image carried the theological freight of the homily. Through the exploration of the image, one quite available to the hearers, the preacher had a solidly doctrinal homily that provided an appropriate challenge to living.[40]

Mystagogical Model

Because of its baptismal practice, the fourth century witnessed the development of mystagogical preaching, preaching directed to the newly baptized, with the goal of probing the initiatory experience more deeply. The catecheses of Ambrose of Milan, Augustine, John Chrysostom and Theodore of Mopsuestia seek to break open the word proclaimed and the word enacted, that is, the sacramental rituals. Reading through these catecheses may leave today's preacher wondering if this model can be rehabilitated for twentieth-century hearers. The publication of William Harmless's excellent volume, *Augustine and the Catechumenate*,[41] gives an affirmative answer. I can do no better than to quote Harmless at length.

> In practice, the art of mystagogy is a good deal simpler than one might think. One way is to begin with a liturgical symbol: for instance, the baptismal water. One then free-associates to gather scriptural stories: the waters of creation, Noah's ark, the Red Sea, Christ walking on the water, the woman at the well, etc. One then repeats the same process, but focuses on how water appears in natural settings; spring rains, snow on mountains, salmon leaping upstream, dolphins swimming in the ocean, etc. One then repeats this a third time, focusing on water experiences in the local culture: turning on tap water, taking a shower, nearly drowning in a lake, polluting a stream with chemicals, etc. In this way, one assembles a whole reservoir of biblical, natural and cultural images. One then probes each in terms of baptism so that it appears either as a type or antitype. For example: "Christ bathes us in baptism's pure waters, not in some polluted stream, for he desires from us not polluted lives, but pure ones"; "Just as salmon struggle up mountain streams to return to their birthplace, so too Christians struggle up a baptismal stream to their birthplace in Christ"; "Both dolphins and Christians swim in depths over their heads, dolphins in the depths of an ocean, Christians in the depths of God's love."[42]
>
> Mystagogy moves by a logic more associative than discursive, more poetic than philosophical. This logic is not its only salient

feature. There is another: a preference for surplus, whether a surplus of cultural images or scriptural echoes or both. The mystagogue tends to let these images and echoes pile up so that the meanings cluster and set off vibrations among themselves. . . . This method is thus a way of telling the truth about mystery: that a mystery can be pointed to, hinted at, even glimpsed, but it cannot be defined or exhausted.[43]

Emotion or Mood Model

The rhetorical effects of a proclaimed text are multiple. Texts communicate an emotional tone and generate certain feelings in the hearers. Tom Long suggests the possibility of allowing the mood of the text to set the mood of the homily.[44] Psalm 150 or Revelation 19 creates a joy-filled, high-pitched mood of thunderous paeans of praise, in contrast to the quiet "come let us reason together" spirit of 1 Corinthians 10:14–22. Psalm 22, used on Good Friday, is a cry of lament, while Mary's Magnificat (Luke 1:46–55) is a shout of praise to the God who ushers in a new age.

An example of this type of preaching can be found in the funeral of Sister Thea Bowman, FSPA. By the time of Thea's death after a lengthy bout with cancer, she had become a well-known educator, catechist and preaching teacher, and not only in the Roman Catholic community; she had been interviewed on CBS's "60 Minutes" by Mike Wallace. The following is a transcribed excerpt of a preaching event which took place as part of the introductory rites of the funeral.

> There's a man whom I'd know gave water
>   the substance of wine.
> There's a woman whom I'd know gave existence
>   the substance of essence.
> There's a man whom I'd know fed five thousand people.
> There's a woman whom I'd know fed us spiritual nourishment.
> There's a man whom I'd know challenged the people
>   of his day.
> There's a woman whom I'd know challenged the people
>   of her day.
> There's a man whom I'd know changed people's name.
> There's a woman whom I'd know allowed us to bear the
>   name "black" and "catholic."

> There's a man whom I'd know whose mother said
>   "My being proclaims the greatness of the Lord."
> There's a woman whom I'd know who is our mother,
>   whose being proclaimed the greatness of the Lord.
> There's a man whom I'd know called forth disciples.
> There's a woman whom I'd know called us forth
>   to discipleship.
> There's a man whom I'd know who asked that this bitter cup
>   be taken away.
> There's a woman whom I'd know who drank
>   of that bitter cup.
> There's a man whom I'd know who is from Galilee.
> There's a woman whom I'd know who is from Canton.
> Now they look into each other's eyes, and this man from
>   Galilee is telling this woman from Canton: "Well done,
>   well done, well done!"

Of course, this transcription does not capture the evident passion of the preacher, nor the rhythm of his speech, nor the applause and acclamations from the congregation. The manner of delivery made this simple proclamation a joyous shout of praise, celebrating a life lived according to gospel values.

Focus Statement Model

In the introduction to this article, I described the movements of homily preparation as pondering, ordering and creating. In a previous article, I attended especially to the first two movements — pondering and ordering.[45] Here I would like to mention that a well-formed "focus statement" — the result of the process of ordering — can provide an initial homiletic outline or form.

In examining the temptation narrative (Mark 1:12–13) using a process of structural exegesis, the article suggested several focus statements. Given the fact that this narrative occurs on the First Sunday of Lent (Year B), when the catechumens are "elected" by the community for the Easter sacraments (when they will become beloved sons and daughters), the preacher may arrive at this focus statement: "When beloved sons and daughters are Spirit-driven into their deserts of temptation, then angels minister to them."

This focus statement easily yields a homiletic form which expresses a life movement — from "being Spirit-driven into deserts of temptation" to "being ministered to angelically." The homily could be arranged into three considerations: How are we Spirit-driven into deserts of temptation? What is the landscape of these deserts? Who are the angels who minister to beloved sons and daughters? Admittedly this is a bare-bones sketch, but it is a clear starting point for the homily.[46]

Conclusion

This article has attempted to provide some models for creating the homiletic manuscript. The models are not to be interpreted as rigid structures, sermonic straightjackets, but rather viewed as heuristic devices to provide some guidance for shaping the sermon. While FIYH provides some assistance for drafting and revising the homiletic manuscript, this article is geared toward helping preachers, once they have a homiletic insight, a sermonic "aha," a focus statement, to move forward in the creative process.

1. The Bishops' Committee on Priestly Life and Ministry (Washington: NCCB, 1982). Hereafter FIYH.

2. In this article I do not intend to discuss the pros and cons of the use of a manuscript while preaching. I find Gerard Sloyan's advice crucial: "If a script is your enemy, do not allow it to get near the pulpit. But if there never was a script, do not let yourself get near the pulpit." Gerard S. Sloyan, *Worshipful Preaching* (Philadelphia: Fortress, 1984), 23.

3. Thomas G. Long makes a useful distinction between focus and function. "A focus statement is a concise description of the central, controlling and unifying theme of the sermon. In short, this is what the whole sermon will be 'about.' A function statement is a description of what the preacher hopes the sermon will create or cause to happen for the hearers. . . . The function statement names the hoped-for change." *The Witness of Preaching* (Louisville: Westminster/John Knox, 1989), 89. Hereafter *Witness*.

4. After having given a class presentation on some ways of creating a homily, Rev. Craig Satterlee, a graduate student in liturgical studies, mentioned how helpful the presentation was and how little attention is generally given to this aspect. His remark spurred this article.

John Allyn Melloh, sm

5. Long, *Witness,* 105.

6. Ibid. Cf. also FIYH, Chapter I.

7. Thomas G. Long, *Preaching and the Literary Forms of the Bible* (Philadelphia: Fortress, 1989), 132. Hereafter *Preaching.*

8. Cf. Robert Alter, *The Art of Biblical Poetry* (New York: Basic Books 1985), 115–118; Walter Vogels, "A Structural Analysis of Psalm 1," *Biblica* 60 (1979): 410–416, for interesting exegetical insights.

9. Alter, 117.

10. Long, *Preaching,* 51.

11. Cf. Walter Vogels, "Structural Analysis and Pastoral Work," *Lumen Vitae* 33 (1978): 482–492, and *Reading and Preaching the Bible: A New Semiotic Approach* (Wilmington, DE: Michael Glazier, 1986), 148–164, for an analysis of Luke 19:1–10.

12. Long, *Preaching,* 132.

13. *De catechizandis rudibus* 22.40. Translation by William Harmless, *Augustine and the Catechumenate* (Collegeville: The Liturgical Press, 1995), 146–147.

14. *Sermo* 214.6. Harmless, *Augustine and the Catechumenate,* 280.

15. FIYH, 19, 20. Emphasis added.

16. CSL, 35.2. Austin Flannery, op, ed. *Vatican Council II: The Basic Sixteen Documents* (Northport, NY: Costello, 1996), 130.

17. Long, *Preaching,* 128.

18. David G. Buttrick, *Homiletic* (Philadelphia: Fortress, 1987), 335–347.

19. I strongly suggest to students that they title each homily. If one can title a homily, there is a good chance that the homily will have a clear focus.

20. Eugene L. Lowry, *The Homiletical Plot: The Sermon as Narrative Art Form* (Atlanta: John Knox, 1980), 12.

21. Lowry, 15.

22. Lowry, 42.

23. Lowry, 42.

24. Lowry, 67.

25. Lowry, 72.

26. Richard L. Eslinger, *A New Hearing: Living Options in Homiletic Method* (Nashville: Abingdon, 1987), 89–93.

27. I believe that I read this years ago but have forgotten where.

28. Eugene L. Lowry, *How to Preach a Parable: Designs for Narrative Sermons* (Nashville: Abingdon, 1989), 38.

29. "Running the story" is following the actual flow of the biblical passage. "Delaying the story" allows the introduction of other material before taking up the biblical sequencing. "Suspending the story" is a temporary leaving of the biblical text in the middle of the story; this technique could be for the purpose of pursuing a related notion. "Alternating the story" typically takes an episodic approach to the biblical passage and fleshes out each aspect with other material.

30. Thomas H. Troeger's *Imagining a Sermon* (Nashville: Abingdon, 1990) is an especially fine preaching resource.

31. FIYH, 25.

32. Elizabeth Achtemeier, *Creative Preaching* (Nashville: Abindgon, 1981), 24.

33. Buttrick, 29.

34. James A. Wallace, *Imaginal Preaching: An Archetypal Perspective.* (New York and Mahwah, NJ: Paulist Press, 1995), 30.

35. Wallace, 32.

36. Wallace, 32–33.

37. Wallace, 33.

38. Wallace, 33–34.

39. The crafting of the image can initially be done in other media. One very effective student homily on the Widow of Nain resulted from her having sketched the burial procession; she showed me the stetch and told me that she could not see the woman's face — and in the sketch it was hidden, head bowed and totally downcast. That image was the central focus of her fine homily.

40. Cf. Augustine's sermons which use the baking metaphor: *Sermo* 229.1; *Sermo* 227, *Sermo* 229A.2. The student homily was a modern revision of Augustine's mystagogical preaching.

41. Cf. note 12. Cf. also my review in *Augustinian Studies.*

42. Harmless, 365–366. Cf. 365–366 for an illustration of preaching on a liturgical text.

43. Harmless, 367.

44. Long, *Preaching,* 134.

45. John Allyn Melloh, "Homily Preparation: A Structural Approach" *Liturgical Ministry* 1 (1992): 21–26.

46. This homily could be fleshed out by using the Antithesis/Paradox model or the Plotting Model or the Narrative Movement model.

As One to Worship God

Throughout our time together at the conference,
poet Kathleen Norris spoke as we gathered for worship.
Here are the thoughts that Kathleen shared with us during the week.

Monday Night

I'd like to welcome you home. That may sound strange, as many of us have just traveled from home to get here. But we have gathered as one to worship God, and that means we're home. Home, as the saying goes, is the place where they have to take you in. And worship is like that; there is no one who is not welcome in God's house. (Now I am speaking as a small-c catholic.)

When we come together like this to pray as one, we come, as God knows us, with all our differences, our strengths and weaknesses, our various experiences and perspectives. And God lets us sing and listen and pray as one.

The miracle of the worshiping body — the body of Christ for that matter — is that it is not a gathering of like-minded people, or those with a high degree of faith or knowledge concerning spiritual matters; I like to think that it resembles Christ's diverse group of disciples in this manner . . .

But when we gather to worship, it's because we're responding to love, because God first loved us. We come to find the God who has promised to meet us here, the God who met Moses on the mountain and promised that worship would be a sign of God's presence to the people. Aidan Kavanagh says of Moses' theophany, "It was a Presence, not faith, which drew Moses to the burning bush. And what happened there was a revelation, not a seminar."

We will have our seminars and our lectures this week; in their own way, they will make us more aware of God's work in our lives, and give us strength for our ministry. But our worship will be other—here, we will not examine and theorize and explain, but experience God's presence through poetry, song and the words of scripture.

I should confess to you that I come here out of the Presbyterian tradition, where worship often does feel like a seminar. And I know of churches within my tradition where people are welcomed to membership and to communion only if the pastor and council of elders are convinced that they have "true saving faith." (Of course the pretense to a uniform agreement on exactly what constitutes "true saving faith" is risky, because even one disagreement can lead quickly to schism.)

As a member of a church that came out of schism, I have a healthy respect for the ability of worship to allow us, as Christians, to celebrate both our unity and our lack of uniformity. Here we are: an unlikely, motley crew that has happened to gathered here, this week, in this church. Let us respond to God's presence among us by welcoming each other home. Let us remain always open to what God wishes to reveal to us. Amen.

Tuesday Morning

According to Genesis, the creation was a daily process. Each day, God spoke more and more into being, and then, it seems, let it all sit until the next day. Our very bodies, our lives, still reflect these daily rhythms of creation, and morning prayer reminds us, powerfully, of our need to renew, remember, recommit to the process of creation in our selves. Those of you who are not "morning people" know how hard this can be. Those of us who are subject to depression know that just getting up in the morning can be the greatest challenge of the day.

Worship, it seems to me, is *primary* theology, the fertile ground out of which our theories and ideas—and to use a dauntingly sober word I seldom use, except in jest, our "hermeneutics"—can grow. Morning worship is also primal, as primal as creation. But it can be

Kathleen Norris

a hard discipline to keep; it can feel useless, not nearly as important, in our workaholic culture, as getting about one's business early in the day. Worship is useless, on the surface, but also absolutely necessary. It places us again in God's creation.

When we despair of worship, when the wonder of God's creation and our place in it is lost to us, it's often because we've lost sight of our true role. We've tried to do too much, we pretend to be in control of things so that we don't feel useless. We lose sight of God's play with creation.

I'll close with a poem by Mark Van Doren, "Morning Worship," in which he finds that, coming up against the limits of language and human creativity, he comes into the presence of the holy, and can take his place again in the blessed dailyness of life.

Morning Worship

I wake and hear it raining.
Were I dead, what would I give
Lazily to lie here,
Like this, and live?

Or better yet: birdsong,
Brightening and spreading —
How far would I come then
To be at the world's wedding?

Now that I lie, though,
Listening, living,
(Oh, but not forever,
Oh, end arriving)

How shall I praise them:
All the sweet beings
Eternally that outlive
Me and my dying?

Mountains, I mean; wind, water, air;
Grass, and huge trees; clouds, flowers,
And thunder, and night.

Turtles, I mean, and toads; hawks, herons, owls;
Graveyards, and towns, and trout; roads, gardens,
Red berries, and deer.

Lightning, I mean, and eagles; fences; snow;
Sunrise, and ferns; waterfalls, serpents,
Green islands, and sleep.

Horses, I mean; butterflies, whales;
Mosses, and stars; and gravelly
Rivers, and fruit.

Oceans, I mean; black valleys; corn;
Brambles, and cliffs; rock, dirt, dust, ice;
And warnings of flood.

How shall I name them?
And in what order?
Each would be first.
Omission is murder.

Maidens, I mean, and apples; needles; leaves;
Worms, and planets, and clover; whirlwinds; dew;
Bulls; geese —

Stop. Lie still.
You will never be done.
Leave them all there,
Old lover. Live on.

Tuesday Night

As I did last evening, I'll begin by saying, "Welcome home." Welcome back to worship. Travel generates a low-level anxiety in many of us. We fear becoming lost, losing our sense of not only where, but who we are. Home is our safe place, the place that gives us room to grow.

But we can also make home *small*; it can be our escape from change, and from a world full of other people who might not respect the myths we've constructed around us. Home in this sense is a place where we'll trade God's purpose "in the fullness of time" in order to feel secure and comfortable in the here and now.

We all know what happens, in worship, when worship leaders grow too much at home. Instead of ministering with music, the cantor emotes and performs; the preacher emotes as well, often indulging

Kathleen Norris

in self-analysis to such a degree that the Word of God is cast aside. A writer friend of mine told me of an Easter Sunday Mass he attended this spring, at which the homily consisted of a lengthy story about a fishing trip.

The pastor had fretted over whether or not to go, and when he overcame his reluctance, he went and had a great time. He reported all of this as an example of one of the "small miracles" available to us in our daily lives. I doubt that this priest meant to suggest that the resurrection is a "small miracle," but that, in effect, is what he said. And my friend went home disedified.

Especially now that our Christian churches threaten to become as polarized as the rest of American society, we need to take special care with our worship, focusing always on Christ, who really does unite all things in heaven and on earth. Sitting with scripture, letting its images and stories work on us, might be a place to start. I can refer you to the story of Emmaus.

I suspect that every age, for the Christian church, has been a time of high risk, of both innovation and resistance to change. Our contemporary, often heated discussion of what constitutes tradition is an ancient one. What can we do when mere myths and ideologies, and fear itself, threaten to diminish our worship? Maybe what poets do— look at what's around us, focus hard on the concrete and specific, and begin to *name*. We may find, as the ancient psalmist did, that contemplating our ultimate fear, the fear of death, can lead us into praise. Here is a modern psalm by Anne Porter, entitled "Leavetaking."

Leavetaking

Nearing the start of that mysterious last season
Which brings us to the close of the other four,
I'm somewhat afraid and don't know how to prepare
So I will praise you.

I will praise you for the glaze on buttercups
And for the pearly scent of wild fresh water
And the great crossbow shapes of swans flying over
With that strong silken threshing sound of wings
Which you gave them when you made them without voices.

And I will praise you for crickets.
On starry autumn nights
When the earth is cooling
Their rusty diminuitive music
Repeated over and over
Is the very marrow of peace.

And I praise you for crows calling from tree-tops
The speech of my first village,
And for the sparrow's flash of song
Flinging me in an instant
The joy of a child who woke
Each morning to the freedom
Of her mother's unclouded love
And lived in it like a country.

And I praise you that from vacant lots
From only broken glass and candy wrappers
Your raise up the blue chicory flowers.

I thank you for that secret praise
Which burns in every creature,
And I ask you to bring us to life
Out of every sort of death

And teach us mercy.

Wednesday Morning

Here we are, again, gathered to praise God, to sing, to sit together in
silence, to receive a blessing—all precious things in this world. When
I first began attending church regularly after some twenty years away,
the fact that I could receive a blessing, just for showing up, seemed
a miracle.

And it still does. Communal worship *is* a miracle, *always*. That
other people are willing to join us like this is simply a wonder. Our
worship makes no sense, culturally speaking; it doesn't seem to be
adding much to the gross national product. In a society in which, we
are told, time is money, worship seems worse than useless, a waste of
time. Alleluia.

Kathleen Norris

In worship, we come together as disparate people to find a unity far greater than the sum of ourselves. We don't have much control over what happens here; recklessly, we let loose the sounds of hymns, the words of psalms, canticles and prayers. We cast them out into the world, into each human heart, to do the work of God. To paraphrase the prophet Isaiah, such a word bears real fruit in God's kingdom. Reaching into our lives, it fulfills the purpose for which God sent it. Isaiah uses the metaphor of rain to convey this, rain that disappears into the ground for a time, so that we can't see it working. And then, it bears abundantly.

Yesterday I stated that worship is primary theology, and I want to make it clear that I mean that literally. The whole reason that I am here today, preaching, is because worship itself converted me. It wasn't theology, studying a catechism or receiving instruction—all that good stuff came later.

I began to learn, or re-learn, my Christian heritage in a traditional, tribal way—by being present at the ceremonies. When I first encountered a Benedictine monastery, I found that the fact that I was so drawn to their worship interested the monks much more than my considerable doubts, and also my ignorance. I remember startling one monk by asking him what Pentecost *was*. I began to learn by attending the liturgies for the feast.

Our worship is never as perfect, as beautiful, as we'd like to make it. And that's a good thing. Our perfectionism would not leave enough room for the Holy Spirit. Perfect worship might not be hospitable enough to welcome a confused, imperfect soul such as myself.

Once, a mistake in worship, a carelessness in the order of worship—a real liturgist's nightmare—proved to be a blessing for me. I'd been struggling for the better part of a week with an essay about the prophet Jeremiah. I'd had the extraordinary experience of listening to him during morning prayer over two months at Saint John's. And then, back home, at Spencer Presbyterian one Sunday morning, I heard Jeremiah's anguished cry: "Is there no balm in Gilead? No physician there?" answered by the children's choir doing a remarkably enthusiastic rendition of "Jesus Wants Me for a Sunbeam," a song I remembered singing as a child. All I could think of was that God definitely did not want Jeremiah for a sunbeam.

I'd been hopelessly stuck in my essay, writing about the paradoxical nature of a call, and what it means to answer a call, as a prophet, a poet, a priest, whatever. Walking home from church, laughing out loud, I knew that I could finish that essay. I'd been led to a place I never expected to be. I looked in an old notebook to discover that the day we had stopped reading from Jeremiah at Saint John's was a feast day, something I'd since forgotten. Here is what I wrote:

> All that fall, when Jeremiah's grief and my own impossible situation cast me into deep loneliness, I was grateful to be sustained by the liturgy that had brought me to Jeremiah and insisted that I listen to him.
>
> And on the feast of Saint John Lateran, in early November, a feast commemorating the dedication of a Roman basilica erected by the Emperor Constantine, and traditionally referred to as "the mother church of Christendom," the words of Psalm 46 — "God is within, it cannot be shaken" — suddenly revealed God to me as a place, both without and within.

In my notebook I had written:

"In naming myself as a 'necessary other,' I finally accept the cross of myself, a burden I've carried ever since childhood, and felt so acutely in my teens: the cross of difference, of being outside, always other. But now, I am free to take it on. It seems appropriate, on this feast."

At morning prayer, we heard these words from the Letter to the Ephesians, chapter 2:

> So you are no longer strangers and aliens, but you are citizens with the saints and also members of the household of God, built upon the foundation of the apostles and prophets, with Christ Jesus as the cornerstone.

"The altar gleamed, bone-white, before the dark wood of the monks' choir, and I could dare to conceive of the church as refuge, a place to find the divided self made whole, the voice of the mocker overcome by that of the advocate. It is still a sinful church — how could it be otherwise? — but the words of its prophets and apostles had led me to this sanctuary, and I could dare to imagine it as home, a place where there is no 'other.'"

Welcome home.

Alan J. Hommerding

Liturgical Music: Traditional Treasure, Contemporary Challenge

Author's note: This session took the form of a guided discussion about liturgical music in the United States during the generation following Vatican Council II. Input came from participants in the session as we discussed changes in liturgy and ecclesiology and new developments and insights since the writing of *Sacrosanctum Concilium* and *Music in Catholic Worship,* among others. This article, while based on the group's discussion, does not literally or comprehensively represent its order nor content

Introduction

Liturgical music in the United States since the promulgation of *Sacrosanctum Concilium* has certainly gone through a time marked by tension, growth, despair, experimentation, alienation, reconciliation and hope. There are few, if any, liturgical musicians who have ministered to God's people through this time who do not have tales to tell. At their worst, these years have been divisive but they have also offered us a dialectic that has spurred us on to new and exciting things.

This dialectic is present to a certain degree in chapter six of *Sacrosanctum Concilium,* which pertains to sacred music. Choirs are to be assiduously developed (114), while the singing of the faithful is to be intelligently fostered (118). Gregorian chant holds pride of place (116) but polyphony and other kinds of sacred music are not to be excluded (116, paragraph 2) and local musical traditions are to be given place in the liturgy as well (119). The pipe organ is held in high esteem (120) but other instruments may be admitted (120, paragraph 2). The treasury of sacred music (mostly for choirs of some ability) is to be preserved and cultivated (114) while composers are to produce works which are singable not only by large choirs but by smaller choirs, and which will promote the participation of all the faithful (121).

Anyone who has been involved with a committee to produce even a parish mission statement knows that any church document is the result of sacrifice and compromise. This certainly characterizes the documents of Vatican II, particularly an early document such as *Sacrosanctum Concilium.* And, while the statements mentioned in the preceding paragraph are by no means mutually exclusive, those who were present during their implementation know that it was not as easy as it was made to seem.

While the chapter on sacred music envisions a "both/and" approach, what actually occurred in the United States tended to be more "either/or," resulting in parishes that offered either the low Mass or the high Mass, either the folk Mass or the silent Mass or the choir Mass; either "hum and strum" or "smells and bells." There were separate worship spaces for separate musical styles, music ministers who would not speak to each other, and people who didn't sing at Sunday noon Mass because they only knew the songs from Saturday night Mass. The list goes on.

Terminology during these years has been slippery. Above all, the terms "traditional" and "contemporary" have been bandied about a good deal. These terms trigger any number of other terms and associations. Some associations given by the group were, on the "traditional" side:

> Music that moves the soul
> Something we've always done
> Organ accompaniment
> Something everybody knows
> Chant
> Four-part/strophic
> Cecilian
> Latin
> Songs associated with a particular generation
>   (pre– vs. post–Vatican II)
> Western European heritage

More reverent
Adoration, Devotions, Benediction, Novena
Written prior to Vatican II
Music that "really says something" vs. "marshmallow music"
Expresses the transcendent

On the "contemporary" side, we've found:

Written since twelve noon today
More upbeat
Scripture-based
More emotional
Dealing with social justice or issues of today
Ethnically diverse
Guitar or a variety of instruments
Spirit-filled, not soul-filled
Expanding the names of God
More in style of folk music
Concern for inclusivity
Vernacular
Cultures appropriating their own music for liturgy
Responsorial format

It became evident that most of these associations were limited in their ability to truly convey a description of a certain style of music, and many of the terms and judgments made had been inadequately thought out or defined. Who is the "we" in "something we've always done"? (Not to mention "always.") And how is it that the emotional "On This Day, O Beautiful Mother" was on the traditional side? "We Gather Together" is folk music, and carols (for many seasons) are a centuries-old example of cultures appropriating their own music for liturgy.

Musical Judgment

The group sang two contemporary (composed recently) pieces—one for assembly and choir, one for assembly—whose composers have definitely been formed and influenced by the church's tradition of chant. These are offered as examples of a both/and approach to chant (though not explicitly Gregorian) in the reformed liturgy.

164

Traditional Treasure, Contemporary Challenge

Luke 1:46–55, adapt.

Becket Senchur, OSB

1. You,— O— God, my soul does mag - ni - fy, And
2. Haugh - ty— hearts you scat - ter to and fro, And
3. Is - ra - el you have with love re - deemed, Ful -

D(add2) D/F♯ Am Dsus D

Ped.

1. all my be - ing finds its joy in you,— Most High! For
2. those who sub - ju - gate the weak you o - ver - throw. But
3. fill - ing what our proph - ets long a - go— had dreamed. Our

G Am Dsus D

1. you have worked most awe - some deeds in me, And
2. those in need, the hun - gry, meek, and poor, You
3. chil - dren shall a - bun - dant bless - ings reap Be -

C G/B Em Am Dsus D

1. hon - ored by all peo - ples shall I ev - er be!
2. shall em - brace and crown with light at heav - en's door!
3. cause your cov - e - nant with us you deigned to keep!

F G Asus A

Alan J. Hommerding

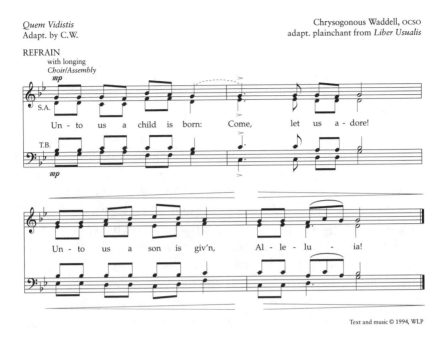

Music in Catholic Worship — *The Three Judgments*

The three judgments — musical, liturgical, pastoral — from the 1983 revision of *Music in Catholic Worship* were summarized for this session as follows: musical — melodies must be accessible, singable and within the range of the assembly; liturgical — the text must be appropriate for liturgical and sacramental celebration, and has to integrate with the particular liturgical action or rite it accompanies; pastoral — the music must effectively serve the needs of the assembly, and should motivate them to action leading from their prayer.

These three judgments serve their purpose well, and give us solid criteria to follow in selecting music for liturgical prayer. But *Music in Catholic Worship* itself states that no set of rules can adequately address every situation. We also need to realize that all the conciliar and post-conciliar documents are landmarks, not endpoints. This realization will help avoid a pseudo-idolatrous or neo-rubricist approach to them.

In addition to knowing what these documents contain, we also need to examine what we have learned in the ensuing generation since *Sacrosanctum Concilium* and the dozen years since the revision of

Music in Catholic Worship. Those who have taken the three judgments out into the parish in pursuit of full, conscious and active participation will have come to new insights, and will have encountered circumstances not envisioned in 1963 or 1983. Documents such as the Milwaukee Report or, in a more limited way, the Snowbird Statement on Liturgical Music are examples of this.

The three judgments can also be put to good use when turned upside-down. The pastoral musician as pedagogue must not only realize the limits of range, melodic complexity, form and format, and so on, of his or her assembly, but must also look for repertoire which will gently expand their voices, minds and hearts to newer limits. We might also ask how a particular piece of music will not only meet particular criteria, but challenge, stretch, enrich, form or re-form the way the assembly understands a particular liturgical rite. Pastorally, we must acknowledge that music inspired by faith in Jesus Christ comes from a multitude of centuries and countries, and can help an assembly move past the limits of its own tastes, geography or heritage into the richness of a truly universal church. A cautionary note must be given here, however: Awareness of a global repertoire must not lead into an eclecticism-driven selection of music for liturgy—an opening hymn from South Africa, gospel-style psalm refrain, gospel acclamation in Spanish, Latin motet at the preparation, and a folk-style setting of the eucharistic acclamations.

Contextual Changes Impacting Liturgical Music

The Impact of Ecclesiology

The vision or image of church held by an individual minister or an entire assembly will definitely impact the way in which they minister and they pray and sing liturgically. A secondary dialectic underlying the dialectics of liturgical music this past generation has been one regarding ecclesiology.

The images of church we inherited were primarily ones of hierarchy (as in "What does the church say about . . ."), worship observed, a building, a sense of duty or obligation, and so forth. None of these

Alan J. Hommerding

are inaccurate in themselves, but their adequacy—particularly in relationship to the biblical foundations of the church—is limited.

A transitional understanding of the church through the eucharistic teaching of Pius XII, re-capturing the Pauline image of church as Body of Christ, was significant for the work of Vatican II and remains important as we grow into a more ready acceptance of church as all those throughout the world who have been baptized: the people of God, the great assembly, or, locally, a community or family.

Asking the question "What does the church say about . . ." becomes entirely different if what is meant by the question is "What does the top-level hierarchy of one particular denomination say about . . ." rather than "What do all baptized people of every Christian denomination throughout the world say about . . ." The impact of this is no less for liturgy and music when we speak of the church offering the great sacrifice of praise, or if we speak of music which the church has always sung.

Changing Images of Ministry

Intimately connected to both inherited and more recent understandings of the church are our perceptions about ministry. Formerly, the church's ministers (though the term itself was seldom used to avoid the taint of Protestantism) were exclusively the ordained and professed religious.

There was, most likely, only one liturgical ministry in the typical Roman Catholic mind: the ordained priest presiding at the altar (more accurately, "saying the Mass"). Servers, musicians and others were viewed most often as his assistants. In particular, the ministry of professed religious, especially women, was a very low-cost reality. Their lifetime commitment was presumed, as well as their rather subservient role and limited authority in a top-down structure.

When we say that focus in ministry has shifted more recently to the concept of service, it is most certainly not to say that those who served the church in generations past did not do so out of a sense of service. Their witness and dedication would instantly invalidate such a statement. However, there was (and remains) a certain sense of the life of service being subjugated to the necessity of structure, and this is where one of the major shifts in focus has occurred.

Less conceptual and more concrete are the new phenomena of parish ministers with outside familial obligations, who need to receive living wages not only for themselves but also for dependents. Also recent is the awareness of the need for ongoing formation and education for those who minister in various ways. (This is quite different from the earlier understanding that once one received ordination or a teaching certificate one was set to minister for life.) An overall paradigm of communication, cooperation and mutual responsibility has most likely been the greatest source of dialectic friction between ordained, religious and lay ministers in this past generation.

Shifts in Understandings of Liturgy

Parallel to shifting ecclesiology and ministerial changes, language surrounding understandings of the liturgy has also been in dialectic motion this past generation. Our inherited understanding of "liturgy" (though the term was used infrequently prior to Vatican II) meant the Mass exclusively, and around it were popular local, ethnic or personal devotions.

The eucharist was regarded primarily as an object, and corporate worship was one more venue for personal piety. To see the liturgy of the church as any one of a number of celebrations, as different sacramental actions of an entire community with eucharist (the activity, not the object) as source and summit of all the church's prayer was an over-arching and—in the truest sense of the word—radical departure for the fathers of Vatican II to take.

None of the shifts or dialectic tensions listed here are new. They have been identified many times before. They do, however, have an important if often unidentified impact for music ministers. Too few music ministers look at these larger contexts too seldom when attempting to work out their ministry within personal or structural contexts. It is extremely easy to see or approach liturgical music as an isolated phenomenon without looking at larger issues surrounding it. A primary example of this was the battles fought over musical styles, one claiming superiority over another to enable assembly participation, when what the assembly really needed was a better understanding of itself as the agent of the liturgical action.

Alan J. Hommerding

Appropriating and integrating these changes in vocabulary and understanding of ecclesiology, ministry and liturgy is going to be the work of a new generation. Bodies as large and organic as the church grow and change slowly. This may frustrate the impatient among us as we stand at the threshold of this next generation of liturgical renewal, but our greatest gift to the next generation is to make sure that these concepts and healthy ways to work within them are handed on.

Liturgical Judgment

At no other time in the history of the church have liturgical reforms been as bound up with changes in doctrine and liturgical scholarship. We can look at two texts for Lent and discuss the manner in which each reflects an inherited or reformed understanding of the season, as well as the re-introduction of the catechumenate to the Lenten liturgy.

> These forty days of Lent, O Lord,
> With you we fast and pray;
> Teach us to discipline our wills
> And follow, Lord, your way.
>
> As thirst and hunger you have known,
> So teach us, gracious Lord
> To die to self and only live
> By your most holy word.
>
> And through these days of penitence,
> And through your Passiontide,
> For evermore, in life and death,
> O Lord, with us abide.
>
> Abide with us, that so, this life
> Of suffering once past,
> An Easter of unending joy
> We may attain at last.

> From ashes to the living font
> Your church must journey, Lord;
> Baptized in grace, in grace renewed
> By your most holy word.

Through fasting, prayer and charity
Your voice speaks deep within;
Returning us to ways of truth
And turning us from sin.

Lent I & II
From desert to the mountaintop
In Christ our way we see;
So, tempered by temptation's might
We might transfigured be.

Lent III
For thirsting hearts let waters flow
Our fainting souls revive;
And, at the well, your waters give:
Our everlasting life.

Lent IV
We sit beside the road and plead
"Come, save us, David's son!"
Now with your vision heal our eyes,
The world's true Light alone.

Lent V
Our graves split open, bring us back,
Your promise to proclaim;
To darkened tombs call out "Arise!"
And glorify your name.

All Sundays
From ashes to the living font,
Your church must journey still,
Through cross and tomb to Easter joy,
In Spirit-fire fulfilled.

Contemporary Challenges: Ecclesial

The challenges currently facing music ministers most frequently expressed by the group fell into three major categories.

Primacy of the Assembly

This relates directly to the shifting concepts of ecclesiology stated above. The realization that all ministries are derived from baptism and that all liturgical ministries come first and foremost from the assembly has not yet been completely grasped. For music ministers, this is the cause of our own failure to realize that the assembly is the first music minister at the liturgy, and that any particularized ministry we may have is subservient to that.

This plays out concretely on the parish level by the continuing domination of soloists or instrumentalists over the entire singing assembly. Occasionally those parts which properly belong to the assembly are usurped by the cantor or choir; or at other times the song of the assembly is obfuscated by a grand yet meandering free accompaniment on the organ or a barrage of instrumentalists that rivals the Hollywood Bowl orchestra. What results is an illusion of mere loudness from somewhere or someone substituting for authentic, hearty singing from the assembly.

Catering to Different Musical Tastes

It is not a new observation that we live in a society driven by individual tastes. However, one is hard pressed to find anywhere in the liturgical documents the criterion of individual taste—be it the taste of a musician, pastor, choir member with a deep checkbook—listed as a means of determining repertoire for liturgy. This phenomenon frequently plays out through the three personae listed above: the musicians' belief that because they are responsible for implementing the music means that their individual taste must be gratified; the hierarchical structure manifesting itself in music that varies from Mass to Mass depending on the personality, mood or taste of the presider; the fallacy that everyone should have an equal voice in determining the music and that the final selection must be reached by consensus. (Alice Parker has pointed out in her book *Melodious Accord* that churches don't deal with the plumbing or any number of other things in this manner.) Or the fallacy that certain voices are more equal than others, depending on their prominence in the parish, bank account, squeaky wheel capability and so on.

Adequate Training and Formation

Ultimately, no amount of quotation from liturgical documents, good will or fervent dedication to the church and Christ will replace or substitute for musical skills. Music is an art and a craft: A certain pitch is a certain pitch and needs to last for a certain duration, words need to be enunciated clearly and on pitch. There are concrete challenges these days: There is a shrinking number of people pursuing music professionally; there are time limitations on part-time or volunteer musicians; there are limited financial resources available at the parish level for the proper training or ongoing training of musicians to ensure that each parish is supplied with capable musicians. Yet a careful reading of the church documents will show that they were written with the assumption that competent musicians are available for parochial music ministry.

On a second level, the issue of how to attain adequate liturgical formation for those who are professional, trained musicians—as well as for volunteers who serve as music ministers, liturgy committee members, and so on—is important as well. Neither a degree in music nor showing up for weekly rehearsals or monthly meetings is any guarantee of liturgical capability. It was noted by several in the group that frequently there does not seem to be an underlying awareness—whether among schooled professionals or volunteer amateurs—that liturgical education, formation and skill training are essential. The first step in addressing this challenge seems to be instilling an awareness or desire among all music ministers to pursue liturgical formation.

Contemporary Challenges: Pastoral

Different ages respond in differing ways to similar realities. We compared the hymn "Faith of Our Fathers," written as a response to social, civil, religious and militaristic persecution during the reign of Elizabeth I, with a more recent hymn responding to some of the same. Here are the original verses of "Faith of Our Fathers," which are usually altered or deleted from current versions:

> Our Fathers, chained in prisons dark,
> Were still in heart and conscience free;

Alan J. Hommerding

How sweet would be their children's fate
If they, like them, could die for thee!

Faith of our Fathers! Mary's prayers
Shall win our country back to thee;
And through the truth that comes from God
England shall then indeed be free.

Though suffering and martyrdom are certainly part of the church's heritage — we still witness their occurrence throughout the world — the need for liturgical music to call or lead people to action must also be a part of the gospel response to issues of nationalism, social and civil strife, oppression and persecution.

PACE MIO DIO

Herman R. Stuempfle, Jr.

Perry Nelson

1. Where ar-mies scourge the coun-try-side, And peo-ple flee in fear;
2. Where an-ger fes-ters in the heart, And strikes with cru-el hand;
3. Where homes are torn by bit-ter strife, And love dis-solves in blame;
4. O God, whose heart com-pas-sion-ate Bears ev-'ry hu-man pain,

1. Where si-rens scream through flam-ing nights, And death is ev-er near:
2. Where vio-lence stalks the trou-bled streets, And ter-ror haunts the land:
3. Where walls you meant for shel-t'ring care Hide deeds of hurt and shame:
4. Re-deem this vio-lent, wound-ing world Till gen-tle-ness shall reign.

O God of mer-cy, hear our prayer: Bring peace to earth a-gain!

Contemporary Challenges: Social, Educational, Technological

Since musicians minister to a church that lives within the world, we cannot ignore the impact that extra-ecclesial influences have on the field of music. When we realize that, at best, most of the people in the pews spend only one hour out of an entire week in liturgical prayer, their experiences of music and corporate prayer from the remainder of their hours and days cannot be discounted. These experiences strongly influence the overall profile of the assemblies we serve.

Music in Society

Music as a social phenomenon has served and continues to serve as a unifying element among different groups within society. Very often groups of a particular age, class or ethnic background will use a specific style of music to define themselves. Youths, particularly adolescents, frequently use music as a means of differentiating or disassociating themselves from a previous generation. This musical and social phenomenon is extremely significant for pastoral musicians, who need to hand on the best of their heritage of liturgical music to the next generation and avoid the ephemeral nature of fads.

Music also has the power to express life experience, and to assist individuals in recalling particular events. "Our song" is most likely the best-known example of this phenomenon in society. In liturgical music, we have found that particular pieces of music will be connected to particular events in the life of the parish or particular members of a parish (psalm 23 and a funeral, for example).

This works in our favor, since liturgy is a repetitive event. The downside is that if we always choose precisely the same piece of music for the same liturgical event (a common seasonal psalm—especially the same setting—year after year) we run the risk of leading our assemblies into an unnecessary impoverishment. Psalm 51 does not explore all the facets of Lent, for example, nor does it adequately connect with the Lenten readings of all three cycles.

Other social phenomena which are currently having an impact on liturgical music include the growing experience that music is not something people make or do, but something we listen to. This growing social passivity in regard to music is definitely going to have to be taken into account and addressed if we are going to continue to foster singing assemblies. Music is also increasingly omnipresent in our society. It is rare for any place of social congress or any form of visual communication not to have music present. "Background" is the most common term by which this music is described. In other words, the people who are walking into our sanctuaries on a Sunday morning are increasingly disposed to think of music as something that occurs while the truly important stuff of life is going on. If our goal as liturgical musicians is a sung liturgy in which music is intrinsic to the entire liturgical action, we will need to explicitly counteract this concept of music as "background."

Education, Domestic and Scholastic

The public, corporate prayer of the church has presumed that some sort of corporate prayer is also taking place in the domestic church. Formal table rituals, oral transmission of family and community history as well as familial and communal music-making were all social realities which were brought to the liturgical activity of the church in ages past. If not extinct, these are currently in decline, and we are seeing the church function as one of the last places where these take place (group song in particular). Several people in the session noted that there is an expectation that the sanctuary and the classroom are going to assume a number of responsibilities that properly belong to the home environment. In the video "When We Sing" (Liturgy Training Publications) I made the observation that when we ask people to sing and to sing together in church we are actually asking them to participate in an aberrant behavior, meaning that we ask them to do something that most of them do nowhere else at any other time during the week. This is not to say that we shouldn't be inviting people to sing in church, but we do need to be aware that we are working in what is, for the most part, the final remnant of community song in our society.

In the discussion about education, a number of participants expressed concern about the ongoing devaluation of the role of the arts and humanities in the academic system. The primary focus of the concern was that when we fail to expose children to the arts we ultimately rob them of another way of becoming a whole human being. Additionally, it was noted that many of the positive group skills which are lauded as part of athletic programs are also present in group music-making. To be part of an instrumental or vocal ensemble is to learn any number of cooperative social skills, training that will benefit any child later in life. Music is also another way to help young people (in truth, people of all ages) to explore the entire human emotional palette. It is shortsighted to think that music for liturgy always needs to be lively and upbeat or—conversely—solemn and somber. The rites of the church express many human emotions, and we will be most effective if we teach our assemblies (of all ages) to use music as one of many venues to access them.

Technology

In the discussion about current technological developments that relate to liturgical music ministry, it was difficult to remember that technological improvement is a historic, not merely recent reality in the realm of music. The piano was an advancement beyond the harpsichord, electric blowers provided better and more consistent wind pressure for organs than hand-pumped bellows, woodwind and brass instruments played significantly better in tune by the end of the eighteenth century, sound systems enabled people to hear better, and so on. (Though it must be noted that every technological advance is not necessarily an improvement.)

Significant mention was made of the fact that current technology is a means by which our society furthers its tendency toward individualization. It is now possible for every member of a household and every room within a household to have its own means of providing music, be it television, radio, CD or tape player, any of which may put the listener into further isolation with the use of headphones. Recent developments in keyboard instruments have now produced instruments that "play" better (or, at least, more precisely) than amateur volunteers or even trained professionals. In this context, it is not unrealistic to wonder if there will follow a loss of sense of ministry and service in the name of technical perfection.

On the positive side, technology has given people exposure to a variety of musical and cultural programs which we can use to engage and educate the people we serve, or the people with whom we share our ministry. A number of participants in the session also mentioned that they have been using tape recordings of new music, weekly responsorial psalms and so on, as a means of training cantors and choir members. Ultimately any technology will be best seen as a gift from God. Like all else we have received from God, its purpose is to serve our needs; our call and challenge is to use it effectively and creatively for the spread of the gospel.

Conclusion

Though liturgical musicians currently face a significant number of substantial challenges, we can continually call to mind what Scott Appleby presents in this book: We are called upon to live and serve in *gaudium et spes,* in hope and joy. Naming the challenges we face is not a source for despair, but rather a realistic way to face the future. In this age, as in any age, it is recognizing our challenges and turning to God in faith which will enable us not only to face these challenges, but to address them creatively, and so increase the treasures of our tradition.

Richard S. Vosko

Worship Environments: Between No More and Not Yet

It has often been said that the buildings we shape will eventually shape us.[1] I am wondering how what seems to be emerging as a "typical church building plan" is shaping the liturgical movement in this country. Although we have achieved a great deal in our efforts to design appropriate environments for worship since the Council, there are still many factors that must be considered or revisited. The renewal of the church is not finished yet.

Surviving the Transition

The Catholic church is in the thick of a major period of transition, and there is still much pain associated with this renewal. Like every post-conciliar period this one is full of transforming experiences. Familiar forms and meanings are gradually being replaced by new ones. To honor a reformed church and its liturgy, the environment for worship is undergoing significant changes. While earlier adaptations and innovations were frequently implemented without understanding or explanation, now there is a renewed interest in creating liturgical spaces that not only function well but also serve as meta-phors for the contemporary church. During this time, zeal, enthusi-asm and creativity are often coupled with confusion, fear and pain.

In the many parishes I work with I have experienced the anger and the joy that accompanies living in a post-conciliar period of church history. I have appealed to these communities to work in a spirit of understanding, patience and respect. I have requested that we walk as companions through this difficult and exhilarating time. Nevertheless, much like a household going on vacation in a car, some members do not want to go at all, some want to go to other places, some want to stop frequently along the way, some want to take dif-ferent roads and some want to keep moving forward.

The Wisdom of the Second Vatican Council

A re-reading of the conciliar documents can be helpful at times. Take the *Pastoral Constitution on the Church in the Modern World,* for example. Most of us usually refer to this major document by its open-ing three words, *gaudium et spes,* referring to the joys and hopes of church renewal. But there is more. In an address to a fiftieth-anniver-sary class of presbyters, Bishop Kenneth Untener reminded everyone that the first sentence continues like this: "The joys and the hopes, the griefs and the anxieties of the people of this age, those who are poor or in any way afflicted, these too are the joys and the hopes, the griefs and the anxieties of the followers of Christ."[2] The document reminds us that we are "passing through a new stage in history"; that "profound and rapid changes are spreading by degrees"; that we are "speaking of a true social and cultural transformation . . . which has repercussions on religious life as well."[3]

Transformation in the life of Christians is nothing new. I would like to think of it as a vocation—a calling to never-ending transforma-tion. Even though some want their religions to serve them as unchang-ing stanchions of traditions, Christian life is synonymous with transformation. In the scriptures we read the metaphors Paul used to describe the radical change which converts experienced. For exam-ple, he uses the word "metamorphosis" in 2 Corinthians 3:18 to mean a radical transformation of one's entire being. He refers to the restructuring of the self to take on the self of Christ in Philippians 3:21; in 2 Corinthians 5:16 he speaks about how the old order is gone while a new order has begun. Transforming experiences cannot happen in a single moment any more than baptism in water signals the moment of conversion. Thirty years of post-Conciliar reform is not enough time. We are not finished yet.

God calls us to ongoing kenosis, a lifelong emptying of the self, like Jesus who emptied himself. The grain of wheat loses its life to bear a special fruitfulness. The church is experiencing a powerful metamorphosis and in doing so it is losing a former life in order to gain a new one. This molting process, of course, takes time. We are in the midst of that time.

The Difference between Change and Transformation

Catholics who are struggling with this time of transition might say that the "changes" are confusing and hurting them. Marist Brother Sean Sammort, borrowing from psychologist Bill Bridges, offers an insight here.[4]

Change and transformation are not the same. There are subtle distinctions. For example, change happens at a point in time while transformation happens *over* time. Change signals a new beginning, while transformation begins with an ending. Change can cause transformation, but the latter enables the spiritual and psychological re-orientations that can help someone find meaning in any changed situation.

For example, job descriptions for military personnel, corporate professionals, salespersons, construction workers and pastoral ministers require occasional moves from one location to another. Although never easy, the moves are accepted as part of the deal. They are not total surprises. They might even lead to promotions. The occupation over time is transformed by the changes made in the life of the person.

When life as a Christian is accepted as a life of ongoing transformation, the changes that are likely to occur over time are perceived as part of the deal. On the other hand, if the Christian life is understood as one that stands firm, a bastion of tradition, and does not transform over time even in the face of social-cultural-religious development, then changes will not be easily tolerated.

We have been so preoccupied with the changes prompted by the Council we have not noticed the impact that the slow and sometimes painful transformation is having on the church. We seem to judge the success of our reform and renewal efforts by the external changes we make along the way, when in reality little transformation is being experienced. Consider for a moment three church building issues that preoccupy some Catholic people: tabernacles, kneelers and images. Are these not accidentals in our religion? Do not these furnishings and objects serve more profound components of the Catholic worship experience? How do we understand the presence of Christ in our life? What postures are appropriate for public and private prayer? How can memory serve us in carrying on the tradition of the church?

According to the psychologist Bill Bridges, a transformation experience has three distinct parts: a difficult process of letting go, a confusing in-between time, and a new beginning. We are in the second stage of transformation, where it is very hard for some to let go of the former models of church architecture and art. The newer models constructed to house the reformed liturgy are often misunderstood and become sources of confusion. We have approached our worship spaces in terms of change but not necessarily in terms of transformation. As newer models begin to take hold, they will actually start reshaping the definition of a worship space and the church itself. We remember Winston Churchill's axiom: "We shape our spaces so they will shape us." So, how we design our churches today will shape the identity of the church tomorrow.

Factors Affecting Transitions and Worship Environments

Although there are many religious, social and cultural factors that have affected transitions in the church, for instance, monasticism, the

Reformation, modernism, feminism, and so on, I will focus on three from the past: imperialism, Scholasticism and the Enlightenment.

Imperialism

The Edict of Milan was a turning point in the history of Christianity. A blessing and a curse, the patronage of the state altered the way everything in the church was done. Once it became politically advantageous to be a Christian those intimate and somewhat autonomous house church groups grew into larger congregations managed by the clergy. Lay participation in the liturgy gradually decreased as the ceremonials became more complex. Like their civic counterparts, the clergy began wearing insignia of rank on their vesture.[5]

Likewise the shape of the Christian place of worship was influenced by the designs of the imperial system. The architectural style of public buildings, that is, the basilica or palace of the king, was the template for the Christian church. The elevated status of the hierarchy slowly led to the eventual clericalization of the church and its buildings. The construction of larger churches separated the clergy from the assembly. There were no seats and the liturgical action took place at a free-standing table which gradually moved from the midst of the nave in some regions to the section occupied by the clergy under the triumphant arch. Eventually, the early basilican style evolved into the medieval cathedral.

What we have to ponder is this: Is imperialism still a system that identifies life in the Catholic church? If not, then how will our worship places express a more non-imperialistic model?

Scholasticism

By the 12th and 13th centuries the clergy had become a wealthy and educated class and the laity appeared to trust the official church, which had become very powerful. The liturgy was regarded as something that belonged to the clergy, and they often used it for personal gain. The laity somehow believed they were not worthy to approach God and relied on the clergy to intervene and win for them divine favors. The cathedrals were designed to be magnificent settings wherein the clergy could ply their trade and preside over the elaborate celebrations of the mass, by now perceived to be an untouchable frightful mystery. The Gothic style of architecture reigned at this time.

The Gothic style is usually distinguished by the difference between its pointed arches and the rounded arches of the Romanesque style. The Gothic style revealed something else, though less tangible—a sense of order, of lightness in materiality and in illumination. Gone were the ponderous piers and internal buttressing. The walls were thin and the windows large. The ambulatory and its chapels were not just mortared together; they somehow flowed in a harmonious rhythm of pointed arches and splendid shafts.[6]

Early Scholasticism was born at the time and in the environment where Early Gothic architecture was born: Suger's S. Denis. High Scholasticism is generally assumed to have begun with the turn of the 12th century, precisely when the High Gothic system achieved its first triumph in Chartres.[7]

The purpose of Early and High Scholasticism was to establish the unity of truth using both reason and faith.[8] The idea was to make faith clearer by an appeal to the imagination and to make imagination clearer by an appeal to the senses. This notion of clarification or *manifestatio* affected everything: literature, speech, music, visual arts (through an exact and systematic division of space) and architecture.[9]

Pre-scholasticism had insulated faith from reason as Romanesque structures conveyed the impression of impenetrable space inside and out. High Scholasticism was governed by the principle of *manifestatio*. High Gothic architecture was dominated—as Suger observed— by the "principle of transparency." Like the High Scholastic *Summa,* the High Gothic cathedral sought to embody the whole of Christian knowledge, theological, moral, natural and historical, with everything in its place.[10]

The Scholastic would look at a High Gothic cathedral as one would look upon a mode of literary composition, from the point of view of *manifestatio.* The many elements used to compose a cathedral were to ensure stability, just like the many elements that constitute a Summa were to ensure validity.[11]

The Gothic style that guided church construction in the Middle Ages served as a resonator of the philosophy that eventually became the handmaid of theology and ultimately shaped the understanding or definition of the church in that period. Still today when one enters a church constructed in that era the verticality, the lightness, the harmony speak aloud of the Christian thinking of that time.

The question for us is this: Is the neo-Gothic style an appropriate expression of the current understanding of the church in the modern world as suggested by the Conciliar and post-Conciliar writings?

The Enlightenment

The secularization of Western European society, culture and thought was already developing two hundred years before the French Revolution. Prompted by the energy of the Reformation and Counter-Reformation, religion by this time was becoming a matter of personal decision. The fragmentation of the universal church into competing churches and the weariness of religious warfare hastened the secularization process.[12]

To some scholars this was the last great building age of Christianity. The constraints that previously caused artists to distinguish between styles suitable for churches and those for palaces and theaters were breaking down. As baroque evolved into rococo, it might have seemed there was more secular splendor than spirituality in the gilt and vivid colors of many churches.[13]

The baroque style and, later, the less frenzied rococo served to emphasize in a very sensual manner the celebration of the Mass believed to be the dramatic re-enactment of the death of Jesus Christ. Everything had emotional and symbolic meaning, and the worshiper, captivated by the riotous and lavish interiors of these churches was, in a way, delivered to heaven. We see that the impact of secularization on the church broke down some of the distinctions between sacred and secular art and architectural forms, allowing the styles incorporated in public spaces to serve the intentions of the church, which was busy putting its own house in order after the Reformation.[14]

As Jim White puts it, "While giving glory to the setting of the liturgy, rococo is highly subjective and individualistic and directed to summoning the emotions. Thus the liturgy tends to be buried in a devotional milieu. One's attention is led hither and yon, to gesticulating saints, to incursions of heavenly hosts, all informative but extraneous to the gathering of the people of God on earth."[15]

Church-Related Factors

Like the historical factors we just explored, there are factors in our own time that can affect the design of church buildings. I believe that, when fully comprehended, these factors could give a new shape to our churches, replacing the typical American plan that has emerged since the Council. Here I would like to examine a few factors, church-related and otherwise, that might affect our understanding of worship and, thus, the environment for worship.

Ecclesiological Factors

A broader definition of the church was affirmed in the Conciliar proceedings. Once thought of as bishops, priests, deacons and the laity who followed the orders of the clergy, the church is now understood as the people of God, the body of Christ, a sacrament of unity. However, not everyone in the church accepts corporate identity and responsibility as an essential prerequisite for church membership.

Richard Gorsuch, a psychologist at the Fuller Theological Seminary in Pasadena, California, says: "People with *extrinsic* religious attitudes have a what's-in-it-for-me attitude and the prime reason to pray is because I have a problem I want God to solve." Dr. David Wulff, a psychologist at Wheaton College, suggests: "People with extrinsic orientations tend to be more dogmatic and prejudiced and to have high levels of anxiety."

David Leege, a sociologist at Notre Dame, reports in the *Study of Catholic Parish Life* that 39% of core Catholics have a basic religious perspective that "focuses on me and my problems." They "are concerned with their own shortcomings, how they act on God or how God acts on them, and on the reward they will receive either in the afterlife or in this life." Another 18% are "communal," focusing on the "common needs of people in their social state." Leege reports that 21% of the core Catholics could be characterized as a mix of these two and 22% could not think in these terms about religion. These findings point out the sobering dominance of individualism!

However, people with an *intrinsic* religious orientation tend to have a positive view of human nature and to have a greater sense of control over the course of their lives and a strong sense of purpose in life. People with this orientation showed greater empathy and less narcissism and depression.

On one hand, tremendous amounts of time, energy and resources are spent celebrating liturgies and creating worship environments in a manner that, it is hoped, will foster the communal nature of the church. On the other hand, studies like these just mentioned indicate that there is still a strong leaning toward individualism.

The question we have to ask is this: To what extent should a church primarily designed to house the celebration of public liturgies be designed for personal prayer?

Liturgical Factors

The *Constitution on the Sacred Liturgy* gave the church direction for understanding itself and how it worships. It was the goal of the Council to intensify the daily growth of Catholics in Christian living; to nurture whatever could contribute to the unity of all who believe in Christ. Hence the Council had special reasons for judging it a duty to provide for the renewal and fostering of the liturgy.[16]

Some short quotations from the CSL offer us a clear picture of what the Mass is.

> The liturgy is considered the exercise of the priestly office of Jesus Christ. In the liturgy, full public worship is performed by the Mystical Body of Jesus Christ, that is, by the head and its members. From this it follows that every liturgical celebration, because it is an action of Christ the priest and of his Body, the church, is a sacred action surpassing all others.[17]
>
> Liturgical services are not private functions but are celebrations of the church, which is the sacrament of unity.[18] It is to be stressed that whenever rites provide for communal celebration, involving the presence and active participation of the faithful, this way of celebrating is preferred over celebration that is individual and quasi-private. This rule applies with special force to the celebration of Mass and the administration of the sacraments, even though every Mass has of itself a public and social nature.[19]

The reference to private celebrations by priests can be a helpful reminder to us that the Mass is perhaps not the time to develop the personal piety endorsed elsewhere in the CSL. These devotions should be drawn up so that they harmonize with the liturgical seasons, accord with the sacred liturgy, are in some fashion derived from it and lead the people to it, since the liturgy by its very nature far surpasses any of them.[20] This suggests to us that the Mass is not really the time to carry out personal devotions. Instead, by engaging in acts of personal piety at other times, the faithful can bring to the Mass a renewed spiritual life.

These references can help us appreciate other ones related to some of the issues. Over time the decorations of the church and the locations of many furnishings and images seemed to attract more attention than the primary symbols of the church. The call for noble simplicity, not extravagance,[21] and the references to the appropriate number and location of images[22] and the location of the tabernacle[23] call for modifications in the plan of the church building in order to help the community focus on primary symbols during the mass.

The question we have to ask here is this: If we agree that there have been developments in the definition of the church and how it understands the manner in which it worships God in the liturgy, do our church buildings reflect it?

Secular Factors

Perceptions of Space and Time

Post-conciliar life in America is characterized by a hectic pace where time is a precious commodity. There just does not seem to be enough time to do everything. This pace also affects our perception of space. John Jackson wrote: "We recognize that certain localities in our life have an attraction which gives us a certain indefinable sense of well-being of which we want to return to, time and time again. So that original notion of ritual, of repeated celebration or reverence, is still inherent . . . What automatically ensues, it seems to me, is a sense of fellowship with those who share the experience and the intrinsic desire to return to establish accustomed repeated ritual."[24]

Jackson's premise is that the event or gathering is what draws people to a space and that, in turn, is what gives a sacred meaning to that place. "People are brought together because of the calendar, not because of the place. What brings us together with people is not that we live near each other, but that we share the same timetable: the same work hours, the same religious observances, the same habits and customs. That's why we are more and more aware of time and the rhythm of the communities. It's our sense of time, our sense of ritual, which in the long run creates our sense of place . . . I believe we attach too much importance to art and architecture in producing an awareness of belonging . . . when what we actually share is a sense of time and not a sense of place."[25]

It is important to understand that houses of prayer are not sacred by themselves or because of any furnishing located inside. Churches become sacred over time because of the activity of the community that worships there. Thus, transformations that occur in the community will be reflected in the arrangement of the space. The primary purpose of the church is to house the worship of the people. If the worship patterns change it makes sense that the environment for worship would also change. Eventually, the community is transformed by the changes in its own identity which then are reflected and affirmed by the environment.

The Media

Changes in the media have always affected the relationship between places and the information that people bring to and receive from those places. Electronic media go a step further, leading to a total dissociation of physical place and social place. When we communicate using the telephone, radio, television and computers, where we are physically no longer determines where and who we are socially. That is, you no longer have to be there when it happens. The telegraph not only defied limits set by distance, but also bypassed the social rite of "passage," that is, the act of moving physically and socially from one position to another.[26]

Electronic media destroy the specialness of place and time . . . Those aspects of group identity, socialization and hierarchy that were once dependent on particular locations and the special experiences available in them have been altered by electronic media.[27]

Richard S. Vosko

When compared to what the entertainment industry offers, most liturgical events tend to be tedious at best and boring at worst. Of course, the liturgy is not intended to be entertaining. However, the manner in which the rites are enacted and the settings for these rites can make a difference, just like liturgical music can. We can no longer overlook the impact of the media (nor the World Wide Web!). This is not what it means for the church to be counter-cultural.

Marshall McLuhan was right when he suggested that the medium is the message. McLuhan remarked that the wheel, as an invention, is the extension of the foot. In a similar way the liturgy can be understood to be an extension of the paschal mystery through time. No one understands how. It is a matter of faith. However, church buildings, because they are metaphors for the church, are tangible expressions of that faith. They too must be extensions of that paschal mystery and not mere containers for focal points and assemblies. This is probably why, although so important to people who can no longer get to mass with the community, the broadcasting of prerecorded liturgies will eventually foster only a virtual-reality understanding of the paschal mystery, suggesting that you do not have to be present for the real thing when it is happening in order to experience it.

The Emerging American Plan

Thus far we have been examining how the design of worship spaces has been affected by various ecclesial and non-ecclesial factors. The teachings of the Second Vatican Council and the reform of the ritual books have together prompted a new understanding of the church and how it worships God. Have the post-conciliar church buildings reflected these teachings or are we pouring old wine into new skins. I suspect that a typical plan for Catholic church buildings is emerging. I fear that what is now being perceived as normative in some areas may not be an adequate reflection of what the church is and how it worships God as a pilgrim community. Let me cite some examples of this emerging plan.

Maintaining Spectator Seating Arrangements

Seating plans that perpetuate a spectatorship model of attending Mass do not foster the active, conscious participation of the assembly. Long churches with innumerable rows of pews tend to keep worshipers at a distance. Sightlines and acoustics often suffer in such buildings. Even newer churches with the so-called fan-shaped seating plan still separate the sanctuary of the clergy from the nave of the assembly.

Although solutions will vary accordingly temporary arrangements made in recent years should be given a final form. "Some of these provisory solutions still in use are liturgically and artistically unsatisfactory and render difficult the worthy celebration of the Mass; the Concilium has ordered that they be corrected."[28]

Although this 1970 instruction from the Congregation for Divine Worship refers only to altars and sanctuaries, the same could be said for the assembly part of the building. Many parishes only make modifications to the sanctuary of the church without taking into consideration how the assembly will be encouraged to participate in the liturgy. The seating arrangement should say that the entire church is invited to be present at the table of the Lord. The only physical way to do this is with a seating plan that places the altar table more in the midst of the assembly.

Building Large Sanctuaries

The altar rails may have been taken out, but new large sanctuaries still create a distance and a physical barrier between the people and the altar table. Undivided attention to the liturgical rites of the church is fostered when the space is not cluttered. Interestingly, although a great deal of furnishings and art not required for the liturgy have been removed from the altar table area, new items have found their way to the platform.

The altar platform (sanctuary) should be large enough to provide space for an altar table, an ambo and a presider's chair only. Occasionally, a chair for a deacon is added. Sometimes even the chair for the priest is placed in the front row of the assembly. Credence tables, chairs for servers, readers and others are best kept off the platform. Brides and grooms do not have to sit "on the altar." Actually, the only reason for having a platform would be to provide good sightlines for the assembly. In some new churches there are no platforms. Spaces that are completely barrier-free will have no steps at all.

Four Focal Points

Since the Council a lot of attention has been given to the proper placement of the altar, ambo, font and chair. Aidan Kavanagh indicates that the altar and font are primary spatial foci of liturgy.[29] More attention could be paid to the manner in which the community celebrates the rites. Then the space and its furnishings should be planned to accommodate the liturgical practice of the community. In hindsight maybe only flexible liturgical settings should have been authorized for the first generation of post-conciliar churches. Kavanagh once said, "Communities do not cohere around lecture halls, but everyone loves a parade!"[30]

Carpeting Worship Spaces

Carpet bedrooms, not churches.[31] Care must be taken not to put too much sound-absorptive material in the church. Adequate acoustical resonance is required to foster the singing of the assembly. Hire the best acoustical consultants (not sound system vendors) before agreeing to the plans for your church.

Installing High Intensity Discharge Lamps

These lamps belong in gyms, not churches. These lamps are often installed as a money-saving endeavor. This presumes that the lights in your church are on all day long. The intensity of these lamps cannot be controlled and the color quality is unpredictable.

Baptismal Fonts near the Altar Table

Fonts do not belong near the altar any more than bathtubs belong in dining rooms. Placing the font of living water near the altar table will dilute the power of both symbols and prevent the assembly's experiencing the water. Further, the procession path for the newly baptized into the church is reduced or removed.

Tabernacles near the Altar Table

A chapel for the reservation of the eucharist will foster private prayer and the adoration of the Body of Christ, sacred food saved in order to be eaten by members of the community who are sick or dying. If the reserved eucharist is not required for the celebration of the eucharist, then would not a distinct chapel for the tabernacle be a more practical setting for encouraging devotion to the sacrament? The issue should not be centered around the location of the tabernacle but how the real presence of Jesus Christ is understood by the faithful.

A Model from the Documents and the Catechism

The emerging typical plan described above suggests that in times of transition trends will develop that are frequently not based on the best understanding of the traditions and current teachings of the church. Further, because worship spaces are primarily designed to house the ritual activity of the faith community, the emerging typical plan is related to the manner in which the community has learned to celebrate rites.

For example, the trend of placing the font near the altar table occurs in parishes where baptism is done during the weekend liturgy in front of the entire assembly "so that everyone can see what is going on." While there is some merit in this explanation for full-view ritual practice, the placement of the font near the altar does not offer the possibility of learning how to celebrate the rites of inititiation in other ways which include processions and foster the understanding that a human being does not necessarily have to see everything in order to participate fully in the celebration. The other senses are frequently dulled when the successful celebration of the rites of the church depends only on seeing and hearing.

Likewise the placement of the altar table at one end of the room, where it is connected to a wall, represents only one approach to the post-conciliar understanding of the environmental implications of the eucharistic rites. Even though the assembly may be arranged on two or three sides of the altar table, the large, distinct platform settings for the ambo, chair and table could still create an atmosphere that suggests the altar does not belong to the assembly.

Are there any guidelines for building and renovating a Catholic place of worship? Although the American bishops have urged that the norms and guidelines found in *Environment and Art in Catholic Worship*[32] "should be followed by pastors and all those engaged in the liturgical arts,"[33] other references may also be found in the ritual books and the catechism of the church. Although many will say that the following references are not to be understood literally, the imagination, like the Scholastic imagination, suggests a very different setting for the celebration of the liturgy than what is being experienced in most post-conciliar church buildings. Basically, these statements imply that the altar table be placed in a central location in the midst of the assembly. The emphasis is added.

> The altar, around which the Church is gathered in the celebration of the Eucharist, represents the two aspects of the same mystery; the altar of the sacrifice and the table of the Lord. This is all the more since the Christian altar is the symbol of Christ himself, present in the midst of the assembly of his faithful, both as the victim offered for our reconciliation and as food from heaven who is giving himself to us. (*Catechism of the Catholic Church*, Part 2, VI, 1383. John Paul II, 1992)

> It should be placed as to be a focal point on which the attention of the whole congregation centers naturally . . . This altar should be freestanding to allow the ministers to walk around it easily and to permit celebration facing the people. (*Ceremonial of Bishops,* 48. ICEL, 1989)

> The anointing with chrism makes the altar a symbol of Christ, who before all others is and is called the "Anointed One." (*Dedication of a Church and An Altar,* Chapter 2, 16. USCC, 1989)

> It is the common table of the assembly, a symbol of the Lord. (*Environment and Art in Catholic Worship,* 71. NCCB, 1978)

> The location of the altar will be central in any eucharistic celebration. . . . (*Environment and Art in Catholic Worship,* 73. NCCB, 1978)

The people of God is called together to share in this table. Thus, the altar is the center of the thanksgiving accomplished in the eucharist. (*The Roman Missal*, General Instruction, 259. 1969)

[The altar] should be placed in a central position which draws the attention of the whole congregation. (*The Roman Missal*, General Instruction, 262)

Above all, the main altar should be so placed and constructed that it is always seen to be the sign of Christ Himself, the place at which the saving mysteries are carried out, and the center of the assembly, to which the greatest reverence is due. (*Instruction on Eucharistic Worship*, 24. Sacred Congregation of the Rites, May 25, 1967, 1969)

[The altar] shall occupy a place in the sacred building which is truly central, so that the attention of the whole congregation of the faithful is spontaneously turned to it. (*Instruction for the Proper Implementation of the Constitution on the Sacred Liturgy*, 91. Sacred Congregation of the Rites, September 26, 1964)

A re-reading of these sources suggests that more conversation about the meaning of and the exact location of the altar table in the nave of the church building would be helpful. That conversation will also focus on the practice of presiding at the liturgy and how the assembly understands what is going on during the proclamation of the eucharistic prayers. In this regard any changes in the environment for worship must flow from a reformed understanding of the liturgical practices of the community. My feeling is that we have settled into well-established plans for our church buildings without seriously considering other liturgical possibilities that are rooted in the ritual books and commentaries.

Conclusions

I have indicated that the changes brought about by the Second Vatican Council will contribute to a slow transformation of the church and that this time of transition is not easy for many people. I have pointed

Richard S. Vosko

out that, throughout the history of the church, the designs of worship spaces were affected by various cultural and ecclesial factors. I have tried to show that the shape of the church is currently affected by new factors (including the Second Vatican Council) and that the environment for worship is also being shaped by these factors. I have suggested that, in most instances, what appears to be an emerging model for Catholic places of worship may not be completely expressive of the church envisioned in the writings of the Council and the post-conciliar reforms. I have proposed that a re-reading of the ritual books and their commentaries, coupled with more conversation about how the rites can be enacted, will create interest for developing new and different models for arranging our worship spaces. There is still much more work to be done. The renewal of the church is not finished yet.

1. Winston Churchill is credited with making this remark when the House of Commons was rebuilt after World War II. He felt the seating arrangement would affect the workings of the political system.

2. *Pastoral Constitution on the Church in the Modern World* (December 7, 1965), 1.

3. *Ibid.*, 4.

4. See *Origins* (August 29, 1991): 21, 12, 187–91.

5. Paula and Tessa Clowney, *Exploring Churches* (Grand Rapids: Eerdmans, 1982), 32.

6. *Ibid.*, 60.

7. Erwin Panofsky, *Gothic Architecture and Scholasticism* (New York: Penguin, 1951), 4 ff.

8. *Ibid.*, 28.

9. *Ibid.*, 38–39.

10. *Ibid.*, 43–45.

11. *Ibid.*, 53.

12. John McManners, *Oxford Illustrated History of Christianity* (New York: Oxford University Press, 1990), 267 ff.

13. *Ibid.*, 237–238.

14. *Ibid.*

15. James White, *Roman Catholic Worship: Trent to Today* (New York: Paulist, 1995), 49–50.

16. *Constitution on the Sacred Liturgy* [CSL] 1.

17. CSL 7.

18. CSL 26.

19. CSL 27.

20. CSL 13.

21. CSL 124 and the *General Instruction of the Roman Missal* [GIRM] 279.

22. CSL 125 and GIRM 278.

23. GIRM 276.

24. John Brinckerhoff Jackson, *A Sense of Place, A Sense of Time* (New Haven: Yale University Press, 1994).

25. *Ibid.,* 160.

26. Joshua Meyrowitz, *No Sense of Place: The Impact of Electronic Media on Social Behavior* (New York: Oxford University Press, 1985), 115–116.

27. *Ibid.,* 125.

28. *Third Instruction on the Correct Implementation of the CSL,* 10. September 5, 1970.

29. Aidan Kavanagh, *Elements of Rite* (New York: Pueblo, 1982), 18.

30. From notes taken in class with Fr. Kavanagh, Summer 1972.

31. Thank you, GIA.

32. This instruction was issued in 1978 by the Bishops' Committee on the Liturgy. Currently, a task group is discussing the strengths and weaknesses of the document.

33. *The Church at Prayer: A Holy Temple of the Lord.* A pastoral statement issued by the American bishops commemorating the 20th anniversary of the *Constitution on the Sacred Liturgy.* NCCB, December 4, 1983.

Jan Michael Joncas

For Better or for Worse: Revising the Roman Rite *Order of Celebrating Matrimony*

Few examples of the intersection between culture and church are more illustrative than the texts and ceremonies associated with Christian marriage. Today, matrimonial traditions, some stretching back nearly 1500 years in the Roman rite, find themselves in transition as the social and ecclesial understandings of what it is to marry transform over time. Changes in understanding marriage both reflect and generate changes in the marriage ritual.

The following is an overview of the texts and ceremonies intended for celebrating marriage in the Roman rite as enshrined in the latest revision of the *Ordo Celebrandi Matrimonium*. After a short introduction situating this document in the ongoing process of liturgical revision, reform and renewal within the Roman rite, seven elements of the latest revision will be highlighted. Finally some possible adaptations of this revision for English-speaking Roman rite Catholics in the United States will be proposed.

Documentation

Contemporary revision of the celebration of marriage in the Roman rite began in response to a mandate of the Second Vatican Ecumenical Council. The Constitution on the Sacred Liturgy, *Sacrosanctum Concilium* [hereafter SC], in its article 77, directed that "the marriage rite now found in the Roman Ritual is to be revised and enriched so that it will more clearly signify the grace of the sacrament and will emphasize the spouses' duties." The body charged with implementing the Council's liturgical reform agenda, the *Consilium ad exsequendam Constitutionem de Sacra Liturgia* [hereafter Consilium], assigned this task to *coetus a studiis* 23.[1] This study group provided a series of drafts that were minutely examined and revised based on decisions by the plenary Consilium. The *editio typica* of the revised marriage rite was officially promulgated in 1969.[2] Immediately this Latin edition was remanded to various bodies for vernacular translation and adaptation for use in local churches.

For the official English version currently approved for use in the United States, these bodies included the International Commission on English in the Liturgy [hereafter ICEL] which proposed a draft translation for its member episcopal conferences, the Bishops' Committee on the Liturgy [hereafter BCL], which modified the ICEL proposal for the particular needs of the United States, and the National Conference of Catholic Bishops [hereafter NCCB], which approved in substance the work of ICEL and BCL. After confirmation by the appropriate Roman authorities, this vernacular edition has been in use in the United States since the early 1970s.

On 19 March 1990 the Congregation for Divine Worship and the Discipline of the Sacraments by the decree *Ritus Celebrandi Matrimonium* promulgated a second edition of the *Order of Celebrating Marriage* for the Roman rite. In 1991 the book containing this *editio typica altera* was published by the Vatican Polyglot Press.[3] Following the procedure mentioned above, ICEL has proposed a draft translation of OCM 1991 which is presently being adapted by the BCL and which will be sent to the NCCB for discussion and approval. Once approved by the NCCB, confirmation from Vatican authorities must be sought before the OCM 1991 can be used by English-speaking worshipers in the dioceses of the United States.

Comparing the rites for solemnizing marriage in OCM 1969 and OCM 1991[4] reveals seven areas of significant change: 1) an expanded and enriched "General Introduction" *(praenotanda);* 2) a new order for solemnizing marriages moderated by a lay officiant; 3) new introductory addresses; 4) new euchology; 5) new guidelines for the liturgy of the word; 6) additional congregational interventions in the marriage rite proper; and 7) new nuptial blessings.

Praenotanda

OCM 1969 provided only 18 articles in its "General Introduction," dividing these articles into four sections. In contrast OCM 1991 provides 44 articles in its "General Introduction," rearranging and supplementing the material found in OCM 1969.

Section 1 of OCM 1969's "General Introduction," entitled "Concerning the importance and dignity of the sacrament of matrimony," comprised articles 1–7. A succinct summary of Catholic teaching on marriage as an irrevocable covenant (rather than dissoluble contract) raised, for the baptized who pledge themselves, to the dignity of a sacrament, appeared in articles 1–4. This summary was based on passages from Ephesians and 1 Corinthians and repeated teachings from *Lumen Gentium* and *Gaudium et Spes.*

Article 5 directed that this summary provide a foundation for pastors' ministry to engaged couples and for preaching at their marriage; it further specified that engaged couples should receive catechesis on marriage, including a review of the fundamentals of Christian belief and practice. Article 6, stressing that marriage should "normally" *(de more)* be celebrated during the eucharist, called attention to core elements of the liturgical celebration: the liturgy of the word, the consent of the couple, the nuptial blessing (designated as "on the bride") and the reception of holy communion. Article 7 exhorted pastors to strengthen and nourish the faith of the engaged, since sacramental marriage "presupposes and demands faith." Clearly OCM 1969's first section gathered quite disparate material under a single heading.

In contrast OCM 1991 strictly limits its first section (articles 1–11) to the importance and dignity of marriage. The sources for this summary of Catholic teaching on marriage are expanded: In addition to the citations found in the 1969 edition, OCM 1991 quotes the Gospel of Matthew, 2 Corinthians, Tertullian's *Ad uxorem,* the 1982 *Code of Canon Law,* and John Paul II's apostolic exhortation *Familiaris Consortio.* The other directives and exhortations of OCM 1969, 5–7, reappear in other contexts in OCM 1991.

Section 2 of OCM 1969's "General Introduction," entitled "Concerning choosing the rite," was in articles 8–11. Article 8 detailed the liturgical formats to be used when celebrating marriages between a Roman Catholic and one baptized in another ecclesial tradition, or between a Roman Catholic and an unbaptized person. Articles 9–10 exhorted pastors to show evangelical concern for all who attend the marriage celebration and to shun any appearance of favoritism. Article 11 offered guidelines on vesture, lectionary and appointments when marriages are celebrated at various times during the church year.

Unlike OCM 1969 (but like most of the other post–Vatican II *editiones typicae*), OCM 1991, 12–27, treats the offices and ministries associated with celebrating marriage in the second section of its *praenotanda.* The roles of bishops (13), presbyters (14–23), deacons (24), lay assistants (25) and other members of the community (26) are specified, with great emphasis placed on pre-marriage preparation. If taken seriously, the blunt statement of article 21 may have some strong impact on pastoral practice:

> If, with every overture reduced to futility, the engaged clearly and expressly commit themselves to reject that which the Church intends when the marriage of the baptized is celebrated, pastors of souls are not allowed to admit them to the celebration; however unpleasant this may be, it is necessary to acknowledge the reality of the situation and to persuade those concerned that it is not the Church, but they themselves who hinder the celebration which they desire by adhering to such attitudes.[5]

It is somewhat surprising that, although article 12 emphasizes the roles played by the engaged couple and their families in preparing for marriage, there is no explicit treatment of others among the baptized who may have a role to play: lectors, acolytes, musicians, godparents, witnesses or "sponsors." In addition, article 27, treating the place in which the ceremony should occur, seems misplaced, more properly situated in OCM 1991's next section on the celebration itself.

OCM 1991, 28–38 gathers and supplements directives on the celebration of marriage from the first two sections of OCM 1969's "General Introduction" in the third section of its *praenotanda*. These directives are divided into two subsections: "Concerning preparation" (28–32) and "Concerning the ritual to be used" (33–38).

With reference to preparing the marriage celebration, OCM 1991 recommends that members of the parish participate since the celebration has a communal character (28a); gives permission for several marriages to be celebrated in the same ceremony or to take place at the Sunday assembly (28b); lists various options to be determined by the spouses and presider: whether the marriage is celebrated within or outside of Mass, the texts of the readings, vows, blessing of rings, nuptial blessing and general intercessions, and the chants sung during the service (29); and provides criteria to determine appropriate music (30) and visual environment (31–32) for the ceremony.

With reference to determining which form of celebration is appropriate, OCM 1991 highlights reasons for choosing marriage within or outside of Mass (33–34, 36); lists four ritual high points for the marriage celebration: the liturgy of the word, the consent of the spouses, the nuptial blessing (here designated as "on the bride and groom") and eucharistic communion (35); and lists the material objects needed for the celebration (38). Article 37 strongly exhorts pastoral discretion in marriage ministry:

> Although pastors are ministers of the Gospel of Christ for all people, nevertheless they should reserve a special attention toward those, whether Catholic or non-Catholic, who never or hardly ever participate in the celebration of Matrimony or of the Eucharist. This pastoral norm applies in the first instance to the spouses themselves.[6]

Section 3 of OCM 1969's "General Introduction," entitled "Concerning preparing particular rituals," was in articles 12–16. These articles presented directives for the content and process by which local territorial bishops' conferences may produce local rituals for celebrating marriage based on the *editio typica*, by adapting or supplementing texts (13), re-arranging the order of constitutive elements (14), or adapting, adding or omitting ceremonies (15–16). The fourth and final section of OCM 1969's "General Introduction," entitled "Concerning the faculty of developing a proper ritual," was in articles 17 and 18. These articles granted permission for local territorial bishops' conferences to develop local rituals for celebrating marriage which are not based on the *editio typica*. Section 3 seems to correspond to the "normal" and section 4 to the "more radical" processes for liturgical revision foreseen in SC 37–40.

OCM 1991 gathers and supplements this material from sections 3 and 4 of OCM 1969's "General Instruction" in the fourth and final section of its *praenotanda* (39–44). Fundamentally the directives appearing in OCM 1969 are repeated. It is somewhat surprising that, although "adaptations" by the local territorial liturgical authority are designated, no mention is made of "accommodations" in the rite made on the authority of the one who presides over it, "accommodations" that are regularly listed in the *praenotanda* of other reformed liturgical books of the Roman rite.

Order of Celebrating Marriage Presided Over by a Lay Officiant

Perhaps the greatest innovation of OCM 1991 occurs in its Chapter Four, which provides an order of service for celebrating marriages presided over by a lay officiant.

The introductory rites consist of the reception of the couple (with no procession or place indicated), a greeting (an ascription of praise based on a phrase from 2 Corinthians without a sign of the cross or trinitarian greeting) and an introduction (one of the introductory allocutions considered below).

A liturgy of the word follows. Although the Lord's Day pattern of a reading from the Hebrew scriptures, psalm, non-gospel reading from the New Testament, gospel acclamation and gospel is permitted, article 125 states that only one or two readings may be proclaimed, but at least one must explicitly speak of marriage.[7] While the lay assistant is not authorized to preach a liturgical homily, article 125 directs that it is fitting that an exhortation be offered or a homily (presumably prepared by the bishop or pastor) be read by the lay assistant at this point.[8]

The marriage rite proper comprises both central and explanatory rites. The central rites include an address to the couple indicating the lay assistant's authorization to witness the marriage, questions before the consent, the consent itself, formal reception of the consent (see "Alternative text for the reception of spouses' consent" below) and an acclamation of praise (see "Congregational interventions in the marriage rite proper" below). These texts by and large reproduce the texts prescribed for ordained presiders. The explanatory rites include a blessing and exchange of rings followed by an optional congregational song of praise. General intercessions seal and conclude the marriage rite proper (see "Model prayers for the general intercessions" below).

When holy communion is distributed as part of the marriage service, the lay assistant first offers a special form of the nuptial blessing (see nuptial blessing D below) followed by the standard communion rite (Lord's Prayer; sign of peace; invitation to communion; communion; silence, psalm or song of praise; prayer after communion). When holy communion is not distributed, the community prays the Lord's Prayer and the lay assistant offers a special form of the nuptial blessing.

In either case the concluding rites comprise a final blessing on the lay assistant and assembly, concluding music and the signing of the marriage register.

Introductory Allocutions

Another innovation in OCM 1991 is the provision of presidential addresses at the beginning of the service "so that spirits might be disposed toward celebrating matrimony" (52). Although the presiding minister may use other texts (presumably prepared beforehand rather than improvised), two sample addresses are provided for marriages of two Christians within or outside of Mass whether presided over by an ordained minister or by a layperson (52 = 87 = 123, 53 = 88 = 124). An adaptation of the second sample address appears when the marriage of a Christian with a catechumen or a non-Christian is celebrated (154).

The first allocution is addressed to the entire assembly. It outlines the structure of the marriage rite, responsive to the word of God in the scriptures and invoking God's blessing on those to be married:

> Brothers [and sisters] most dear, exulting we come together into the Lord's house to accomplish this celebration on the day in which N. and N., here present, intend to establish their house. Indeed this hour is of singular importance for them. Therefore with affection of soul and our friendship as well as fraternal prayer let us assist them. One with them let us attentively hear the word that God speaks to us today. Then with the holy church let us suppliantly ask God the Father through Christ our Lord that he might kindly receive these marrying servants of his, bless them and make them always one.[9]

The alternative allocution is addressed to the couple themselves. It seems less an opening address and more an invocation on the couple; as such it seems redundant, ritually duplicating portions of the nuptial blessing and the blessing at the conclusion of the service:

> N. and N., the church takes part in your joy and welcomes you with a full heart, along with your relatives and friends on the day on which before God our Father you establish a sharing of [your] entire life among yourselves. May the Lord hear you on the day of your joy. May he send to you assistance from heaven and may he/it protect you. May he grant to you [that which is] in conformity with your heart['s desires] and may he fulfill all your requests. [10]

For marriages of a Christian with a catechumen or a non-Christian, this alternative allocution is enriched and modified, presenting the presider with an opportunity for gentle evangelization (additions and modifications are highlighted):

> N. and N., the church takes part in your joy and welcomes you with a full heart, along with your relatives and friends on the day on which . . . you establish a sharing of [your] entire life among yourselves. *For believers, God is the font of love and faithfulness because God is love. Therefore let us attentively*

Jan Michael Joncas

hear his word and suppliantly entreat him that he may grant to you [that which is] in conformity with your heart['s desires] and may fulfill all your requests.[11]

Euchology

Opening Prayers

In addition to four collects reproduced from OCM 1969 with slight modifications in typography, layout, order and text,[12] OCM 1991 provides two further collects for use as opening prayers.

Collect E (OCM 1991, 227) is based on a prayer found in the *Verona collection of libelli missarum* [hereafter Ve], also known as the "Verona" or "Leonine" Sacramentary (1109):[13]

> Be present, Lord, to our supplications and kindly assist your institutions that you have established for the propagation of the human race so that what is joined together with you as author may be preserved with you helping. Through [our] Lord.[14]

If the nuptial blessing is omitted in marriages celebrated between a Christian and a catechumen or non-Christian, OCM 1991 directs that this collect be prayed over the bride and groom as a substitute (174).

Collect F (OCM 1991, 228) is based on a prayer found in the *Old Gelasian Sacramentary* [hereafter GeV] (1450):[15]

> God, you who blessed the beginning of the developing world with multiplied offspring, be favorable toward our supplications and pour out the grace of your blessing upon these servants of yours (N. and N.) so that in conjugal yoking-of-life they may be joined with equal affection, common outlook and mutual holiness. Through [our] Lord.[16]

Alternative Text for the Reception of the Spouses' Consent

Immediately after the vows the officiant formally receives the couple's matrimonial consent. In addition to the text in OCM 1969, OCM 1991 presents a new composition inspired by biblical texts:

> May the God of Abraham, the God of Isaac, the God of Jacob, the God who joined the first humans in paradise confirm and bless this consent of yours which you have manifested before the Church so that what [God] himself has joined, no human being may separate.[17]

This text is clearly related to the blessing said by the priest at the conclusion of the nuptial mass after the *"Benedicamus Domino"* or *"Ite, missa est"* in *Missale Romanum* [MR] 1570.[18]

Proper Insertions in Eucharistic Prayers II and III

OCM 1969 gives a single proper *Hanc igitur* for insertion into Eucharistic Prayer I; this text is a conflation of material from Ve and GeV with the Gregorian Sacramentary. OCM 1991 retains this proper *Hanc igitur* for Eucharistic Prayer I but also offers two new insertions for Eucharistic Prayers II and III:

> Indeed remember, Lord, N. and N., whom you have commanded to come to this day of marriage, so that your grace may abide [in them] in mutual love and peace [Eucharistic Prayer II].[19]

> Strengthen, we pray, in the grace of matrimony N. and N., whom you have happily led to the day of marriage, so that they may always preserve in life the covenant which they have established in your sight, with you protecting [it].[20]

Model Prayers for the General Intercessions

Unlike OCM 1969, OCM 1991 provides two model forms for the general intercessions in its Appendix. They are notable for the order in which the intercessions are offered, the concision and biblical inspiration of their language and the universality of their scope. They clearly follow the directive in OCM 1991, 103 that the individual invocations "should be congruent with the nuptial blessing, but should not reduplicate it."

Model I provides three intercessions for the newly married couple, an intercession for the church and those afflicted by need and an intercession for those sacramentally married:

Brothers most dear, recalling the special gift of grace and love by which God has deigned to perfect and consecrate the love of our kin, N. and N., let us commend them to the Lord:

1. That Christ's faithful, N. and N. now united in holy matrimony, would be worthy to enjoy eternal health and salvation, let us pray to the Lord: We ask you, hear us.

2. That he would bless their covenant, as he was disposed to sanctify the wedding feast in Cana of Galilee, let us pray to the Lord:

3. That he would grant to them perfect and fruitful love, peace and assistance, so that they might bear good witness to the name of Christian, let us pray to the Lord:

4. That the Christian people would grow in virtue from day to day and that the assistance of heavenly grace would be conferred on all who are afflicted by various needs, let us pray to the Lord:

5. That the grace of the sacrament would be renewed in all the married here present by the Holy Spirit, let us pray to the Lord:

Kindly pour forth the Spirit of your love, Lord, onto these spouses, so that one heart and one spirit may be produced in them, and that nothing might later separate what you have yoked, and nothing may afflict those whom you have filled with your blessing. Through Christ our Lord.[21]

Model II offers intercessions for the spouses, their relatives and friends, those preparing for marriage and other forms of dedicated life, for families to live in peace, for deceased relatives, and for the unity of Christians in the well-being of the church:

Brothers [and sisters] most dear, let us support this new family with our prayers so that the mutual love of these spouses would increase day by day and that God would kindly assist all families in the world.

1. For the new spouses here standing and for the good of their family, let us pray to the Lord: R. We pray you, hear us.

2. For their neighbors and friends and all those who were of aid to these spouses, let us pray to the Lord. R.

3. For young people who are preparing themselves for undertaking matrimony, and for all those whom the Lord has called to another state of life, let us pray to the Lord. R.

4. For all families in the world and for peace to be established among men [and women], let us pray to the Lord. R.

5. For all members of our families who have departed from this world and for all the dead, let us pray to the Lord. R.

6. For the church, the holy People of God, and for the unity of all Christians, let us pray to the Lord. R.

Lord Jesus, who are present in our midst when N. and N. covenant their union, receive our prayer and fill us with your Spirit. You live and reign unto the ages of ages. Amen.[22]

Final Blessing

In addition to the blessing texts intended for use by ordained officiants at the conclusion of the marriage service reprised almost verbatim from OCM 1969, OCM 1991 provides a final blessing text for a lay officiant to use:

> May God fill us with joy and hope in believing. / May the peace of Christ exult in our hearts. / May the Holy Spirit deepen his gifts in us.[23]

The lay officiant and the assembly are directed to sign themselves during the recitation of this text and the assembly indicates its assent with "Amen."

The Liturgy of the Word

Prior to the Second Vatican Council, marriages celebrated according to the Roman rite could be solemnized without any formal proclamation of sacred scripture or preaching if the marriage took place outside of Mass. If marriage was celebrated during the Nuptial Mass, a single set of scriptural readings was provided for proclamation (Ephesians 5:22–33 as the epistle and Matthew 19:3–6 as the gospel) with a limited number of psalm verses to be chanted between these scriptural proclamations according to the season. (Outside of Lent and Eastertide the Gradual and Alleluia were from Psalm 127/128:3 and Psalm 19:3/20:2; in Lent the Tract was from Psalm 127/128:4–6; in Eastertide the Gradual was replaced by Psalm 19:3/20:2 and Psalm 133/134:3).

Jan Michael Joncas

In conformity with SC 35.1's declaration that "[i]n sacred celebrations there is to be more reading from holy Scripture and it is to be more varied and apposite," OCM 1969 provided a list of 35 scriptural pericopes from which the readings to be proclaimed during the liturgy of the word might be chosen.

Fifteen passages from the Hebrew Bible appeared: seven responsorial psalms and eight selections from other books. Twenty passages from the New Testament were offered: ten selections from the gospels and ten from other books. Whether marriage is celebrated during or outside of Mass, the Sunday-and-solemnity pattern for scriptural proclamations (non-psalm reading from the Hebrew Bible, responsorial psalm, non-gospel reading from the New Testament, gospel acclamation, gospel) could be employed, but the earlier pattern of an "epistle" reading—which might be from the Hebrew Bible or from the non-gospel readings of the New Testament—and a "gospel" reading with interspersed biblical chants could also be used (OCM 1969, 21, 41). A single scripture reading could be proclaimed when marriage is celebrated between a Catholic and a non-baptized person (OCM 1969, 56). OCM 1969 also directed that a homily be given following the proclamation of the scriptures in marriages during or outside of Mass.

OCM 1991 modifies the prescriptions for celebrating the liturgy of the word given in OCM 1969. First, since the Neo-Vulgate translation of the Bible is used in OCM 1991, some of the verse references have been modified and some of the titles for the individual pericopes have been changed. Second, while all of the pericopes provided in the earlier book are retained in the latter, OCM 1991 adds five new pericopes to the pool given in OCM 1969: one from the Hebrew Bible (Proverbs 31:10–13, 19–20, 30–31) and four from the New Testament (Romans 15:1b–3a, 5–7, 13; Ephesians 4:1–6; Philippians 4:4–9; Hebrews 13:1–4a, 5–6b). Third, OCM 1991 asserts that at least one of the readings chosen must explicitly speak of marriage (OCM 1991, 55, 90, 125, 156). The readings that fulfill this criterion are marked with an asterisk in the Appendix: eight from the Hebrew Bible (one psalm and seven selections from other books), two from the apostolic letters and three from the gospels. Fourth, the Sunday-and-solemnity pattern for the scriptural proclamations is highlighted for marriages celebrated during Mass (OCM 1991, 55), but fewer proclamations seem suggested for marriages outside of Mass: OCM 1991, 125 declares that "one or two readings could be proclaimed, as would be deemed appropriate" for marriages witnessed by a lay assistant and OCM 1991, 156 states that "one or two readings could be proclaimed; but if circumstances suggest it, there could be only one reading proclaimed."[24] Finally, preaching crowns the proclamation of the scriptures in every marriage liturgy of the word, but the liturgical homily is reserved to an ordained person (OCM 1991, 57, 91).

In marriage ceremonies presided over by a lay assistant, the gospel is introduced with a greeting different from that given by a deacon or priest ("Hear, brothers, the words of the holy Gospel according to N.") and the assistant may offer an "exhortation" or read a homily prepared by the bishop or pastor (OCM 1991, 125, cf. 156–157.).[25]

Congregational Interventions in the Marriage Rite Proper

OCM 1991 provides two new opportunities for the assembly to actively intervene during the solemnization of matrimonial consent. The first is a community ratification of the couple's matrimonial consent in addition to the formal reception by the officiant:

> *[The officiant] invites those present to praise God:*
> Let us bless the Lord.
> *All respond:*
> Thanks be to God.
> *Another acclamation could be done.*[26]

The second is an optional hymn or canticle of praise to be sung by the assembly as its own acknowledgement of the covenant event.[27] OCM 1991 provides no sample texts. Presumably chants based on scriptural texts would have pride of place, but ecclesiastical compositions would not be forbidden.

Jan Michael Joncas

Nuptial Blessings

Four sets of nuptial blessings appear in OCM 1991, exhibiting the most extensive euchological revision in the document.

Nuptial Blessing A

Intended for use by an ordained officiant at the marriage of two Christians whether celebrated within or outside of Mass, Nuptial Blessing A revises the ancient blessing over the bride in the Roman rite. The form in which it appeared in the *Missale Romanum* 1570 served as the foundational text for the revision appearing in OCM 1969:

> Let us pray.
> Lord, be pleased with our supplications, and kindly assist those institutions of yours which you have ordered for the propagation of the human race: so that, what has been joined together with you as source may be preserved with you assisting. Through Christ.
> Let us pray.
> God, who have made all things from nothing by the might of your power; who, having arranged the foundations of the universe, created the inseparable help of woman for man, formed to the image of God, so that you bestowed the beginning of the female body from male flesh, teaching that what it pleased [you] to be established from one [principle] would never be lawful to be put asunder:
> God, who have consecrated conjugal union by so excellent a mystery that you have pre-signified the sacrament of Christ and of the Church in the covenant of marrying people;
> God, through whom woman is joined to man, and society is given its arrangment principally by this blessing, which is the only one neither washed away through the pain of original sin nor through the punishment of the Flood:
> Look kindly upon this female servant of yours, who, about to be joined in marital partnership, seeks to strengthen herself by your protection: May this union be for her [one] of love and peace:
> Faithful and chaste may she marry in Christ, and may she remain an imitator of the holy women. May she be dear to her husband as [was] Rachel; wise, as [was] Rebecca; long-lived and

faithful, as [was] Sarah. May that author of lies [i.e., Satan] control nothing in her conduct. Bound by faith, may she remain [faithful] to your commandments. Joined to one spouse, may she flee from any unlawful contacts. May she fortify her weakness with the strength of discipline. May she be of reserved sincerity, respectable modesty [and] well-taught in heavenly doctrines. May she be fruitful in offspring. May she be tested and innocent. And may she come to the rest of the blessed and to the heavenly kingdoms.

And may they both see their children's children [literally, "the sons of their sons"] even to the third and fourth generation, and may they come to a desirable old age. Through the same Lord.[28]

Despite its antiquity, this text was vigorously criticized by the members of study group 23. The initial collect was judged ritually redundant and was replaced by a more extended invitation to prayer. Contemporary exegesis of the Genesis creation accounts challenged the implication of the first paragraph of the blessing prayer proper that only men are created in the image of God. Since the Roman rite presumes that the exchange of matrimonial consent begins the marriage and since the nuptial blessing occurs after the exchange of matrimonial consent, the reference to the bride "about to be joined" to her husband had to be modified. The concluding petitions for the couple seem tagged onto the petitions for the bride and interrupt the chronological flow of its thought. But most substantively, the almost exclusive concentration on the bride had to be balanced with equal prayer for the groom and for the couple if the text was to reflect the teachings of the Second Vatican Council on marriage.

Thus OCM 1969's version of Nuptial Blessing A, though clearly based on the MR 1570 original, recast the prayer in significant ways. Changes from the nuptial blessing in MR 1570 have been highlighted in the following translation:

> 33. *Let us suppliantly pray to the Lord, brothers [and sisters] most dear, that he would mercifully pour out upon this female servant of his, who has been wed to this husband in Christ, the blessing of his grace: and that he would make those who have been joined by holy covenant (and by the sacrament of the Body and Blood of Christ) unified in one love.*

Jan Michael Joncas

And all pray in silence for a short time. Then the priest, with hands extended, continues:

God, who have made all things from nothing by the might of your power; who, having arranged the foundations of the universe and *having made human beings* [literally "man"] to the image of God, created the inseparable help of woman for man, so that *they should not be two but one flesh,* teaching that what it pleased [you] to be established *as one* would never be lawful to be put asunder:

God, who have consecrated conjugal union by so excellent a mystery that you have pre-signified the sacrament of Christ and of the Church in the covenant of marrying people;

God, through whom woman is joined to man, and society is given its arrangement principally by this blessing, which is the only one neither washed away through the pain of original sin nor through the punishment of the Flood:

Look kindly upon this female servant of yours, who, *having been joined* in marital partnership, seeks to strengthen herself through your *blessing:* May *the grace* of love and peace be *in her:*

And may she remain an imitator of the holy women, *whose praises are proclaimed in the Scriptures.*

May the heart of her husband, who (acknowledging that she is equal in status and a co-heir to the life of grace) should offer her the honor that is due her and should cherish her always with that love by which Christ cherished the Church, trust in her.

And now we pray you, Lord, that these servants of yours might remain bound in faith and the commandments and, joined to a single spouse, they might be notable for the integrity of their conduct; united by the strength of the gospel, may they give good witness to Christ before all; (may they be fertile in off-spring, may they be parents of tested virtue; may they both see their children's children [literally "the sons of their sons"]); and, *having come at last* to a desirable old age, may they come to the life of the blessed and to the heavenly kingdoms. Through *Christ our* Lord.[29]

Note that the stereotyped invitations to prayer have been omitted; an extended invitation to prayer, rather than a collect, is prefixed to the blessing prayer proper; according to OCM 1969, 34, only one of the three invocatory paragraphs of the blessing prayer proper (the one corresponding to the reading proclaimed earlier in the service) need be publicly pronounced; the reference to the creation of woman from man has been adapted to reconize the equal status of males and females before God; the list of virtuous women from the Hebrew Bible has been subsumed into a general category; reference to some of the allegedly female virtues has been omitted and replaced by a section that prays for the bride's activity in the church; and references to parenting in the final paragraph may be omitted if it is clear that the couple will never play that role.

Although this recasting of the traditional Roman rite Nuptial Blessing was generally well received, further criticisms also appeared. First, both the invitation and the blessing text remain focused on the bride, although some mention is made of the groom and the couple. Second, while the texts distinctly connect marriage to the activity of God the Father (by appropriation) in creation and Christ as Bridegroom in relation to the Church, the activity of the Holy Spirit is not explicitly acknowledged. Third, instead of subsuming the scriptural models of virtue for the bride into a single category, listing scriptural models for the groom could enrich the prayer.

Repeating most of OCM 1969's prayer verbatim, OCM 1991 recast some elements of Nuptial Blessing A to respond to these criticisms. Modifications of the OCM 1969 text have been highlighted in the following translation:

> 73. Let us suppliantly pray to the Lord, brothers [and sisters] most dear, most that he would kindly pour out upon *these servants of his, who are wedded* in Christ, the blessing of his grace, and that he would make those he has joined by holy covenant (and by the sacrament of the Body and Blood of Christ) unified in one love. . . .

> 74. . . . God, who have made all things from nothing by the might of your power; who, having arranged the foundations of the universe and having made human beings [literally, "man"] to *your* image, created the inseparable help of woman for man, so that they should not be two but one flesh, teaching that what it pleased you to be established as one, would never be lawful to be put asunder:

Jan Michael Joncas

God, who have consecrated conjugal union by so excellent a mystery that you have pre-signified the sacrament of Christ and of the Church in the covenant of marrying people;

God, through whom woman is joined to man, and society is given its arrangement principally by this blessing, which is the only one not washed away through the pain of original sin or through the Flood:

Look kindly upon *these servants of yours,* who, *having been joined* in marital partnership, seek to strengthen *themselves* with your blessing: *send forth upon them the grace of the Holy Spirit, so that, with your love diffused in their hearts, they may remain faithful in the conjugal covenant.*

May the grace of love and peace be *in your female servant N.,* and may she remain an imitator of the holy women whose praises are proclaimed in the Scriptures.

May the heart of her husband, who (acknowledging that she is equal in status and a co-heir to the life of grace) should offer her the honor that is due her and should cherish her always with that love by which Christ cherished the Church, trust in her.

And now we pray you, Lord, that these servants of yours might remain bound in faith and the commandments and, joined to a single spouse, they might be notable for the integrity of their conduct; united by the strength of the gospel, may they exhibit good testimony to Christ before all; (may they be fertile in offspring, may they be parents of tested virtue; may they both see their children's children [literally, "the sons of their sons"]); and, having come at last to a desirable old age, may they come to the life of the blessed and to the heavenly kingdoms. Through Christ our Lord.[30]

The invitation now requests prayer for both spouses rather than for the bride alone, followed by prayer for the couple. The blessing prayer proper now exhibits an explicit epiclesis, praying that the grace of the Holy Spirit be poured out upon the couple first, and only then turning to individual petitions for each of the spouses. Both the invitation and the formal blessing are printed with musical notation, suggesting that a chanted form of the Nuptial Blessing is normative. (As far as I am able to determine, OCM 1991 rescinds the permission given in OCM 1969 to use only one of the three invocatory paragraphs corresponding to the reading proclaimed.)

Nuptial Blessing B

Intended for use by an ordained minister at the marriage of two Christians whether celebrated within or outside of eucharist, Nuptial Blessing B is a new composition created for OCM 1969 primarily by two members of study group 23, Louis Ligier and Secundo Mazzarello:

120 . . . *The priest, standing turned toward the groom and bride, says with his hands joined:*

Let us pray to the Lord over these spouses, who, undertaking marriage, come to the altar so that (as sharers in the Body and Blood of Christ) they might be joined forever in mutual love.

And all pray in silence for a short time. Then the priest, with hands extended, continues:

Holy Father, who have created humanity to your image as male and female so that man and woman, joined in unity of flesh and heart, might fulfill their responsibility in the world:

God, who, for the sake of revealing the plan of your love, have willed that that covenant of mutual love between spouses which you have deigned to enter with your people be so designed that, having received the status of a sacrament, the nuptial mystery of Christ and the Church could appear in the conjugal partnership of your faithful:

Upon these servants of yours (N. and N.) we pray, kindly extend your right [hand]. Be present, Lord, that as they begin in the partnership of this sacrament, the gifts of your love may be shared between them and that, displaying the sign of your presence to one another, they may be one in heart and one in spirit. Grant also, Lord, that they might sustain by their activity the household which they build and that they might prepare their children [literally, "sons"], having been formed by evangelical discipline, to be members of the heavenly family.

Deign to heap your female servant N. with your blessings so that, fulfilling the responsibilities of a wife and a mother, she might nurture her household with chaste love and adorn it with pleasant grace.

[Deign] also to shower your male servant N. with heavenly blessing so that he might persevere worthily in the responsibilities of a faithful husband and a generous father.

Jan Michael Joncas

Grant, holy Father, that those who have been joined by partnership before you may seek to come to your table and rejoice to share in the heavenly banquet in the future. Through Christ.[31]

Two major criticisms of this text have arisen since it was promulgated. First, while both God the Father and Christ are explicitly mentioned in the prayer, the action of the Holy Spirit is underplayed. Second, the attempt to differentiate the separate responsibilities of the spouses may betray a sexist bias. (The officially approved English translation heightens the disparity of responsibilities: "Give your blessings to N., your daughter, so that *she may be a good wife [and mother], caring for the home, faithful in love for her husband, generous and kind.* Give your blessings to N., your son, so that *he may be a faithful husband [and a good father].*" While one might argue that the emphasis placed on the wife's role exalts her status in a culture that degrades women, the text as heard in North American liturgical assemblies suggests that the husband has fewer responsiblities for maintaining the household than does the wife.)

OCM 1991 reproduces this second nuptial blessing with minor retouches. First, both the invitation to prayer and the blessing prayer proper are provided with musical notation, suggesting that the preferred method of execution for these texts is in chant. Second, the permission to omit one of the invocations of the prayer appears to have been rescinded. Third, the optional phrases concerning parenthood are clearly marked with parentheses and one of these phrases is repositioned in a way that does not affect the English translation. Fourth and most importantly, OCM 1991 adds a phrase to the central petition of the prayer that transforms it into a genuine epiclesis:

Upon these servants of yours (N. and N.) we pray, extend your [right] hand and pour out the power of the Holy Spirit in their hearts. . . . [32]

Finally, OCM 1991 adds "our Lord" and the congregational response "Amen" to the conclusion of the prayer.[33]

Nuptial Blessing C

Nuptial Blessing C, newly composed for OCM 1969 after the April 1967 meeting of study group 23, appears in OCM 1991 in three

versions: one for use by an ordained officiant at *sacramental* marriages (that is, between two Christians) whether celebrated within or
outside of Mass, a second for use by an ordained officiant at *non-
sacramental* marriages (that is, between a Catholic Christian and a
catechumen or non-Christian), and a third for use by a lay officiant at
non-sacramental marriages.

Version One

[121.] *The priest, standing turned toward the groom and bride,
says, with hands joined:*
   Suppliant, let us invoke with our prayers, brothers [and sisters]
most dear, God's blessing upon these spouses, so that he himself
might kindly support with his help those whom he has joined by
the sacrament of wedding.
   *And all pray for a short time in silence. Then the priest, with
hands extended, continues:*
   Holy Father, creator of the entire world, who have created
man and woman to your image and have willed that their union
be filled to overflowing with your blessing, we humbly pray to
you for this bride, who today is joined to her husband in the
sacrament of marriage.
   May your copious blessing come down upon her, Lord, and
upon her partner for life so that, when they are made fruitful
by the mutual gift of marriage, they might adorn their family
with children [literally, "sons"] and enrich your Church.
   Joyful, may they praise you, Lord [and] sorrowing, may they
seek you; may they rejoice that you are present to them in [their]
work so that you might help them, may they know that you
are present in their [times of] need so that you might sustain
them; may they pray to you in the holy assembly, may they
show themselves your witnesses in the world; and having
achieved a prosperous old age, with this circle of friends by
which they are surrounded, may they come to the heavenly
kingdoms. Through Christ.[34]

OCM 1991 lightly recasts version one of Nuptial Blessing C.
Modifications of the OCM 1969 prayer are highlighted in the following translation:

243. The priest *(or deacon)*, standing turned toward the groom and bride with hands joined, *invites those present to pray:*

Suppliant, let us invoke with our prayers, brothers most [and sisters] dear, God's blessing upon these spouses, so that he himself might kindly support with his help those whom he has joined by the sacrament of wedding.

And all pray for a short time in silence.

244. Then the priest *(or deacon)*, with hands extended *over the spouses,* continues:

Holy Father, creator of the entire world, who have created man and woman to your image and have willed that their union be filled to overflowing with your blessing, we humbly pray to you for *these your servants,* who today are joined in the sacrament of marriage.

May your copious blessing come down upon *this bride N.,* Lord, and upon her partner for life, *N., and may the power of your Holy Spirit inflame their hearts from above* so that, when they are made fruitful by the mutual gift of marriage, they might adorn their family with children [literally, "sons"] and enrich your Church.

Joyful, may they praise you, Lord [and] sorrowing, may they seek you; may they rejoice that you are present to them in [their] work so that you might help them, may they know that you are present in their [times of] need so that you might sustain them; may they pray to you in the holy assembly, may they show themselves your witnesses in the world; and having achieved a prosperous old age, with this circle of friends by which they are surrounded, may they come to the heavenly kingdoms. Through Christ *our Lord. R. Amen.*[35]

OCM 1991 provides musical notation for both the invitation and the blessing prayer proper, suggesting that these texts would be normatively chanted. It indicates that the ordained officiant could be either a bishop or presbyter *(sacerdos)* or a deacon. It calls for the bride and groom to be mentioned by name. Most importantly, it rewords the opening petitions so that they apply to the couple throughout and it adds a reference to the Holy Spirit, thus providing an explicit epiclesis.

Version Two

In articles 64–65, OCM 1969 adapted Nuptial Blessing C for use in marriages between a Catholic Christian and a non-Christian to reflect the non-sacramental character of this covenant marriage. Modifications of version one are highlighted in this translation:

> 65 . . . Suppliant, let us invoke by our prayers, brothers [and sisters] most dear, God's blessing upon these spouses so that he might kindly support by his help those whom he has joined in the *partnership* of wedding. . . .
>
> Holy Father, creator of the entire world, who have created man and woman to your image and have willed that their union be filled to overflowing with your blessing, we humbly pray to you for this bride, who today is joined to her husband in the *covenant* of marriage.
>
> May your copious blessing come down upon her, Lord, and upon her partner for life so that, when they are made fruitful by the mutual gift of marriage, *they might be notable for the integrity of their conduct (and be parents of well-tested virtue).*
>
> Joyful, may they praise you, Lord [and] sorrowing, may they seek you; may they rejoice that you are present to them in their work so that you might help them, may they know that you are present in their need so that you might sustain them; and having achieved a prosperous old age, with the crown of friends by which they are surrounded, may they come to the heavenly kingdom. Through Christ *our Lord. R. Amen.*[36]

Major modifications of version one include: omitting and rearranging some words in the invitation to prayer; changing the reference to the "sacrament" of marriage to the "covenant" of marriage; changing the text about producing children to enrich the church; omitting the text about praying in the liturgical assembly and witnessing in the world; and adding "our Lord" and the congregational response "Amen" to the conclusion of the prayer.

OCM 1991 lightly retouches version two of Nuptial Blessing C. Modifications of OCM 1969's version two are highlighted in this translation:

> 171 . . . *Now upon these spouses let us, suppliant, invoke* God's blessing so that he *himself* might support by his help those whom he has joined in the partnership of wedding. . . .

Jan Michael Joncas

172 . . . Holy Father, creator of the entire world, who have created man and woman to your image and have willed that their union be filled to overflowing with your blessing, we humbly pray to you for *these servants of yours,* who today *are* joined in the covenant of marriage.

May your copious blessing come down upon *this bride, N.,* Lord, and upon her partner for life, *N., and may the power of your Holy Spirit inflame their hearts from above* so that, when they are made fruitful by the mutual gift of marriage, they might be notable for the integrity of their conduct (and be parents of well-tested virtue).

Joyful, may they praise you, Lord [and] sorrowing, may they seek you; may they rejoice that you are present to them in their work so that you might help them, may they know that you are present in their need so that you might sustain them; and having achieved a prosperous old age, with the crown of friends by which they are surrounded, may they come to the heavenly kingdoms. Through Christ our Lord. R. Amen.[37]

In its recasting of version two of Nuptial Blessing C, OCM 1991 modifies the invitation to prayer to make it less verbose; restructures the blessing proper so that intercession is made for the couple before prayers for the individual spouses; and adds an explicit epiclesis.

Version Three

Foreseeing situations in which a lay assistant might moderate the marriage between a Catholic Christian and a catechumen or non-Christian, OCM 1991 provides a third version of Nuptial Blessing C which prefixes an ascription of praise to the text we have just considered:

173. *Blessed are you, Lord God, creator and preserver of the human race, who have in the partnership of man and woman left an authentic image of your love.*

Upon this bride N., *we pray,* Lord, and upon her partner for life, N., may your copious blessing come down so that, when they are made fruitful by the mutual gift of marriage, they might be notable for the integrity of their conduct (and be parents of well-tested virtue).

Joyful, may they praise you, Lord [and] sorrowing, may they seek you; may they rejoice that you are present to them in their work so that you might help them, may they know that you are present in their need so that you might sustain them; and having achieved a prosperous old age, with the crown of friends by which they are surrounded, may they come to the heavenly kingdoms. Through Christ our Lord. R. Amen.[38]

Nuptial Blessing D

Also appearing for the first time in OCM 1991 is a nuptial blessing intended to be prayed by a lay officiant in marriages between two Christians. The rubric prefixed to the text indicates that the lay officiant is to pray the prayer with joined hands and prescribes vocal interventions by the assembly during the prayer, both signs clearly differentiating this prayer from the three prayers proper to ordained officiants.

139. *Then the assistant says with hands joined:* Now let us suppliantly invoke the blessing of God upon these spouses so that he might kindly nurture with his help those whom he has joined by the sacrament of marriage. *And all pray for a certain space of time in silence.*

140. *Then the assistant, with hands joined, says over the kneeling spouses the prayer of nuptial blessing, with all participating:*
Blessed are you God, the Father almighty, who willed to elevate humanity [literally, "man"], created by the gift of your piety, to such dignity that in the partnership of man and woman you have left an authentic image of your love.
All: Blessed be God.
Assistant: Blessed are you God, the only-begotten Son, Jesus Christ, who in the conjugal covenant of your faithful willed to reveal the mystery of your love in the church for whom you handed yourself over that it might be holy and immaculate.
All: Blessed be God.
Assistant: Blessed are you God, the Holy Spirit, Paraclete, worker of all sanctification and maker of unity, who dwell within the children [literally, "sons"] of delight so that they should take care to preserve unity in the bond of peace.
All: Blessed be God.
Assistant: Grant, Lord, to your servants, N. and N., whom you have joined in the sacrament of matrimony, to be united in

mutual love, so that, when they are fruitful by the gift of marriage, they may enrich the human family with children [literally, "sons"], be present in the holy church, and show themselves your witnesses in the world. Through Christ our Lord.

All: Amen.

(Or:)

Look, Lord, upon these servants of yours, N. and N., and be present, so that trusting in you alone, they may receive the gifts of your grace, preserve charity in unity, and may merit to come, after the course of this life, to the joys of eternal happiness, one with their children. Through Christ our Lord.

All: Amen.[39]

Nuptial Blessing D offers new possibilities for the development of marriage euchology. The verbal interventions by the community enhance the possibilities of their full, conscious and active participation in this element of the liturgy. (A parallel might be made between Nuptial Blessings A–C and Eucharistic Prayers I–IV in comparison to Nuptial Blessing D and the second Eucharistic Prayer for use in Masses with Children.) While I understand the desire to differentiate this prayer from those offered by ordained officiants, I question the rubric that the lay officiant should pray the ascriptions of praise with hands joined; perhaps the entire assembly could be invited to pray with hands uplifted (rather than stretched out over the couple) during these texts. Unlike Nuptial Blessings A–C in OCM 1991, Nuptial Blessing D is not set to musical notation. The ascriptions of praise with their congregational interventions could be enhanced if they were to be chanted.

Possible United States Adaptations

Since OCM 1991 indicates that local territorial authorities may adapt its texts and ceremonies to local cultures, I conclude by listing some areas in which Roman rite weddings in the United States might be inculturated.

Modifications of the Ordo

In recent years the insights of anthropologists on the structure and content of "rites of passage" have enriched our thinking about certain liturgical rites. For example, the *Rite of Baptism of Infants* presents a clear four-station structure (rites at entryway, ambo, font, altar) with processional movement among the stations as a spatial enactment of the passage ritual aimed at infant initiates, parents, godparents and the assembly. I recommmend a similar structuring of the marriage ritual to underscore its status as a rite of passage.

The introductory rites would be held at the entryway of the church where the presider and other church ministers would greet the assembly, identifying the various ritual actors: bride and groom, principal witnesses (best man and maid or matron of honor, who can testify to the assembly about the engaged couple's readiness to undertake Christian marriage), marriage sponsors (a married couple involved in the engaged couple's preparation who can testify on behalf of the worshiping assembly), godparents (whose presence bespeaks Christian marriage as a specification of the vocation assumed in baptism), parents, family members and other supporters. The ritual questions establishing the engaged couple's freedom and intent to undertake marriage would lead to a procession by the entire group to the space around the ambo. The opening prayer would conclude the procession and signal the opening of the liturgy of the word.

The liturgy of the word would proceed according to the revised Roman rite Lord's Day eucharistic structure: reading from the Hebrew Bible, normatively proclaimed by a lector; psalm or canticle from the Hebrew Bible, normatively sung by a cantor or choir and assembly; New Testament non-gospel reading, normatively proclaimed by another lector; gospel acclamation, sung by cantor or choir and assembly as the Book of the Gospels is borne in procession to the ambo; gospel reading, normatively proclaimed by the deacon; homily or reflection, normatively by the officiant.

The marriage rite proper would then consist of the exchange of consent (central ritual sign in word and gesture) formally received by the officiant and assembly; blessing and exchange of rings (explanatory ritual sign in word and gesture); nuptial blessing (solemnization of marriage covenant by officiant); hymn or canticle of praise (congregational confirmation of the solemnized marriage covenant); and prayers of the faithful.

After the marriage rite proper the liturgy of the Lord's table following the revised Roman rite Lord's Day eucharistic structure (preparation and presentation of gifts, eucharistic prayer, fraction rite, communion rite and dismissal) could be celebrated; alternatively the assembly could recite the Lord's Prayer and be dismissed.

Modifications of Texts

I have already indicated the modifications I would recommend in the OCM 1991 nuptial blessings. But new texts appropriate for particular cultures and local churches should also be developed as examples of ritual creativity. Of an increasing number of examples I will cite only five: two nuptial blessing texts, one in English and one in Irish, which appeared in the 1980 Irish marriage ritual, and three French texts, two shared in the French and Canadian marriage rituals and one unique to French-speaking Canada.

An English-language original text appears in the Irish marriage ritual as "Nuptial Blessing IV":

> We call God our Father. Let each of us now ask him, in silence, to bless his children as they begin their married life.
>
> *All pray silently for a short while. Then the priest extends his hands and continues:* Father, from you every family in heaven and on earth takes its name. You made us. You made all that exists. You made man and woman like yourself in their power to know and love. You call them to share life with each other, saying, "It is not good for man to be alone." (You bless them with children to give new life to your people, telling them: "Increase and multiply, and fill the earth.")
>
> We call to mind the fruitful companionship of Abraham, our father in faith, and his wife Sarah. We remember how your guiding hand brought Rebecca and Isaac together, and how through the lives of Jacob and Rachel you prepared the way for your kingdom.
>
> Father, you take delight in the love of husband and wife, that love which hopes and shares, heals and forgives.

We ask you to bless N. and N. as they set out on their new life. Fill their hearts with your Holy Spirit, the Spirit of understanding, joy, fortitude and peace. Strengthen them to do your will, and in the trials of life to bear the cross with Christ. May they praise you during the bright days, and call on you in times of trouble. (May their children bring them your blessing, and give glory to your name.) Let their love be strong as death, a fire that floods cannot drown, a jewel beyond all price. May their life together give witness to their faith in Christ. May they see long and happy days, and be united forever in the kingdom of your glory. We ask this through Christ our Lord. R. Amen.[40]

One might critique this text for its anamnesis which only presents Hebrew Bible patriarchal types for Christian marriage and for the use of the masculine generic in its quotation of Genesis, but it should be lauded for the balancing of male and female scriptural models, the absence of "division of labor" for the spouses and some memorable poetic phrases.

An Irish-language original text appears in ICM 1980 as "Beannú an Phósta"; here is an English translation:

Let us ask God to send his blessing on N. and N. and unite them in love.

All pray silently for a while.

God our Father, you created the universe. You made a human person from the soil of the earth and into the nostrils you blew the breath of life, thus making a living being. And you said: It is not good that this person be alone; I will make a worthy helpmate to match. And, causing a deep sleep to fall on him, you took a rib and covered it in flesh. This you made into a woman, and brought her to the man, who said: This at last is bone of my bone and flesh of my flesh! She shall be called woman because she was called into being from man. For this reason, a man leaves father and mother and holds fast to his wife and they come to be one flesh. You blessed them and said[:] Be fruitful and multiply and fill the earth and subdue it.

Therefore, Lord God, grant your generous blessing to your servants here, N. and N. Bless them as you blessed Abraham and Sarah, Isaac and Rebecca, Zachary and Elizabeth, Joachim and Anne. Protect them, Lord, as you protected Noah from the flood, [t]he three in the fiery furnace, Isaac from the sword, and the people of Moses from slavery in Egypt.

Look kindly on N. May she live in peace with you and follow the example of those women who are praised in the Scriptures. May she have the cheerfulness of Rachel and the wisdom of Rebecca and a long life of faithfulness like Sarah. May she be blessed in her looks and in her speech. May she be blessed in her health and in her beauty. May she be blessed in love and in grace.

May N. put his trust in her, and may she be a companion to him. May he always esteem her and love her as Christ does the Church.

Father, keep this couple strong in faith and true to your commands. May they be faithful to each other, examples of Christian living, and witnesses to Christ. May they see their children's children. And after a long and happy life together, [m]ay they find joy in the company of your saints in heaven. We ask this through Christ, our Lord.

People: Amen.[41]

This original nuptial blessing presents many scriptural types (the recounting of the Genesis story might even be considered excessive) and echoes a long tradition of Celtic blessings. More problematic, however, is the absence of an explicit epiclesis, the relative lack of New Testament references, and the unequal "division of labor" between the spouses.

The first French-language original nuptial blessing is intended to be used only when the spouses actually receive communion:

Brothers [and sisters], ask of God that he might bless these new spouses who wish to receive together the body and blood of Jesus Christ.

All pray for a few moments in silence. Then the priest, with his hands extended, continues:

Lord our God, you have called N. and N. by their names so that in giving themselves to one another they might become one flesh and one spirit: give them the body of your Son through whom their unity will be realized.

You are the source of their love and you have placed in them the desire for goodness that animates them: give them the blood of your Son who will sanctify their love and their joy.

In receiving the bread of life and the cup of blessing, let them undertake to give their life for others; let them raise in faithfulness to the Gospel the children who are born of their love; let them seek before all things the Kingdom of God and his justice; let them be useful to the world where they are living; let them show themselves welcoming to those who are poorer; let them always be able to give you thanks and let them come one day to renew their covenant in communing together in the risen body of Jesus Christ.

It is through Him that we pray to you: as he has sanctified the wedding of Cana and purified his Church in offering himself for her, we know that he intercedes before you for our friends N. and N., today, tomorrow and all the days of their life unto eternity.
All: Amen.[42]

This blessing clearly presumes a ritual context in which the nuptial blessing is closely linked to sacramental communion, praying that the fruits of holy communion will enrich the married life of the new spouses; it would therefore be inappropriate if this blessing text were to be repositioned to the end of the marriage rite proper as I suggested above. While there are no explicit references to the Hebrew Bible, two New Testament references are woven into the final paragraph of the prayer in a quasi-anamnesis. Perhaps the strongest contribution this text makes is its forthright articulation of the social responsibilities undertaken by Christian spouses. Less happy are its lack of an explicit epiclesis and the absence of a clear cue to evoke the assembly's "Amen."

A second French-language original text is intended for use at marriages outside of Mass, especially when a Catholic marries a non-Catholic baptized person:

Lord our God, creator of the universe and of all that lives there, you have made man and woman in your likeness, and so that they might be associated with your work of love, you have given them a heart capable of loving.

You have willed that today, in this church, N. and N. would unite their life. You now will that they would establish their household, that they would seek to love each other each day henceforth and would follow the example of Christ, he who has loved humans even to his death on a cross.

Bless, protect and strengthen the love of these new spouses: may their love sustain their fidelity; may it make them happy and cause them to discover (in Christ) the joy of a gift totally given to the one whom one loves.

May their love, like your love, Lord, become a source of life; may it make them attentive to the requests of their brothers, and may their household be open to others.

In founding themselves upon their love (and upon the love of Christ) may they take an active part in the construction of a world that is more just and fraternal and may they thus be faithful to their calling as human beings (and as Christians).

All: Amen.[43]

While there are no explicit scriptural citations in this text, both the Genesis creation narrative (human beings created in God's likeness) and Christ's saving Passion (with an oblique reference to the kenosis hymn in Philippians) are evoked. Like the first French-language prayer we noted above, there is a strong sense of the spouses' social responsibilities. Problems include the absence of a formal call to prayer (a text supplied in the Canadian version of the marriage ritual), an explicit epiclesis and an ending that would clearly evoke the assembly's "Amen."

A third French-language original text appears in the Canadian *Rituel du Mariage:*

Brothers [and sisters], again today placed in the presence of the wonderful mystery of marriage, let us give thanks to God our Father; and so that he would choose to bless through the length of their life the new spouses, let us pray to the Lord:

All pray a few moments in silence. Then the priest, with hands extended, begins the blessing:

Father very good, you have created man and woman so that they might form together your image in the union of flesh and of heart and so that they might thus accomplish your work in the midst of the world.

We ask you to bless N. and N.: through the length of their life, may they be given the grace of your love and may they be for one another a sign of your presence.

Look upon N. *(the bride):* that your Spirit might establish in her clearness of vision, warmth of welcome, constancy in affection and joyous serenity.

Look as well upon N. *(the groom):* by the power of your Spirit in him may he be happy, constant and resourceful, as well as generous with confidence in the future.

Yes, Lord, bless their love (and bless them in their children). Protect them with peace in the days of joy as in the days of sorrow.

Finally, God our Father, give to these two, after a long life, the joy of being your companions one day at the table in your Kingdom in company with all those whom they love in Christ Jesus, our Lord.

R. Amen.[44]

This text reads as a fusion of Nuptial Blessings B and C from OCM 1968. The text follows Nuptial Blessing B's structure: a formal invitation to prayer; silent prayer by the assembly; address to God the Father; request for God's blessing on the couple; request for blessing on the bride; request for blessing on the groom; request for final fulfillment of the couple; ending evocation of the assembly's "Amen." The text also echoes certain phrases from Nuptial Blessing C, especially the reference to days of joy and days of sorrow. Drawbacks to the prayer include the "division of labor" among the spouses and the lack of biblical references (except for the Genesis reference in the address to God).

In addition to nuptial blessing texts generated for particular language groups and cultures, other new texts might include: the minor presidential prayers (opening prayer / blessing of the rings / prayer over the gifts / prayer after communion or concluding prayer); opening allocutions (especially if the texts acknowledge and incorporate parents, godparents, sponsors, witnesses, and others); texts for the exchange of consent (especially if such texts eliminate precedence between the spouses); texts for the assembly's reception of the couple's consent or hymns of praise and thanksgiving; wedding prefaces to be used with Eucharistic Prayers II or III. Perhaps following the pattern of the two "thematic" Eucharistic Prayers for Masses of Reconciliation, a Eucharistic Prayer for Nuptial Masses might be written.

Modifications of Ceremonies

Here I concentrate on the ceremonial enhancement of the marriage rite proper and its climactic nuptial blessing. The active engagement of the assembly in the marriage rite proper could be enhanced by inviting parents, godparents or witnesses to lay hands on the shoulders of the bride and groom as a sign of solidarity throughout the marriage rite proper. During the nuptial blessing the rest of the assembly could be invited to extend hands toward the couple as the officiant recites the prayer text. The lasso ceremony popular in some Hispanic marriage celebrations or the wrapping of the couple's hands in the priest's or deacon's stole as in some Slavic traditions might ritually bind the couple during the marriage rite proper. Since sacramental Christian marriage is conceptualized as a particular activation of the Christian discipleship assumed in baptism and confirmation, perhaps anointing the couple (even with chrism) might be appropriate, especially if the anointing is followed by handlaying. Crowning the couple, whether with garlands of flowers or circlets of precious metal, might link Western and Eastern forms of celebration. Kenneth Stevenson has suggested that a large canopy be held over the couple during the recitation of the blessing prayer, yoking Jewish and Christian marriage ceremonies.[45]

The major form of ceremonial development I have witnessed over the last thirty years in United States Roman rite marriage ceremonies is the lighting of the wedding or unity candle. Strong arguments can be made both for and against the incorporation of this ceremony. The United States Bishops' Committee on the Liturgy has surveyed various individuals and institutions for their descriptions of and attitudes toward this ceremony with a view to its possible inclusion in the marriage ritual to be published for the dioceses of the United States in the wake of OCM 1991.

In conclusion, I note that modifications of ordo, texts and ceremonies cannot by themselves guarantee a pastorally effective celebration of Christian marriage, faithful to the heritage and open to the Spirit's presence. Rites of betrothal and engagement carefully correlated with structures of matrimonial catechesis (perhaps developed along the lines of the periods and rites of the catechumenate) are strongly needed to counter-balance cultural understandings of marriage that are actively opposed to the Christian vision. Rites of anniversary celebration carefully correlated with structures of matrimonial mystagogy (perhaps developed after the models appearing in the Rite of Christian Initiation of Adults) are strongly needed to sustain married couples in the unfolding of the covenant they have vowed. But perhaps these reflections will assist pastoral ministers and Christian spouses at the sacramental interface of culture, church and worship.

Select Bibliography

English Language

Joncas, J. M. "Solemnizing the Mystery of Wedded Love: Nuptial Blessings in the Ordo Celebrandi Matrimonium 1991," *Worship* 70/3 (May 1996) 210–237.

Martínez, G. "Greco-Roman Cultural Symbols and Ritual Creativity Today: An Approach to Marriage," *Questions Liturgiques* 65 (1984) 39–50.

Martínez, G. "Marriage: Historical Developments and Future Alternatives," *American Benedictine Review* 37 (1986) 370–395.

Martínez, G. "The Newly Revised Roman Rite for Celebrating Marriage," *Worship* 69 (March 1995) 127–142.

Matovina, T. M. "Marriage Celebrations in Mexican American Communities," *Liturgical Ministry* 5 (Winter 1996) 22–26.

Stevenson, K. W. *To Join Together: The Rite of Marriage, Studies in the Reformed Rites of the Catholic Church,* 5 (New York: Pueblo, 1987).

Weiss, J. E. "Marriage Rites," *Liturgical Ministry* 5 (Winter 1996) 1–9.

Other Languages

Cecolin, Romano. "Il Lezionario del nuovo «Ordo celebrandi Matrimonium». Alcune annotazioni di carattere biblico-liturgico." *Rivista Liturgica* LXXIX (1992) 635–658.

"Commentarium." [in French] *Notitiae* 26 (1990) 310–327.

Lessi-Ariosto, Mario. "Aspetti rituali della celebrazione del Matrimoni nella «editio typica altera»." *Rivista Liturgica* LXXIX (1992) 692698.

Lodi, Enzo. "La benedizione nuziale. Sua valenza teologico-liturgica." *Rivista Liturgica* LXXIX (1992) 659–691.

Triacca, Achille Maria. "Linee teologico-liturgiche in vista di una rinnovata celebrazione del Matrimonio." *Rivista Liturgica* LXXIX (1992) 599–634.

Jan Michael Joncas

1. For accounts of the work of study group 23 see: A. Bugnini, *La riforma liturgica (1948–1975),* Biblioteca «Ephemerides Liturgicae» «Subsidia», 30 (Roma: CLV Edizioni Liturgiche, 1983) 676–686; C. Braga, "La genesi del''Ordo Matrimonii'," *Ephemerides Liturgicae* 93 (1979) 247–257; K. W. Stevenson, *To Join Together: The Rite of Marriage, Studies in the Reformed Rites of the Catholic Church,* 5 (New York: Pueblo, 1987) 127–132.

2. The Latin text appears as *Rituale Romanum ex decreto sacrosancti Oecumenici Concilii Vaticani II instauratum auctoritate Pauli Pp. VI promulgatum Ordo Celebrandi Matrimonium. Editio typica* [hereafter OCM 1969] (Urbs Vaticana: Typis Polyglottis Vaticanis, 1969).

3. *Rituale Romanum ex decreto sacrosancti Oecumenici Concilii Vaticani II renovatum auctoritate Pauli Pp. VI editum Ioannis Pauli Pp. II recognitum Ordo Celebrandi Matrimonium. Editio typica altera* [hereafter OCM 1991] (Urbs Vaticana: Typis Polyglottis Vaticanis, 1991).

4. I will not treat the rites for betrothal or engagement and for anniversary celebrations contained in Appendices to OCM 1991.

5. "Si vero, omni conatu ad irritum redacto, nupurientes aperte et expresse id quod Ecclesia intendit, cum Matrimonium baptizatorum celebratur, se respuere fatentur, animarum pastori non licet eos ad celebrationem admittere: quamvis id aegre ferat, debet rem ipsam agnoscere atque iis, quorum interest, persuadere non Ecclesiam, sed eos ipsos celebrationem, quam quidem petant, in talibus rerum adiunctis impedire." OCM 1991, 5.

6. "Etsi pastores ministri Evangelii Christi sunt pro omnibus, specialem tamen animadversionem servent erga eos, qui celebrationem Matrimonii vel Eucharistiae, sive sint catholici sive acatholici, numquam vel vix umquam participant. Norma haec pastoralis in primis valet pro ipsis sponsis." OCM 1991, 8.

7. "Fieri possunt una vel duo lectiones, prout opportunum visum fuerit. Semper eligatur saltem una lectio quae explicite de Matrimonio loquitur." OCM 1991, 47.

8. "Convenit ut assistens adhortationem tradat aut homiliam legat ab Episcopo vel parocho significatam." OCM 1991, 47.

9. "Ad hanc celebrationem peragendam, fratres carissimi, / in domum Domini exsultantes convenimus, / N. et N. circumstantes / in die qua domum suam condere intendunt. / Illis vero hora daec singularis est momenti. / Quapropter animi affectu nostraque amicitia / necnon oratione fraterna eis assistamus. / Verbum quod Deus nobis hodie loquitur / una cum eis attente audiamus. / Deinde cum Ecclesia sancta, / per Christum Dominum nostrum, / Deum Patrem suppliciter deprecemur, / ut hos famulos suos nupturientes / benignus suscipiat, benedicat unumque semper faciat." OCM 1991, 12.

10. "N. et N., Ecclesia in vestro gaudio partem habet / et magno corde vos recipit, / una cum parentibus et amicis vestris, / in die qua coram Deo Patre nostro /

totius vitae consortium inter vos constitutis. / Exaudiat vos Dominus in die laetitiae vestrae. / Mittat vobis auxilium de caelo et tueatur vos. / Tribuat vobis secundum cor vestrum / et impleat omnes petitiones vestras." OCM 1991, 12.

11. "*N. et N.,* Ecclesia in vestro gaudio partem habet / et magno corde vos recipit, / una cum parentibus et amicis vestris, / in die qua totius vitae consortium inter vos constituitis. / Pro credentibus, Deus fons est dilectionis et fidelitatis, / quoniam Deus caritas est. / Quapropter verbum eius attente audiamus, / eumque suppliciter deprecemur, / ut tribuat vobis secundum cor vestrum / et impleat omnes petitiones vestras." OCM 1991, 56–57.

12. OCM 1969, 106 = OCM 1991, 223 prefixed with a rubric that this collect is not to be used when it will be incorporated into the first form of the nuptial blessing; OCM 1969, 107 = OCM 1991, 225 with an optional addition of the couple's names.

13. The prayer appears in formulary XXXI *"Incipit Uelatio Nuptialis"* positioned in the month of September. The formulary appears to consist of a Mass set (opening prayer [1105], prayer over the gifts [1106], *Hanc igitur* insertion into the Roman Canon [1107] and post-communion prayer [1108]) and a nuptial blessing (1110). Formula 1109, from which OCM 1991 Collect E is adapted, may have served as a prayer over the people or as an introductory prayer before the nuptial blessing: "Adesto, domine, supplicationi[bu]s nostris, et institutis tuis, quibus propagationem humani generis ordinasti, benignus adsiste: ut quod te auctore iungitur, te auxiliante seruetur: per." Leo Cunibert Mohlberg, Leo Eizenhöfer and Petrus Siffrin, *Sacramentarium Veronense (Cod. Bibl. Capit. Veron. LXXXV[80]),* 3rd ed., *Rerum Ecclesiasticarum Documenta, Series Maior, Fontes* 1 (Roma: Herder, 1978) 140.

14. "Adesto, Domine, supplicationibus nostris, / et institutis tuis, / quibus propaginem humani generis ordinasti, / benignus assiste, / ut quod te auctore coniungitur, / te auxiliante servetur. / Per Dominum." OCM 1991, 73.

15. This text appears as part of formulary LII *"Incipit Accio Nuptialis"* in Liber Tertius of the GeV. The formulary consists of two collects (1443 [= Ve 1109] and 1444 [= Ve 1108]: alternative opening prayers? a stational prayer followed by the opening prayer of the Mass? an opening prayer followed by an *oratio super sindonem*?), a prayer over the gifts (1445: entitled *secreta*), a preface (1146), two *Hanc igitur* insertions in the Roman Canon (1447 [= Ve 1107] to be used on the day of the wedding and 1448 for use on anniversaries), the nuptial blessing (1451 [= Ve 1110], a post-communion blessing on the spouses (1454) and a post-communion (1455). OCM Collect F is adapted from the introductory prayer before the nuptial blessing (1450); note that in its original form it invokes God's blessing on the bride rather than the couple: "Deus, qui mundi crescentis exordio multiplicata prole benedicis, propiciare supplicacionibus nostris et super hanc famulam tuam opem tuae benedictionis infund, ut in iugali consortio affectu conpari, mente consimili, sanctitate mutua copulentur: per". Leo Cunibert Mohlberg, Leo Eizenhöfer and

Jan Michael Joncas

Petrus Siffrin, *Liber Sacramentorum Romanae Aeclesiae Ordinis Anni Circuli (Cod. Vat. Reg. lat. 316/Paris Bibl. Nat. 7193, 41/56) (Sacramentarium Gelasianum)*, 3rd ed., *Rerum Ecclesiasticarum Documenta, Series Maior, Fontes* 4 (Roma: Herder, 1981) 209.

16. "Deus, qui mundi crescentis exordio / multiplicatae proli benedicis, / propitiare supplicationibus nostris, / et super hos famulos tuos (N. et N.) / opem tuae benedictionis infunde, / ut in coniugali consortio / affectu compari, mente consimili, / sanctitate mutua copulenter. / Per Dominum." OCM 1991, 73.

17. "Hunc vestrum consensum, quem coram Ecclesia manifestatis, Deus Abraham, Deus Isaac, Deus Iacob, Deus qui protoplastos coniunxit in paradiso, in Christo confirmet ac benedicat, ut quod ipse coniungit, homo non separet." OCM 1991, 18–19, 34, 49–50, 59–60.

18. "Deus Abraham, Deus Isaac, et Deus Jacob sit vobiscum: et ipse adimpleat benedictionem suam in vobis: ut videatis filios filiorum vestrorum usque ad tertiam et quartam generationem, et postea vitam aeternam habeatis sine fine: adjuvante Domino nostro Jesu Christo, qui cum Patre et Spiritu Sancto vivit et regnat Deus, per omnia saecula saeculorum. R. Amen." MR 1570 "Missa votiva pro Sponso et Sponsa".

Note that this blessing text repeats in slightly modified form the concluding petitions of the nuptial blessing intended for both spouses. Most probably it was removed in OCM 1969 as a ritual duplication.

19. "Recordare quoque, Domine, N. et N., quos ad diem nuptiarum pervenire tribuisti: ut gratia tua in mutua dilectione et pace permaneant." OCM 1991, 76.

20. "Conforta, quaesumus, in gratia Matrimonii N. et N., quos ad diem nuptiarum feliciter adduxisti, ut foedus quod in conspectu tuo firmaverunt, te protegente, in vita semper conservent." OCM 1991, 77.

21. "251. Fratres carissimi, speciale gratiae et caritatis donum recolentes, quo Deus amorem fratrum nostrorum N. et N. perficere et sacrare dignatus est, eos Domino commendemus:

Ut christifideles N. et N., nunc Matrimonio in sanctitate coniuncti, perpetua salute et sanitate gaudere valeant, Dominum deprecemur. R. Te rogamus, audi nos. . . .

Ut foedus eorum benedicat, sicut in Cana Galilaeae nuptias sanctificare disposuit, Dominum depredemur. R.

Ut eis perfectus et fecundus amor, pax et auxilium tribuatur, et bonum testimonium de nomine christiano perhibeant, Dominum deprecemur. R.

Ut populus christianus de die in diem in virtute proficiat et omnibus qui variis premuntur necessitatibus supernae gratiae auxilium conferatur, Dominum deprecemur. R.

Ut omnibus coniugibus hic praesentibus a Spiritu Sancto renovetur gratia sacramenti, Dominum deprecemur. R.

Spiritum tuae caritatis, Domine, in hos sponsos benignus effunde, ut cor unum fiant et anima una, quatenus nihil prorsus separet, quos tu coniunxisti, nihil afflictet, quos tua benedictione implevisti. Per Christum Dominum nostrum. R. Amen." OCM 1991, 93–94.

22. "252. Fratres carissimi, hanc novam familiam nostris presequamur precibus, ut mutuus amor istorum coniugum in dies percrescat atque Deus omnibus in mundo familiis benignus succurrat.

Pro novis sponsis hic astantibus et pro bono eiusdem familiae, Dominum deprecemur. R. Te rogamus, audi nos. . . .

Pro eorum propinquis et amicis cunctisque qui ipsis sponsis adiumento fuerunt, Dominum deprecemur. R.

Pro iuvenibus, qui ad Matrimonium ineundum se praeparant, et pro omnibus, quos Dominus ad aliam vitae condicinem vocat, Dominum deprecemur. R.

Pro omnibus in mundo familiis et pro pace inter homines firmanda, Dominum deprecemur. R.

Pro cunctis familiarum nostrarum membris, quae ex hoc saeculo transierunt cunctisque defunctis, Dominum deprecemur. R.

Pro Ecclesia, Populo sancto Dei, ac pro omnium christianorum unitate, Dominum deprecemur. R.

Domine Iesu, qui in medio nostri ades, dum N. et N. unionem suam obsignant, suscipe orationem nostram nosque tuo reple Spiritu. Qui vivis et regnas in saecula saeculorum. R. Amen." OCM 1991, 94–95.

23. "Deus repleat nos guadio et spe in credendo. / Pax Christi exsultet in cordibus nostris. / Spiritus Sanctus in nos sua dona profundat." OCM 1991, 55.

24. "125. . . . Fieri possunt una vel duo lectiones, prout opportunum visum fuerit. . . . 156. . . . Fieri possunt una vel duae lectiones. Si vero ex adiunctis opportunius evadat, potest una tantum lectio fieri." OCM 1991, 47, 57.

25. "125. . . . Lectio evangelica sic introducitur: Audite, fratres, verba sancti Evangelii secundum N. Convenit ut assistens adhortationem tradat aut homiliam legat ab Episcopo vel parocho significatam." OCM 1991, 47.

26. "65 [=99 *(minister)*=133 *(assistens)*=164 *(ille qui praeest)*]. *Sacerdos ad Dei laudem adstantes invitat:* Benedicamus Domino. Omnes respondent: Deo gratias. *Alia acclamatio proferri potest.*" OCM 1991, 19, 34, 50, 60.

27. "68 [=102=136=168]. *Tunc a tota communitate proferri potest hymnus vel canticum laudis.*" OCM 1991, 19, 35, 51, 61.

28. "Oremus . . . Propitiare, Domine, supplicationibus nostris, et institutis tuis, quibus prepagationem humani generis ordinasti, benignus assiste: ut, quod te auctore jungitur, te auxiliante servetur. Per Dominum.

Oremus. Deus, qui potestate virtutis tuae de nihilo cuncta fecisti: qui dispositis universitatis exordiis, homini ad imaginem Dei facto, ideo separabile mulieris

Jan Michael Joncas

adjutorium condidisti, ut femineo corpori de virili dares carne principium, docens quod ex uno placuisset institui, numquam licere disjungi:

Deus, qui tam excellenti mysterio conjugalem copulam consecrasti, ut Christi et Ecclesiae sacramentum praesignares in foedere nuptiarum:

Deus, per quem mulier jungitur viro, et societas principaliter ordinata, ea benedictione donatur, quae sola nec per originalis peccati poenam, nec per diluvii est ablata sententiam:

respice propitius super hanc famulam tuam, quae maritali jungenda consortio, tua se expetit protectione muniri:

sit in ea jugum dilectionis, et pacis:

fidelis et casta nubat in Christo, imitatrixque sanctarum permaneat feminarum: sit amabilis viro suo, ut Rachel: sapiens, ut Rebecca: longaeva et fidelis, ut Sara: nihil in ea ex actibus suis ille auctor praevaricationis usurpet: nexa fidei, mandatisque permaneat: uni throno juncta, contactus illicitos fugiat: muniat infirmitatem suam robore disciplinae: sit verecundia gravis, pudore venerabilis, doctrinis caelestibus erudita: sit foecunda in sobole, sit probata et innocens: et ad beatorum requiem atque ad caelestia regna perveniat:

et videant ambo filios filiorum suorum, usque in tertiam et quartam generationem, et ad optatam perveniant senectutem. Per eundem Dominum." MR 1570 "Missa votiva pro Sponso et Sponsa" [paragraphing added].

29. "33 . . . Dominum, fratres carissimi, suppliciter deprecemur, ut super hanc famulam suam, quae huic sponso nupsit in Christo, benedictionem gratiae suae clementer effundat: et quos foedere sancto coniunxit (Christi Corporis et Sanguinis sacramento) una faciat caritate concordes.

Et omnes per breve tempus in silentio orant. Deinde sacerdos, manibus extensis, prosequitur:

Deus, qui potestate virtutis tuae de nihilo cuncta fecisti, qui, dispositis universitatis exordiis et homine ad imaginem Dei facto, inseparabile viro mulieris adiutorium condidisti, ut iam non duo essent, sed una caro, docens quod unum placuisset institui numquam licere disiungi;

Deus, qui tam excellenti mysterio coniugalem copulam consecrasti, ut Christi et Ecclesiae sacramentum praesignares in foedere nuptiarum:

Deus, per quem mulier iungitur viro, et societas, principaliter ordinata, ea benedictione donatur, quae sola nec per originalis peccati peonam nec per diluvii est ablata sententiam:

Respice propitius super hanc famulam tuam, quae maritali iuncta consortio, tua se expetit benedictione muniri: sit in ea gratia dilectionis et pacis, imitatrixque sanctarum permaneat feminarum, quarum in Scripturis laudes praedicantur.

Confidat in ea cor viri sui, qui, parem sociam et gratiae vitae coheredem agnoscens, eam honore debito prosequatur eoque diligat semper amore, quo Christus suam dilexit Ecclesiam.

Et nunc te, Domine, deprecamur, ut hi famuli tui nexi fidei mandatisque permaneant, ut, uni thoro iuncti, morum sint integritate conspicui; Evangelii robore communiti, bonum Christi testimonium omnibus manifestent; (in sobole sint fecundi, sint parentes virtutibus comprobati; videant ambo filios filiorum suorum) et, optatam demum senectutem adepti, ad beatorum vitam et ad caelestia regna perveniant. Per Christum Dominum nostrum." OCM 1969, 14–15.

30. "73 . . . Dominum, fratres carissimi, suppliciter deprecemur, ut super hos famulos suos, qui nupserunt in Christo, benedictionem gratiae suae clementer effundat, et quos foedere sancto coniunxit (Christi Corporis et Sanguinis sacramento) una faciat caritate concordes.

74 . . . Deus, qui potestate virtutis tuae de nihilo cuncta fecisti, qui dispositis universitatis exordiis et homine ad imaginem tuam facto, inseparabile viro mulieris adiutorium condidisti, ut iam non duo essent, sed una caro, docens quod unum placuisset institui numquam licere disiungi;

Deus, qui tam excellenti mysterio coniugalem copulam consecrasti, ut Christi et Ecclesiae sacramentum praesignares in foedere nuptiarum;

Deus, per quem mulier iungitur viro, et societas, principaliter ordinata, ea benedictione donatur, quae sola nec per originalis peccati peonam nec per diluvii est ablata sententiam.

Respice propitius super hos famulos tuos, qui, maritali iuncti consortio, tua se expetunt benedictione muniri: emitte super eos Spiritus Sancti gratiam, ut, caritate tua in cordibus eorum diffusa, in coniugali foedere fideles permaneant.

Sit in famula tua N. gratia dilectionis et pacis, imitatrixque sanctarum remaneat feminarum, quarum in Scripturis laudes praedicantur.

Confidat in ea cor viri sui, qui, parem sociam et gratiae vitae coheredem agnoscens, eam honore debito presequatur eoque diligat semper amore, quo Chrisus suam dilexit Ecclesiam.

Et nunc te, Domine, deprecamur, ut hi famuli tui nexi fidei mandatisque permaneant, et, uni thoro iuncti, morum sint integritate conspicui; Evangelii robore communiti, bonum Christi testimonium omnibus manifestent; (in sobolo sint fecundi, sint parentes virtutibus comprobati; videant ambo filios filiorum suorum) et, optatam demum senectutem adepti, ad beatorum vitam et ad caelestia regna perveniant. Per Christum Dominum nostrum." OCM 1991, 20–21, 26–27.

31. "120 . . . *Sacerdos, stans ad sponsum et sponsam conversus, dicit, manibus iunctis:*

Super hos sponsos, qui, matrimonium ineuntes, ad altare accedunt, ut, (Christi Corporis Sanguinisque participes,) mutua semper dilectione nectantur, Dominum deprecemur.

Et omnes per breve tempus in silentio orant. Deinde sacerdos, manibus extensis, prosequitur:

Pater sancte, qui hominem ad imaginem tuam conditum masculum creasti et feminam, ut vir et mulier, in carnis et cordis unitate coniuncti, munus suum in mundo adimplerent:

Deus, qui, ad amoris tui consilium revelandum, in mutua dilectione sponsorum foedus illud adumbrari voluisti quod ipse cum populo inire dignatus es, ut, sacramenti significatione completa, in fidelium tuorum coniugali consortio Christi et Ecclesiae nuptiale pateret mysterium: super hos famulos tuos (*N.* et *N.*) dexteram tuam, quaesumus, propitiatus extende.

Praesta, Domine, ut, in huius quod ineunt sacramenti consortio, inter se amoris tui dona communicent, et, praesentiae tuae signum invicem ostendes, cor unum fiant et anima una. Da etiam, Domine, ut domum, quam aedificant, opere quoque sustentent, filiosque suos, evangelica disciplina formatos, caelesti familiae tuae praeparent cooptandos.

Hanc famulam tuam *N.* tuis digneris benedictionibus cumulare, ut, uxoris et matris munera complens, casta suam domum dilectione refoveat, et gratia decoret affabili.

Hanc etiam famulum tuum *N.* caelesti, Domine, benedictione presequere, ut mariti fidelis officia digne persolvat et providi patris.

Concede, Pater sancte, ut, qui coram te coniugio copulati ad mensam tuam accedere cupiunt, caeleste aliquando convivium participare laetentur. Per Christum." OCM 1969, 35–36.

32. "Super hos famulos tuos (*N.* et *N.*) dexteram tuam, quaesumus, propitiatus extende et in eorum corda Spiritus Sancti virtutem effunde. . . ." OCM 1991, 82.

33. "Per Christum Dominum nostrum. R. Amen." OCM 1991, 83.

34. "Pater sancte, mundi conditor universi, qui virum atque mulierum ad imaginem tuam creasti, eorumque societatem tua voluisti benedictione cumulari; te pro hac sponsa humiliter deprecamur, quae hodie viro suo nuptiarum iungitur sacramento.

Super eam, Domine, eiusque vitae consortem benedictio tua copiosa descendat, ut, dum mutuo connubii dono fruuntur, familiam ornent filiis, ditent Ecclesiam.

Laeti te laudent, Domine, te maesti requirant; te in laboribus sibi gaudeant adesse ut faveas, te sentiant in necessitatibus adstare ut lenias; te in coetu sancto precentur, tuos in mundo se testes ostendant; et adepti prosperam senectutem cum hac qua circumdantur amicorum corona ad caelestia regna perveniant. Per Christum." OCM 1969, 36–37.

35. "243. *Sacerdos (vel diaconus), stans ad sponsam et sponsum conversus, manibus iunctis, adstantes invitat ad orandum:* Precibus nostris, fratres carissimi, super hos sponsos, Dei benedictionem supplices invocemus, ut ipse suo foveat benignus auxilio, quos ditavit connubii sacramento. . . .

244. *Deinde sacerdos (vel diaconus), manibus extensis super sponsos, prosequitur:*

Pater sancte, mundi conditor universi, qui virum atque mulierem ad imaginem tuam creasti, eorumque societatem, tua voluisti benedictione cumulari; te pro his famulis tuis humiliter deprecamur, qui hodie nuptiarum iunguntur sacramento.

Super hanc sponsam *N.*, Domine, eiusque vitae consortium *N.*, benedictio tua copiosa descendat, et virtus Spiritus Sancti tui corda eorum desuper inflammet, ut, dum mutuo connubii dono fruuntur, familiam ornent filiis ditentque Ecclesiam.

For Better or For Worse

Laeti te laudent, Domine, te maesti requirant; te in laboribus sibi gaudeant adesse ut faveas, te sentiant in necessitatibus adstare ut lenias; te in coetu sancto precentur, tuos in mundo se testes ostendant; et, adepti prosperam senectutem cum hac qua circumdantur amicorum corona, ad caelestia regna perveniant. Per Christum Dominum nostrum. R. Amen." OCM 1991, 83–84, 86–87.

36. "Pater sancte, mundi conditor universi, qui virum atque mulierem ad imaginem tuam creasti, eorumque societatem tua voluisti benedictione cumulari: te pro hac sponsa humiliter deprecamur, quae hodie viro suo iungitur foedere nuptiarum.

Super eam, Domine, eiusque vitae consortem benedictio tua copiosa descendat, ut, dum mutuo connubii dono fruuntur, morum sint integritate conspicui (et parentes virtutibus comprobati).

Laeti te laudent, Domine, te maesti requirant; te in laboribus sibi gaudeant adesse ut faveas, te sentiant in necessitatibus adstare ut lenias; et adepti prosperam senectutem cum hac qua circumdantur amicorum corona ad caelestia regna perveniant. Per Christum Dominum nostrum. R. Amen." OCM 1969, 25–26.

37. "171 . . . Nunc super hos sponsos, Dei benedictionem supplices invocemus, ut ipse suo foveat benignus auxilio quos ditabit connubii consortio. . . .

172 . . . Pater sancte, mundi conditor universi, qui virum atque mulierem ad imaginem tuam creasti, eorumque societatem tua voluisti benedictione cumulari: te pro famulis tuis humiliter deprecamur, qui hodie iunguntur foedere nuptiarum.

Super hanc sponsam N., Domine, eiusque vitae consortem N. benedictio tua copiosa descendat et virtus Spiritus Sancti tui corda eorum desuper inflammet, ut, dum mutuo connubii dono fruuntur, morum sint integritate conspicui (et parentes virtutibus comprobati).

Laeti te laudent, Domine, te maesti requirant; te in laboribus sibi gaudeant adesse ut faveas, te sentiant in necessitabius adstare ut lenias; et, adepti prosperam senectutem cum hac qua circumdantur amicorum corona, ad caelestia regna perveniant. Per Christum Dominum nostrum.

R. Amen." OCM 1991, 62–63.

38. "Benedictus es, Domine Deus, creator et conservator generis humani, qui in viri mulierisque consortio veram reliquisti tui amoris imaginem.

Super hanc sponsam *N.*, quaesumus, Domine, eiusque vitae consortem *N.* benedictio tua copiosa descendat, et virtus Spiritus Sancti tui corda eorum desuper inflammet, ut, dum mutuo connubii dono fruuntur, morum sint integritate conspicui (et parentes virtutibus comprobati).

Laeti te laudent, Domine, te maesti requirant; te in laboribus sibi gaudent addesse ut faveas, te sentiant in necessitatibus adstare ut lenias; et, adepti prosperam senectutem cum hac qua circumdantur amicorum corona, ad caelestia regna perveniant. Per Christum Dominum nostrum. R. Amen." OCM 1991, 63.

39. "139. *Tunc assistens prosequitur, manibus iunctis:* Nunc super hos sponsos Dei benedictionem supplices invocemus, ut ipse suo foveat benignus auxilio

quos ditavit connubii sacramento. *Et omnes per aliquod temporis spatium in silentio orant.*

140. *Deinde super sponsos genuflexos assistens dicit, manibus iunctis, orationem benedictionis nuptialis, omnibus participantibus:* Benedictus Deus, Pater omnipotens, qui hominem pietatis tuae dono creatum, ad tantum voluisti dignitatem extolli, ut in viri mulierisque consortio veram relinqueres tui amoris imaginem. *Omnes:* Benedictus Deus.

Assistens: Benedictus Deus, Filii Unigenite, Iesu Christe, qui in fidelium tuorum coniugali foedere tuae patere voluisti dilectionis mysterium in Ecclesiam, pro qua teipsum tradidisti ut esset sancta et immaculata. *Omnes:* Benedictus Deus.

Assistens: Benedictus Deus, Spiritus Sancte Paraclite, omnis sanctificationis operator et unitatis effector, qui filios dilectionis inhabitas, ut solliciti sint servare unitatem in vinculo pacis. *Omnes:* Benedictus Deus.

Assistens: Serva, Domine, hos famulos tuos N. et N., quos Matrimonii sacramento coniunxisti, in mutuo amore concordes, ut, dum connubii dono fruuntur, humanam familiam ornent filiis, sanctam ditent Ecclesiam et tuos in mundo se testes ostendant. Per Christum Dominum nostrum. *R.* Amen.

Vel: Respice, Domine, super hos famulos tuos N. et N., et praesta, ut in te solum confidentes, gratiae tuae dona percipiant, caritatem in unitate servent, et post huius vitae decursum ad aeternae beatitudinis gaudia, una cum prole sua, pervenire mereantur. Per Christum Dominum nostrum. *R.* Amen." OCM 1991, 52–53.

40. *The Roman Ritual revised by decree of the Second Vatican Council and published by authority of Pope Paul VI: The Celebration of Marriage approved for use in Ireland/Gnás an Phósta* [hereafter ICM 1980] (Dublin: Veritas Publications 1980) 35–36.

41. English translation as found in Padraig McCarthy, *A Wedding of Your Own,* 2nd ed. (Dublin: Veritas 1988) 198–199; the Irish-language original may be found in ICM 1980, 80–81. I am grateful to Fr. Paul Kenny of the Irish Church Music Association for these references.

42. "*59. Cette formule ne peut être employée que pour des époux qui communient.*

Frères, demandons à Dieu de bénir ces nouveaux époux qui vont recevoir ensemble le corps et le sang de Jésus Christ.

Tout prient quelques instants en silence. Puis le prêtre, les mains étendues, reprend:

Seigneur notre Dieu, tu as appelé par leur nom N. et N., pour qu'en se donnat l'un à l'autre ils deviennent une seule chair et un seul esprit; donne-leur le corps de ton Fils par qui se réalisera leur unité.

Tu es la source de leur amour et tu as mis en eux le désir de bonheur qui les anime; donne-leur le sang de ton Fils qui sanctifiera leur amour et leur joie.

En recevant le pain de vie et la coupe de bénédiction, qu'ils apprennent à donner leur vie pour les autres; qu'ils élèvant dans la fidélité à l'Évangile les enfants qui naîtront de leur amour; qu'ils recherchent avant toutes choses le Royaume de

Dieu et sa justice; qu'ils soient utiles au monde où ils vivront; qu'ils se montrent accueillant aux plus pauvres; qu'ils puissent toujours te rendre grâce, et viennent souvent renouveler leur alliance en communiant ensemble au corps ressuscité de Jésus Christ.

C'est par Lui que nous te prions: Puisqu'Il a sanctifié les noces de Cana, et purifié son Église en se livrant pour elle, nous savons qu'Il intercède auprès de Toi pour nos amis *N. et N.,* aujourd'hui, demain et tous les jours de leur vie, jusque dans l'éternité.

Tous: Amen." *Rituel pour la célébration du mariage à l'usage des diocèses de France,* 3e èdition [hereafter FRCM] (Paris: Éditions Brepols, 1970) 55.

The same text appears as "Bénédiction Nuptiale 5" in the Canadian *Rituel du Mariage* [hereafter CRM] (Ottawa, ON: Service des Éditions, 1983) 90–91.

43. "60. . . . Seigneur notre Dieu, créateur de l'univers et de tout ce qui vit, tu as fait l'homme et la femme à ta ressemblance; et pour qu'ils soient associés à ton oeuvre d'amour, tu leur as donné un coeur capable d'aimer.

Tu as voulu qu'aujourd'hui, dans cette église, *N. et N.* unissent leur vie. Tu veux maintenant qu'ils construisent leur foyer, qu'ils cherchent à s'aimer chaque jour davantage et suivant l'exemple du Christ, lui qui a aimé les hommes jusqu'à mourir sur une croix.

Bénis, protège et fortifie l'amour de ces nouveaux époux: que leur amour soutienne leur fidélité; qu'ils les rende heureux et leur fasse découvrir (dans le Christ) la joie du don total à celui que l'on amie.

Que leur amour, semblable à ton amour, Seigneur, devienne une source de vie; qu'ils les garde attentifs aux appels de leurs frères, et que leur foyer soit ouvert aux autres.

En s'appurant sur leur amour (et sur l'amour du Christ) qu'ils prennent une part active à la construction d'un monde plus juste et fraternel et soient ainsi fidèles à leur vocation d'hommes (et de chrétiens).

Tous: Amen." FRCM, 56.

This text also appears as "Bénédiction Nuptiale 5" in CRM, 92–93 with the following invitation prefixed to the prayer text: "Frères, demandons à Dieu de bénir ces nouveaux époux: qu'il donne sa force à ceux qu'il a unis dans le mariage" ("Brothers [and sisters], ask God to bless these new spouses: that he would give his power to those whom he has united in marriage").

44. "143 . . . Frères, remis en présence, aujourd'hui encore, du mystère admirable du mariage, rendons grâce à Dieu notre Père; et pour qu'il veuille bénir tout au long de leur vie les nouveaux époux, prions le Seigneur.

Tout prient quelques instants en silence. Puis le prêtre, les mains étendues, commence la Bénédiction:

Père très bon, tu as créé l'homme et la femme pour qu'ils forment ensemble ton image dans l'unité de la chair et du coeur et qu'ils poursuivent ainsi ton oeuvre au milieu du monde.

Jan Michael Joncas

Nous te prions de bénir N. et N.: tout au long de leur vie, qu'ils se donnent la grâce de ton amour et qu'ils soient l'un pour l'autre un signe de ta présence.

Souviens-toi de N. (l'épouse): que ton Esprit soit en elle clarté du regard, chaleur de l'accueil, constance dans l'affection et joyeuse sérénité.

Souviens-toi aussi de N. (l'époux): par la force en lui de ton Esprit qu'il soit heureux, constant et inventif, aussi généreux que confiant dans l'avenir.

Oui, Seigneur, bénis leur amour (et bénis-les dans leurs enfants). Garde-les dans la paix, aux jours de joie comme aux jours d'épreuve.

Enfin, Dieu notre Père, donne-leur à tous deux, après une longue vie, la joie d'être un jour tes convives à la table de ton Royaume, en compagnie de tous ceux qu'ils aiment, dans le Christ Jésus, notre Seigneur.

R. Amen." CRM, 88–89.

45. Stevenson, *To Join Together,* 196.

Victoria M. Tufano

Christian Initiation: Well Begun, Not Nearly Half Done

It is now 24 years since the promulgation of the Rite of Christian Initiation of Adults in Latin, 22 years since its publication in English and 8 years since the revised, adapted and expanded text for use in the United States was published.

When the rite was first promulgated in English in the second half of 1972, the new lectionary had been in use in this country for barely four years; the complete new sacramentary had just been published in English after years of gradual changes, numerous inserts and no little confusion; and the new rite of penance had been promulgated in Latin but not yet in English. At that time, an ordinary Catholic who had even heard the word "catechumen" only knew it because someone had taught them that the first part of the Mass was known as the "Mass of the Catechumens," but no one had ever seen one, at least not to their knowledge, and no convert knew that she or he had actually been one.

It remained to be seen how this ritual would be received here. After all, the common wisdom said, the restoration of the catechumenate was for "mission countries." The United States was already a predominantly Christian country and so there was no need for it here. Most of the energy of diocesan liturgy commissions and offices at the time was obliged to go toward catechizing for the new rite of penance and working through the questions regarding the age of confirmation. But a few people understood, or at least intuited, that what had happened in the promulgation of a new order for initiating adults was, or at least could be, an event of great significance.

In 1973, the Federation of Diocesan Liturgical Commissions (FDLC) focused its national meeting on Christian initiation. By educating its membership, this body no doubt paved the way for the future hold that the rites of Christian initiation would take in this country, much as the FDLC would do in the 1980s with the *Order of Christian Funerals*. In 1974 the Murphy Center for Liturgical Research, later to be known as the Notre Dame Center for Pastoral Liturgy, focused its annual June conference on Christian initiation.

The proceedings of that conference were published as *Made, Not Born: New Perspectives on Christian Initiation and the Catechumenate* (University of Notre Dame Press, 1976). Like everything liturgical that came out of Notre Dame then and since, at least from the theology department and the Center, the various papers presented at that conference 22 summers ago rooted the questions in historical research. On page 138 of the book, however, the text of the talk given by the late and sorely missed Ralph Keifer, "Christian Initiation: The State of the Question," raised the question of whether this rite could be celebrated in any meaningful way in the church as it was at that time, and in the American culture. In his own unique way, Ralph defined the state of the question in this way:

> It is ironic that we have so often cried out to Rome to turn radical, so often expecting in turn obscurantism, time-serving and conservatism of a conventional sort, that we have not been able to perceive radical revision and drastic change when Rome presents us with it. . . .
>
> What has Rome done? First of all, it has restored the baptismal focus of the paschal season from Lent through Pentecost, designing a lectionary and a sacramentary which are only fully intelligible when the paschal celebration revolves around the baptizing of adults whose catechumenate has been brought to a head during Lent and whose initiation is the central event of the liturgical year. . . .

Second, such a revision represents a radical change of sacramental symbols and priorities. Instead of being an occasional hurried service for infants and an exceptional one for a few adults, but nonetheless hurried and as private as possible, Christian initiation has become not merely a public event in the church, but the public event. . . .

Third, such drastic revision and innovation represents a departure in pastoral priorities and perspectives . . . The new initiatory perspective rejects the pastoral assumption that an implicit faith, appropriated in and through a Christian culture, is an acceptable standard for lay life. The norm of pastoral care becomes . . . the radical transformation of life and values, publicly celebrated as a corporate responsibility.

Fourth, the new perspective signals the end of a divorce between liturgy and life, between private devotion and public function, between active ministers and inert laity. It assumes that the liturgy will be a manifestation of the real life lived by the church, a life marked by sufficient conversion to be worth celebrating, sufficient conversion and catechesis to perceive that the proclamation of the wonderful works of God is possible because they occur among us, sufficient conversion to assure that the laity are not passive recipients of hierarchical grace but that ministry made sacramental in orders is a mirror of the priestly service of the entire people of God. The real nature of ministry as collegial, shared and mutual is revealed in the preparation of catechumens (138–39).

Keifer then takes note of two situations that work against the vision of the rite: the continuation of the practice of confirmation apart from baptism and "the confusion of catechesis with education and the simultaneous confusion of education with the dissemination of information" (142). Toward the end of the article, Keifer notes,

The attempt to reform the rites of initiation has issued in the promulgation of rites which are, historically and culturally speaking, a massive rejection of the presuppositions both of pastoral practice and of most churchgoers regarding the true meaning of church membership. This is a revolution quite without precedent, because the Catholic church has never at any time in its history done such violence to its ritual practice as to make its rites so wholly incongruous with its concrete reality. Such an act is either a statement that rite is wholly irrelevant or a statement that the church is willing to change, and to change radically, that concrete reality. Such an approach is either suicide or prophecy of a very high order.

Our task here is to look back on the 22 years since Ralph Keifer defined the state of the question as he saw it to see what has become of the practice of Christian initiation. Then, perhaps, we can make a statement about the state of the question in 1996.

As the editor of *Catechumenate* magazine and the various other Christian initiation materials that Liturgy Training Publications puts out and as a team member for institutes of The North American Forum on the Catechumenate, I have something of a privileged vantage point from which to view the Christian initiation scene in this country, and to some extent internationally. It is also a perilous position in that it would be easy to mark the success of Christian initiation by the number of subscriptions or books sold or by the number of people who attend Forum institutes. To do so would be the grossest kind of inculturation into American consumer culture. It would reduce Christian initiation to a product.

But I would submit that there has been a far more subtle kind of inculturation into the American scene. Perhaps the best symbol of it is the chart that has been reproduced in numerous places. On the first night of a Beginnings & Beyond institute, all the participants who are newcomers to Christian initiation sit with me and get a crash course on the language and structure of the order of Christian initiation. One of the first things I put up on the overhead projector is a chart, a detailed grid of the steps and stages, the periods and the rites that make up the initiation process.

This chart can represent the American "can-do" attitude with which we have approached Christian initiation. We have taken the somewhat bare-bones structure presented by the rite and created a model in our own image and likeness. Which is not a bad definition of inculturation. The church in the United States, perhaps more than any other church, has poured an enormous amount of energy into "doing" Christian initiation, and this energy already has borne great fruit.

I enumerate some of the blessings that have come to us in part or in whole through the implementation of the rites of initiation.

Well Begun

1. The emphasis on catechesis "accommodated to the liturgical year and solidly supported by celebrations of the word" (*Rite of Christian Initiation of Adults,* 75.1) has caused the lectionary to be taken seriously as a basis for Christian formation and prayer not only for catechumens but for all Christians. Bible-study groups, prayer groups, small faith communities and individuals have begun to use the lectionary as the basis for study, faith-sharing, "breaking open the word" and *lectio divina.* As more and more Christian communions adopt lectionaries based on the Roman *Lectionary for Mass,* particularly the *Revised Common Lectionary,* this has become a great source of unity. Increasingly, Christians separated by denominational differences are hearing, praying over and preaching the same scriptures each week. Perhaps this unity around the word is a necessary step to unity at the table. Would this have happened without the implementation of the RCIA? Probably, but not as soon as it has.

2. The implementation of the *Rite of Christian Initiation of Adults* has expanded the notion of ministry beyond the ordained and the professional staff. The importance of ministries of hospitality, of witness, of prayer, of sponsorship, of catechesis and of the assembly have been highlighted. Not only has the ministry of the parish to the catechumens been emphasized, but also the formation of catechumens for ministry. In parishes where the full vision of the catechumenate had taken hold, former catechumens are active in every aspect of parish ministry. One measure of how well the catechumenate process is forming people for mission might be how many former catechumens minister outside the liturgical and catechumenal circles.

This is, however, a place where, though we have begun well, we are not yet done. Rather than preparing the catechumens for the life of mission that baptism inaugurates, many parish catechumenates are treating baptism as the end of the process. In other situations, neophytes join the Christian initiation team or take on liturgical ministries, but are never encouraged to participate in any of the other ministries of the parish.

3. The implementation of the Christian initiation process has reintroduced the basic sacramental symbols of water, oil, touch, light,

Victoria M. Tufano

white garments and the human person. As these symbols are used lavishly in the various rites of initiation, and as mystagogical preaching and catechesis help the community assimilate their meanings, the power of these symbols is opened up for the entire assembly. This enhances the use of these symbols in other sacraments and sacramentals, such as infant baptism, anointing of the sick and various blessings at home and in church.

4. The renewal of Christian initiation has focused attention on the importance of preaching for the formation of catechumens and the entire Christian assembly. As catechesis focuses on the word preached, many preachers have become more conscientious. In some places, catechists and preachers prepare together for the work they will do with the Sunday scriptures.

5. Christian initiation has reintroduced the ancient pattern of catechesis based on word and symbol that is transformed by ritual and brought to meaning by mystagogy. This has begun to reshape the way that we prepare for all the sacraments, from infant baptism to marriage to anointing of the sick, and the way that pastoral care is given following these and other rites, such as Christian burial. We know, for example, from the work of Richard Rutherford, that in the year following the death and burial of a loved one, a bereaved person will return in memory to the rituals and texts of the rites of Christian burial for comfort and to make sense of the loss. This is a form of mystagogy that could form the basis of pastoral care.

6. Christian initiation has offered a reintegration of the various aspects of church life. Rather than seeing prayer, catechesis, apostolic action and communal life as discrete areas of parish life, it unites them into a whole (see RCIA, 75). It restores the vision of the pioneers of the liturgical movement, who always saw the goal of the renewal of the liturgy to be the renewal of the life of the church. In particular, it breaks down the barrier that somehow grew up between "social-justice types" and "liturgy types."

It has also brought liturgists and catechists together to try to overcome the artificial split between their two disciplines. This has been a great blessing and a great struggle for both catechists and liturgists. It has meant a lot of listening and a lot of humility on both sides. It has been made more difficult by the large and lucrative industry that has grown up around the publication of catechetical materials, which has made it difficult to separate religious education, sacramental catechesis and catechesis for initiation. In fairness, you may wish to note that this observation is coming from someone trained as a liturgist who works for a liturgical publisher. Also in fairness, I must note that many good folks within the catechetical publishing world are struggling with this.

Not Nearly Half Done

Lest we come to believe that the *Rite of Christian Initiation of Adults* has inaugurated the parousia, I think it would be useful for us to list some of the things we have yet to be fulfilled of the great promise of the restoration of the initiation process.

I return to the chart that I mentioned earlier. Aside from being a useful tool for explaining the steps and stages of initiation to beginners at the beginning of a Beginnings & Beyond institute, this chart is a great symbol of the American "know-how" that has implemented Christian initiation in this country. Throughout the whole rest of the institute, and in many of the books and articles on initiation, we tend to talk about RCIA teams, precatechumenate teams, catechumenate teams, retreat teams, mystagogy teams, catechists, sponsors and godparents, hospitality ministers, spiritual directors, prayer partners and various other ministries. In the course of all this, it sounds like it takes a cast of thousands organized in a corporate, urban/suburban model to "do the initiation right."

I sometimes see the look of despair on the faces of people from small parishes. They are thinking, "There's no way. The same six people are already doing all the work in my parish. We can't take this on." Many have decided it takes a big parish, a huge organization and lots of people to implement the RCIA. Others, from black, Hispanic or rural parishes, for example, have decided that this will not translate into their cultural situation. I think this points us toward some of the work that we have left to do.

1. Christian communities whose cultures are other than corporate and urban will have to look to their own gifts and geniuses to implement the rite in a way that makes sense for those communities. This is probably done by focusing on images and analogies of Christian initiation from human life.

I often parallel the Christian initiation process to the process of meeting, falling in love and getting married. Much like the initiation process, the process that leads to marriage is one of steps and stages, each step forging a deeper relationship through the sharing of ideas, dreams, experiences, values and beliefs. As the relationship progresses to deeper levels, the movement is celebrated by signs of love (gifts, special dinners or other events, the handing on of heirlooms), which themselves serve to deepen the relationship. As the relationship grows, its circle widens, so that what began as something private between two individuals gradually expands to the community of friends and family who celebrate the wedding and, ideally, support and strenghten the marriage.

Another story I tell is of a cousin of my mother. He had been raised by his two unmarried Italian aunts. When he brought his non-Italian fiancée home to meet them, he was somewhat concerned that they might not accept her. Like people of all nationalities, Italians can be clannish. The two aunts, however, welcomed her with open arms, took her into their home and taught her how to cook, speak and "live" Italian. Most people who met her after she had been married for a few years assumed that she had been born Italian. I use this as an example of how Christian initiation is about learning the way of life of a people by living with them and coming to incorporate their beliefs, their ways and even their history as one's own.

A third image that I often use for Christian initiation is that of apprenticeship. When one first learns to do carpentry or electrical work or pottery or knitting, there are things one must know about wood or currents or glazes or wool. But the real learning usually comes from being with a master, observing them and trying out the skill under their watchful eye. Like these disciplines, Christian initiation is more about learning to do than about learning facts. It is about incorporating knowledge into flesh and blood, mastering the skill of faithful Christian living.

2. The dominant culture has much to learn from other cultures, for example, from African Americans and Native Americans about the role of elders in initiating; from the youth culture about using media to interpret experience; from Hispanic Americans about the importance of hospitality and establishing relationships before getting down to business.

3. We have always to remember that before the rite there is the church. The ritual text must always be read in the context not only of the Roman Catholic church but also this local church. So, to use an example from a recent issue of *Catechumenate* ("Implementing the Vision of Christian Initiation in the Rural Community," parts 1 and 2, Joanna Case and Michael Clay, March and May, 1996), how do you ritually introduce someone who is seeking to be received as a catechumen in a community where everyone not only knows everyone else but is related to just about everyone else?

4. In addition to the church, there is the individual. Although many parishes have begun to be open to receiving catechumens and candidates on God's schedule, many are still working on a school-year model.

5. After years of treating baptized candidates like catechumens, an awareness is developing of the need to spend time and energy helping the baptized, both those in the pews and those who wish to be received into full communion, to value their baptism. I strongly recommend Ron Oakham's *One at the Table: The Reception of Baptized Christians* (Chicago: LTP, 1995) for a serious treatment of this topic.

Finally, it occurs to me that many of the things I list as "successes" have to do with the word and with the initiation rituals. We have yet to place the same emphasis on the eucharist and on mystagogy. It also occurred to me that just as we are relearning our initiation rites, we are in danger of losing the ongoing rite of initiation, the eucharist. Will we miss it? If the implementation of the Christian initiation process can raise the awareness not only of the catechumens but of the whole assembly regarding their priestly role in the great act of offering thanks and praise, then perhaps we will protest with one voice when we are offered communion services in place of eucharist.

Catherine Dooley, OP

Liturgical Catechesis for Confirmation

It is an understatement to say that the age for confirmation is a controversial pastoral question! The issue of the sequence of the rites of initiation has been researched and studied from scriptural, theological, historical and liturgical perspectives only to reach an impasse. In 1994, the National Conference of Catholic Bishops (NCCB) determined that the sacrament of confirmation is to be conferred between the ages of seven and eighteen within the limits determined by the diocesan bishops. The result throughout the United States is a wide variety of practice and a fair amount of polarization on the question of confirmation.

Many liturgists and catechists support the reestablishment of the ancient sequence of baptism, confirmation and eucharist as the order of initiation not only for adult catechumens and unbaptized children of catechetical age, but even for those baptized as infants. In this view, confirmation is a sacrament of initiation and its meaning is derived from its relationship to baptism and eucharist. Confirmation completes baptism but eucharist is the sacrament of completion for Christian initiation. In confirmation the individual is sealed with "the inexpressible gift of the Spirit," becoming more completely the image of the Lord in order to bear witness to him, to build up the body of Christ and to the living-out of this relationship in a life of service to others.

Other authors favor delaying the sacrament until the individual has the maturity of faith to comprehend confirmation and participate in its reception. Delaying the sacrament to late teen-age years provides the opportunity for a more extended catechesis. The difficulty involved in adequately preparing children at the age of seven simultaneously for the reception of three sacraments—confirmation, penance and eucharist—is another reason given for a later age of reception. Diocesan and parish leaders who do celebrate confirmation before or with first communion acknowledge that catechesis is sometimes difficult since most of the resources for confirmation are written for adolescents and youth. Consequently, catechists often draw from a number of sources to put together an instructional program in whatever fashion they can.

On a pastoral level, it is clear that the question is not about the age for confirmation but rather it is the twofold issue of appropriating the meaning of confirmation as a sacrament of initiation and ensuring the Christian formation of those baptized as infants. I propose that the situation will remain at an impasse until the vision offered us in the Vatican II and post-Vatican II liturgical and catechetical documents is implemented. In this essay, I will briefly review the principles of those documents and suggest a model of liturgical catechesis for confirmation.

In this model the content of catechesis for confirmation as initiation comes out of the theological understanding of the sacrament as found in the ritual texts, symbols and symbolic actions, scriptures and historical background that uncovers and discloses the significance of confirmation. The method of catechesis is participation in word and symbol since it is the act of celebrating that captivates the imagination, shapes attitudes and outlooks, and transforms actions.

Principles of Liturgical Catechesis

In recent decades, documentary sources such as the *Constitution on the Sacred Liturgy* [CSL] 48, other liturgical and catechetical

Catherine Dooley, OP

documents such as *Eucharisticum mysterium* [EM] 14, the *National Catechetical Directory, Sharing the Light of Faith* [NCD] 36, the apostolic exhortation of Pope John Paul II, *Catechesis in our Time* [CT] 23, the *Catechism of the Catholic Church* [CCC] 1074–1075, the revised *Rite of Baptism for Children*, the *Rite of Confirmation* and particularly the *Rite of Christian Initiation of Adults* [RCIA] 75, provide a future direction by calling for a sacramental and liturgical catechesis based on the following principles.

Mystery of Faith through Rites and Prayers

The celebration of the rites and prayers is a starting point for catechesis. As the *Constitution on the Sacred Liturgy* states: "The church wants the faithful to have a good understanding of the mystery through the rites and prayers and thus to take an intelligent, devout and active part in the sacred action" (48). It is the mystery of faith which is to be understood well and this understanding comes from prayerful celebration.

Active Participation

The purpose of liturgical catechesis is to lead communities and individual members of the faithful to maturity of faith through full and active participation in the liturgy which effects and expresses that faith in the conscious living-out of a life of justice. In preparing for the celebration of confirmation, emphasis should be placed on confirmation as a parish celebration that involves the active participation of the community and a diversity of ministries. It is important to underline that active participation, the right and duty of the Christian people by their baptism, is, however, more than acting as cantors and lectors, communion ministers or ministers of welcome, more than participating in processions or responding to prayers. Active participation is relationship. As Mark Searle noted:

> To participate is to allow oneself to become caught up in the eternal relations of the Son to the Father, a relationship which was enacted in the incarnate life and death of the Son of God and is summarized in the term "paschal mystery." It is a relationship to which we are introduced when we were first engrafted on to the living body of the church in baptism, which

we live out day by day in persevering obedience to the Spirit and which we rehearse as a people in the weekly celebration of the eucharist on the Lord's Day.[1]

Paschal Mystery

This relationship "summarized in the term paschal mystery" is the heart of all baptismal catechesis. The dying and rising of Jesus Christ is not only the cornerstone of Christian faith; it is the paradigm of Christian life, both for individuals and for a community of faith. Christians die to themselves to live for Christ. The church proclaims and celebrates this paschal mystery in the liturgy in order to live from it and to carry on Christ's saving work in the world.

The various aspects of the one paschal mystery unfold throughout the liturgical year, beginning with the Easter Triduum and continuing through the cycles of seasons and feasts. Sunday is the preeminent day on which the assembly is gathered to call to mind the death and resurrection of Jesus Christ in the hope of his coming again. In order to make concrete the relationship of the paschal mystery and initiation, sacraments are celebrated on Sundays within the Easter season or on other days and feasts throughout the year that have inherent paschal significance. Since confirmation is a sacrament of initiation, the Easter season is the most appropriate time for celebration.

Initiation is the Responsibility of the Community

Sacramental and liturgical catechesis takes place in the midst of the community. The liturgical documents speak of the ministry of the whole community in the sacramental celebration and in the handing on of the faith of the church. The solemn affirmation of the *Rite of Baptism for Children* is, "This is our faith, the faith of the church, the faith we are proud to profess in Christ Jesus" (59). The *Rite of Confirmation* is clear that it is the responsibility of the people of God to prepare the baptized for confirmation but Christian parents have a particular responsibility and concern for the initiation of children into the sacramental life (3). Since all who are to be initiated should be confirmed at a common celebration (RC, 11), attention should be given especially to the significance of the celebration for the local church.

Catherine Dooley, OP

The whole people of God, represented by the families and friends of the candidate and members of the local community, will be invited to take part in the celebration and express its faith in the fruits of the Holy Spirit (RC, 4). The RCIA affirms the role of the community and states that initiation is a gradual process taking place within the community of the faithful" (RCIA, 4).

In the past, sacramental preparation was almost solely the responsibility of the school or parish religion classes. The complementary education that takes place within these settings continues to be greatly valued but sacramental initiation of children as an endeavor akin to the catechumenate takes place in the midst of the community and through the liturgical rites and prayers. The challenge, of course, is to raise the parish community's awareness of its responsibility for handing on the faith to the catechumen and to the baptized children seeking full initiation.

Ongoing Conversion

The RCIA and other revised sacramental rites teach that the sacraments are not isolated moments but are celebrated as part of one's life within the framework of the liturgical year. Initiation, conversion and the Christian life are ongoing and gradual processes. This insight, encapsulated in the image of journey in the RCIA, leads to the understanding that commitment is part of all the initiation sacraments and is not identified only with confirmation. Moreover, sacramental celebration marks only one moment in the larger reality of continuing conversion. Sacraments are not limited to the moment of celebration but are interwoven with the events that have taken place before and after the celebration. The mystery of God experienced and celebrated in the sacrament is linked to the mystery of God experienced in daily life. Initiation is to be lived out in a life of service to others and the baptismal commitment to a covenanted relationship with Christ is continually renewed in the celebration of the eucharist.

Interrelationship of the Sacraments

The *Constitution on the Sacred Liturgy* provided for the revision of the rite of confirmation so that the intimate connection of this sacrament with the whole of Christian initiation may appear more clearly

(71). The *Rite of Confirmation* emphasizes the celebration of confirmation within Mass in order to highlight the basic connection of confirmation with all of Christian initiation. "The newly confirmed therefore participate in the Eucharist which completes their Christian initiation" (RC, 13). The sacraments as interrelated, as an organic whole, in which "the Eucharist occupies a unique place as the 'sacrament of sacraments,'" and "all the other sacraments are ordered to it as to their end" (CCC, 1211). The commitment made in baptism and confirmation is renewed and repeated in the eucharist.

> Baptism is the way the eucharist begins (with rebirth and forgiveness of sins), and the eucharist is the way baptism is sustained in the lives of the faithful. These two sacraments are thus fundamental to the whole sacramental system: the other sacraments make sense only to the extent that each of them relates to baptism (in particular, confirmation, penance, and anointing of the ill) and to eucharist (in particular, ordination and marriage).[2]

Theologically, this understanding of the relationship of the sacraments places confirmation in its proper context as a sacrament of initiation, as a sign of the "unity of the paschal mystery, the close link between the mission of the Son and the outpouring of the Holy Spirit" (RCIA, 215). Pastorally this configuration of sacraments does not inflate the sacrament of confirmation while overshadowing and diminishing the meaning of baptism and eucharist. Rather it puts emphasis where it properly belongs and helps us to understand that baptism and eucharist are the primary sacraments of commitment and mission.

The Nature and Purpose of Liturgical Catechesis[3]

The nature and purpose of liturgical catechesis flows from these basic sacramental and liturgical principles. The purpose of liturgical catechesis is to enable believers to come to a full, conscious and active participation that expresses and deepens relationships: relationship to God and to one another in Christ through the Spirit.

Catherine Dooley, OP

Liturgical catechesis prepares communities to enter into the liturgical symbols and rituals so children and young people, consonant with their age and personal development, can experience the paschal mystery which is at the heart of the liturgy. When children authentically participate in the liturgy, they will come to a sense of identity and belonging to the Christian community.

Central symbols such as the assembly itself, the water, wine, oil, bread, a laying on of hands, the reading and preaching of scriptures and the sign of the cross are integral to the liturgy itself. Liturgical catechesis aims to uncover the meaning of the words and actions so that children and young people may gradually realize that when they participate in the sacramental actions they are actually participating in the saving action of Christ which the sacrament signifies. These words and actions speak most forcefully when they "are expressed in the cultural richness of the people of God who celebrate" (CCC, 1158).

Taking inspiration from the RCIA, liturgical catechesis is a gradual process of conversion within a catechetical and liturgical process. There are three phases within this one process: preparation for, celebration of and reflection upon the liturgical action.

Catechesis for the Liturgy

The preparation for the liturgy is essential for the building up of a lexicon of images, rituals, symbols, gestures, music and sacred space in order to be open to the mystery of God within the liturgy.

In preparing for the celebration of the sacrament, the starting point of catechesis is the community that celebrates and the human values that underlie the liturgical celebration including "community activity, exchange of greetings, capacity to listen and to seek and grant pardon, expression of gratitude, experience of symbolic actions a meal of friendship and festive celebration" (DMC, 9).

Liturgical catechesis enables the children and young people to reflect on the rites and prayers of the liturgy in the light of these values in order to attend to the ways in which the liturgy reveals the presence of God in their lives. The purpose is to lead the assembly to express its faith and enter into relationship with the loving God and one another in and through the liturgical and sacramental ritual.

The Word of God

Liturgical catechesis takes place within a celebration of the word of God that accords with the liturgical season and attends to the readings, prayers, symbols and gestures intrinsic to the meaning of the sacraments. This celebration has a simple format of an opening song, a reading from scripture and a responsorial psalm. This is followed by the catechetical reflection and closing prayer. Celebrations of the word include ritual actions such as marking with the cross, anointing, lighting the candles, blessing with the baptismal water so that the children experience the ritual action in other contexts.

The RCIA, the *Rite of Baptism for Children* and the *Rite of Confirmation* include a list of biblical readings that may be the basis of these celebrations of the word. The readings provide a synthesis of how the church views the sacraments of initiation. The aim of the preparation is to come to a deeper awareness of the meaning and implications of the Holy Spirit in the life of the candidates through prayer and reflection on the readings suggested by the church. Chapter 5 of the *Rite of Confirmation* provides many options for readings from the Hebrew scriptures, gospels and other readings from the Christian scriptures.[4]

Each of the gospel readings, for example, offers a particular understanding of the gift of the Holy Spirit. The gospel of Mark (1:9–11) teaches that through the Spirit, Jesus is the beloved Son of God. In the context of the confirmation rite, it assures the confirmed that they too share in the same Spirit as Jesus does. In the reading from Luke (4:16), the account of Jesus in the synagogue in Nazareth when he begins his public ministry gives an insight into the implications of the gift the Holy Spirit. Like Jesus, those who receive the Spirit are sent to continue the mission of Jesus to bring about the kingdom of God. The gift of the Spirit is not only for the benefit of the one confirmed but for the building up of the community. It is the empowerment to continue Jesus's saving work. The confirmands rejoice in the Holy Spirit with Jesus (Luke 10:21–24), aware that the work they accomplish through the Spirit is the gift of God. The reading from John (7:37–39) underlines that the Spirit is a gift that the risen Christ bestows upon believers. Other readings from the gospel of John, taken from the farewell discours, name the Holy Spirit as the Paraclete, the intercessor, the one who will enable the disciples to understand what Jesus has taught and said. Other gospel readings suggested do not refer directly to the Holy Spirit but focus on responsible service and the willingness to join together with Jesus in the giving of oneself. The word proclaimed and reflected upon enables the confirmands to come to an understanding, appreciation and thanksgiving for the Gift of the Holy Spirit who gives joy, strength, and courage for witness.

The liturgical celebration incorporates many of the scriptural images of the Holy Spirit into the ritual texts: paraclete, Spirit of promise, Spirit of adoption, Spirit of truth, water, fire, wind, cloud, light, dove, finger and hand of God, anointing and seal (CCC, 694–701). These images provide another rich source for catechesis on the Holy Spirit which is directed to the imagination and allows the young people to attend to the language of the liturgy. For example, reflection on the blessing of the baptismal water traces the working of the Spirit in saving history and gives insight into the action of the Holy Spirit in baptism.

The Spirit can be likened to the wind. In Hebrew the word for spirit, *ruah,* means moving air or wind. The term includes all the movements of wind from the gentle breeze that often comes in early evening to the mighty gale that erodes the shores and even the rocks. Jesus said:

> The wind blows where it wills; you hear the sound but you do not see where it comes from nor where it is going. But you know it is passing by when you see its effects. So it is with everyone who is born of the Spirit. (John 3:8)

The scriptural analogy of the spirit and wind can be traced from Genesis (1:1), where in the beginning a mighty wind swept over the face of waters; to Exodus (14:21), where a strong east wind blows back the waters of the sea so that slaves can be free; to Ezekiel (37:1–14), where the wind rushes through the valley of the dry bones, breathing life into the people; to Acts, where the mighty wind of Pentecost not only shakes the house but shakes the disciples out of their fear, impelling them to preach the good news. Christians pray, "Come, Holy Spirit, and renew the face of the earth," words taken from Psalm 104, in which the psalmist recognizes that the presence of the Spirit brings life; the absence of the Spirit means death. Exploring the images enables the confirmands to see differently, to "move from the visible to the invisible, from the sign to the thing signified, from the 'sacraments to the mysteries'" (CCC, 1075).

Ritual Texts

Catechesis for confirmation should also attend to the ritual texts, such as the renewal of baptismal promises, the sacramental formulas, the blessing of the chrism and the prayer accompanying the laying on of hands. For example, the prayer said with the laying of hands on the confirmands asks that those to be confirmed might have the spirit of wisdom and understanding, the spirit of right judgment and courage, the spirit of knowledge and reverence and be filled with the spirit of wonder and awe in God's presence.

The gifts of the Holy Spirit are the names given to the experience of being led by the Spirit through and with one's own talents and gifts. The gifts of the Spirit are active because the Spirit is present in the love or charity shown one to another in very ordinary ways. There is nothing greater than the ordinary actions of reaching out to others who are sick or lonely or suffering with the fragility of age, of working to obliterate prejudice or to care for the environment. This is the work of the Spirit today. The Holy Spirit is "the principle of every vital and truly saving action in each part of the Body of Christ; the Spirit works in many ways to build up the whole Body in charity" (CCC, 798).

Catechesis through the Liturgy

The second phase of the process is catechesis through the liturgy. "A sacramental celebration is woven from signs and symbols" (CCC, 1145), and these symbolic actions are already a language that is accompanied and given life by the word of God and the response of faith (CCC, 1153). Liturgy conveys its meaning not through explanation but through participation. Liturgy is action; the words and symbols enact that which is spoken.

In the context of the liturgy, when we give thanks, when we ask for pardon, when we praise, these words not only describe attitudes of gratitude, contrition and awe but effect these attitudes. It is by participating in the liturgical word and action that individuals come to discover or perceive the relationship being celebrated. The catechumen or young person may not yet be able to articulate meaning, but participation provides an intuitive way of knowing that is foundational for reflection and integration in the future.

Liturgical language uses plural forms, "we" and "us"; creates a common identity and makes an assembly out of a previously disparate group of participants. It is in and through the repeated pronouncement of these words that the community is constituted.[5]

Repetition is key in evoking the meaning contained in a liturgical ritual. "Repetition is never simply what it proclaims itself to be — never merely 'the same' again. The reiteration of 'the same' is always a new act in a new time; newness disguises itself beneath sameness."[6] The repetition of the celebrations of the same events year after year, the proclamation of sacred texts and the performance of ritual gestures enable the child to come to remember and celebrate the saving presence of God in past events as an action that is made present and lived now and into the future.

Ritual is frequently a means of social transformation. It shapes the way we think because it encourages us to interpret reality in certain ways. The public nature of ritual not only unites participants but embodies and promotes the struggle for justice. Catechists must continually be aware of the power that liturgical ritual has to nurture and shape the child's attitudes, values and actions.

Conclusion:
Catechesis from the Liturgy of Confirmation

In the weeks following the celebration, the community, neophytes and newly confirmed, within the context of the celebration of the word, reflect together on the reality of the Holy Spirit. This is a period of integration which aims to bring together the experience of the liturgy, the scriptural images and the meaning for their own lives.

The symbols and gestures essential to the meaning of confirmation — the anointing with chrism and the laying of hands — are central to the catechesis. The liturgical actions are related to scriptural images and historical background and are seen within the context of baptism and eucharist. The laying on of hands signifies the biblical gesture that invokes the gift of the Holy Spirit. The anointing with chrism and the accompanying words express clearly the meaning of the sacrament: "Be sealed with the gift of the Holy Spirit." The concept of sealing can be traced to the sources of identity and covenant. Owners marked their possessions with a distinctive seal so that they could be identified. In ancient Rome, soldiers were tattooed to indicate that they belonged to the emperor. In modern times, Jews were branded with numbers. The meaning of seal as covenant comes from the use of a seal to impress a mark on wax for official documents. The seal certified the action or transaction and guaranteed authenticity. It was a sign of covenant, of entering into a reciprocal relationship.

The catechesis probes the meaning of identity and covenant. What does it mean in the here and now to be "sealed"? What does it mean here and now to be anointed with chrism? To be sealed with the gift of the Holy Spirit is to be promised the presence of the Spirit who conforms those who have been marked with the chrism and the cross more closely to Christ. To be sealed with the gift of the Holy Spirit is to be claimed as God's own. To be sealed is to respond to the prompting of the Spirit to bring "good news to the poor, heal the brokenhearted, proclaim liberty to the captives and release to the prisoners" (Luke 4:18).

The follow-up is the most important phase of the catechesis and, unfortunately, the one most likely to be omitted. Post-sacramental catechesis or mystagogy enables the one confirmed as well as the whole community to understand that catechesis does not end with the sacramental celebration or completion of initiation but is lifelong and ongoing. Preparation for the sacrament does not need to carry the burden of the total catechesis. The most effective catechesis follows the celebration because participation in the sacramental ritual brings insight. What has been experienced can be appropriated when it has been reflected upon and articulated.

Catechesis from the liturgy of confirmation is an ongoing process because sacraments of initiation are but the beginning of the Christian life. The sacramental rites and texts are a rich and inexhaustible source for reflection and transformation. In opening oneself to the symbols of the liturgy, one opens oneself to the power of the Spirit.

Catherine Dooley, OP

1. Mark Searle, "The Mass in the Parish," *The Furrow* 37 (1986): 621–622.

2. Aidan Kavanagh, "Theological Principles for Sacramental Catechesis," *Living Light* 23 (1987): 316.

3. For the application of this process to other sacramental celebrations, see Catherine Dooley, "Mystagogy: Ministry to Parents," 97–104, and Jane Marie Osterholt, "A Proposed Method of Liturgy and Catechesis," 27–42, in *Catechesis and Mystagogy: Infant Baptism* (Chicago: Liturgy Training Publications, 1996); Catherine Dooley, "Mystagogy: A Model for Sacramental Catechesis," in *The Candles Are Still Burning,* ed. M. Grey, A. Heaton, D. Sullivan (London: Geoffrey Chapman, 1995), 58–69.

4. Eugene Laverdiere, "Confirmation: Light from the Liturgical Readings," *Hosanna* 1:2 (1983): 24–27.

5. See Paul Connerton, *How Societies Remember: Themes in Social Sciences* (New York: Cambridge University Press, 1989) on the role of commemorative ceremonies (ritual) in the formation of the identity of a community.

6. Stephen Buickland, "Ritual, Bodies and 'Cultural Memory'" in *Liturgy and the Body,* eds. Louis-Marie Chauvet and Francois Kabasele Lumbala, Concilium (1995/3): 54.

Toinette M. Eugene

Between
"Lord, Have Mercy!"
and "Thank You, Jesus!"

Pastoral Issues for Liturgical Renewal

Liturgical change has not been well received by some cultural anthropologists and sociologists of religion. Most, of course, have ignored this somewhat quiet revolution and its ramifications, but a few have reacted strongly. The renowned anthropologist Victor Turner, for example, lamented the loss of the dignified pre-conciliar Mass and the emergence of "relevant" liturgical experimentation.[1] Since the turn of the century, the study of religious ritual worship has been closely tied to issues of social change. Two general approaches have predominated, which model broadly the concerns of maintaining "tradition" on one hand, but movement in "transition" on the other.

The first approach, rooted in W. Robertson Smith's study of Semitic sacrifice,[2] has been developed with great sophistication by Victor Turner and Mary Douglas, among others.[3] This approach has focused on the role of ritual worship in the maintenance of social groups. It therefore tends to analyze religious ritual as the expressive deployment of the symbolic structures that undergird a group's common worldview. In this way religious ritual is seen to act as a mechanism of continuity to resist force that could fray the fabric of the community. Edward Foley has described this approach as an aspect of the "mythic tradition" utilizing the framework of theologian John Dominic Crossan.[4]

A second approach has focused on how groups change and grow through ritual worship. Within this perspective, liturgical ritual action is seen as integral to the way in which the ideas and traditions of a social group are adapted to changing circumstances. This approach is probably rooted in Durkheim's analysis of cult, but articulated most recently and persuasively in the work of Clifford Geertz.[5] According to this perspective, liturgical or ritual worship is seen to facilitate meaningful social change by fusing a community's "general conceptions of the order of existence" with the actual circumstances of its daily life.[6] This approach closely parallels Foley's use of the parabolic narration tradition as explained by Crossan. In this tradition, liturgical ritual action would call us to confront the present, disallow us from living in an ideal and nonconfrontational world, challenge the reconciliation with which we are comfortably living and bring us to a new tradition in a future that is realistic yet full of hope.[7]

The first approach casts liturgical ritual as a mythic mechanism of continuity, a way of countering change. The second approach regards liturgical or religious ritual as affording parabolic opportunities for change via adaptation or integration. Examples abound to support both approaches, but as theoretical formulations of the basic dynamics of ritual, one wonders if both can be correct. Of course, the apparent contradiction between these approaches is largely a matter of emphasis. Yet their stark polarization highlights the fact that our most influential theories of liturgical ritual use it to solve *other* questions, particularly those raised by bifurcations of culture and society, of stasis and change.[8]

The pressure to change visited upon our cultures, our church and even our worship increases each year. But the resistance to change increases as well. How do we hold tradition and transition in balance? What changes are inevitable or desirable? What forces and factors are changing the face of our cultures, our church and our worship?

The concomitant questions that emerged first began to express themselves for me in dichotomous tension: How do we live with the growing tension we feel between change and resistance to change? When something is clearly dying and something is coming to birth for us as church, how do we keep our pastoral balance while living with these dynamics of conversion, of metanoia, of renewal? How do we embrace change as life-giving and grace-filled?

Confession

These kinds of dichotomies remind me of an experience that is inevitable for me whenever I return to my home church in Oakland, California. Like a good and lifelong Catholic who loves and appreciates at least selected aspects of our tradition, I should begin my account of renewal by starting with confession. Let me begin my confession as a recollection of the memories of the tribe from which I have sprung. As we struggle with the tension of traditions and transitions, I choose to begin by first reflecting on a dichotomous proverb from the prophetic book of "Mama Said," a book from which many womanist theologians and ethicists obtain their lessons on the practicalities of ministry situations that call for prophetic/pastoral care that is both loving and liberating in marvelous ways![9]

Whenever I go home to preach in my home parish, a black Roman Catholic church in Oakland, California, there is always the African American religious and cultural ritual of greeting the mothers of the church. These elders in the assembly of the faithful are embodied as those wizened and wise older women who have grown down smaller with the passing of the years because they have borne the heat and the burden of the day. I always look forward to an exchange with Mother Camille. She always says to me, "Why, chil', girl, how you all doin'?" and I say, "Well—just fine, Mother Camille. And how 'bout you?" She looks me in the eye, and she says with a straight face, "Why, baby, I'm somewhere between 'Lord, Have Mercy!' and 'Thank You, Jesus!'"

Mother Camille then says to me, as I am processing up the aisle to proclaim the Good News, "Girl, you go now!" (which I take to be a message of commission). Then she winks and hands me a wadded-up dollar bill—the widow's mite—and she says, tongue in cheek, "Now, girl, don't you give this to Father, he don't need it!" (a message of affirmation and autonomy for me). And finally, she says, "Now, don't you embarrass us!" (a paradoxical message for me containing both admonition and tender affection).

I will use this bit of African American folk wisdom, "being somewhere between Lord, Have Mercy and Thank You, Jesus" in order to develop some paradigms that may be of use when dealing with change and renewal as one of many examples of diverse cultural contexts and communities where leadership in pastoral life encounters stages, difficulties and development in our own unique ecclesial traditions and transitions.

True confessions are good for the soul and vitally important for the religious community in an era of reclaiming identity and integrity in an era of change, when complicity and conspiracy are emblematic of the sickness and sinfulness of our American society. As Scott Appleby has reminded us, liberalism alone is unable to articulate or demonstrate the kind of moral values that must undergird any serious movement of spiritual, liturgical or social transformation which can occur somewhere between honoring older traditions and newer transitions.[10] I confess then that the critical link between personal responsibility and pastoral, ecclesial or societal change seems to be noticeably missing on the ideological left—a place where I sometimes have chosen to reside in self-righteous splendor.

On the ideological right, conservatism and traditionalism still deny the reality of cultural, racial and religious diversity, where change, growth and development must go on unless the living liturgy and life of the church opt to accept ennui, entropy and eventually theological, social, spiritual and finally demographic death. I confess that I sometimes have envied the self-righteous morality of those who profess ideological "righteousness."

Because I deal with and struggle with cultural, religious and social diversity in painful and poignant ways every day of my life—not because I want to but because I have to—I need to begin by confessing who I am as well as who I want to be. I want to confess that my most significant academic degrees were received and my best dissertation was written in the School of Hard Knocks. As Zora Neale Hurston, premier African American anthropologist and author in the literary era of the Harlem Renaissance, would say, "Ah done been in sorrow's kitchen and Ah licked de pots clean."[11]

Can we say confessionally and experientially with her that we know the taste of disappointment, despair, deprivation delivered only and intentionally because of religious denomination, race, class, gender or sexual orientation? Can you taste it? Can you smell it? Can you feel it? Can you choose to be in solidarity with it? That means taking it on, taking it up—the way one reverently picks up a fallen flag (a rainbow one, perhaps, rather than a papal or national one), or the way one takes up and embraces like a friend the frame of an old rugged cross.

I need to confess that even though I am black, I am also by birth and academic training and denominational tradition, a Western Catholic Christian. Because of that I have inherited, and sometimes even handed on like bread gone stale, the pernicious dualism that our dichotomous Western Christianity has held sacred between God, the church and the world—a theological, social, pastoral and liturgical split that has made a big difference and a big deal between that which is sacred and profane, between sexuality and spirituality, between justice and peace—big differences which the church historically has used to dull the edges of human and divine experience. And so I am compelled to cry out with Mother Camille and with the countless others who suffer most from this dichotomy, "Lord, have mercy!" *Kyrie eleison.*

Finally, I confess that I am longing to stand more closely in solidarity with those whose radical vision, politics and spirituality I have come to trust: those who know, through the experience largely of suffering and struggle, that we meet the sacred in relation to one another, and who understand that any power that we or others use in ways that are not mutually empowering is abusive.[12] I look to such radical women and men, of whatever color, religion, class, sexual preference or orientation, to confirm in me a joyful commitment to live responsibly in this one, holy, catholic and apostolic church as well as within our diverse, pluralistic, ecologically and ecumenically fragile world.[13] And so I am empowered to cry out with Mother Camille and those many nameless but fortunate others who actually and regularly live in the interstices where I would like to remain, "Thank you, Jesus!" *Deo gratias.*

Toinette M. Eugene

Dealing with pastoral issues involving theological, liturgical and social change means more than just welcoming or recruiting more women or people of color to ministerial and liturgical leadership. Dealing with change means dealing with and honoring human differences, confronting the racism, classism, elitism and liturgical literalism that limits our pro-action and reaction. It means dealing with whatever limits our ability to sit and listen longer than what we claim as our inalienable right to stand and preside, to preach, to share in decision-making that affects the whole People of God. Dealing with pastoral issues involving real and lasting conversion, ongoing metanoia, requires the confession that "It's me, it's me, it's me, O Lord, standing in the need of prayer!" Lord, have mercy!

Convictions

We have already observed that the pressure upon our cultures, our church and on our liturgical lives to implement change increases each year. But the resistance to change increases as well. How do we hold authentic tradition and transition in balance? What changes are inevitable or desirable? What forces and factors are changing the face of our cultures, our church and our worship? It is this last question that I choose to investigate more thoroughly by way of parables and myths of change and conversion, in order to offer some concluding reflections on pastoral strategies, suggestions and scriptural recollections that move us toward real pastoral renewal.

It is this inquiry about forces and factors on which I want to focus. It is in the presence of our enemies as well as our friends (Psalm 23) that I want to sit at the table of liturgical renewal that is also intended to be the Table of Justice/Love.[14] It is in this locus where myth and parable intersect that I want to invite our continued efforts at investing in the experience of the disciples on the road to Emmaus, who, in the midst of critical and seemingly tragic change in their lives, chose to receive and respond to both the myth and parable of tradition and transition that "set their hearts on fire" as he — Jesus the resurrected one — talked with them explaining the scriptures and manifesting his presence in the "breaking of the bread." (Luke 24:13–35)

Because of my confessions, I stand convicted, not as a criminal, but by the love of God for me and for all who struggle to deal with issues of liturgical change in the midst of cultural and social diversity. I am convicted and convinced by this experience to honor diversity, and to utilize diversity as a way to enter joyfully into the reign of God which is ritually enacted and embodied in the midst of the believing assembly of faith.

Stemming from my African American cultural heritage, I want to draw upon the gift of the griot, the one who is entrusted as steward and minister with the memories of the tribe. I want to recall and recount for you both some stories and some dreams — myths and parables about change and conversion, about death and resurrection, about justice/love and liberation among those who claim both leadership and membership in the chosen people of God. We need to remember and to recite the myths and parables, the prophetic and pastoral passages that stem from sacred scripture. We need to engage not only in the narratives, but also in the iconoclastic actions like those of the woman who anointed Jesus's feet with her hair, like the Syro-Phoenician woman who dared to engage Jesus in a dialogue homily about who gets cake and who gets crumbs; like the woman of Samaria who demanded and got from Jesus a drink of living water.

We need to remember and to revive again the religious rituals engaged in by Harriet Tubman who, like the magi of old, followed the light of the North Star to find and bring liberation to her people. We need to be reminded of the dreams, desires and models offered by Mother Henriette Delille and the other mother foundresses of the historically black religious orders who served the poor and the disenfranchised as well as debated and dialogued with those who disparaged their vocation to reform and reclaim the whole church. Catherine of Siena, important doctor of the church that she is, is not the only "uppity religious woman" witness we can cite, imitate and re-imagine ourselves richly to resemble!

We need to know of and share dreams like that of Father Augustus Tolton, first African American priest and of Blessed Pierre Toussaint, beloved Haitian immigrant hairdresser and healer in eighteenth-century Harlem. We need to celebrate and emulate the legendary but true tales of holy Thea Bowman and of Archbishop James

Patterson Lyke (now of happy and sacred memory), who struggled mightily and publicly lobbied for much-needed changes in our liturgy. They predicted and prefigured renewal for us in their own unique black Catholic way through remodeling diocesan styles of ordained and lay leadership, and in initiating and molding innovative forms of what might be described broadly as forms of prophetic/pastoral care. Their lives are paradigms of ways and means to restore vibrance and health to an ailing ecclesial community suffering from the phobias and failures of cross-cultural aversion, of subtle and not-so-subtle xenophobia and of sexist and racist resistance to the contribution of the "others," the strangers, the "newcomers" in our midst.[15]

Pulitzer prize–winning author Alice Walker has a story that lends itself to the kind of moral imagination needed to envision and model the kinds of pastoral care of which the church might make use as we continue to journey and claim the beauty of our traditions and employ the ministries that will best encourage, empower and embody the communities of the faithful. Her story invites us joyfully to accept, experience, experiment and ultimately implement the kinds of change that are needed in order for the Spirit to continue to renew the face of the earth. Alice Walker writes this in her journal:

April 17, 1984
The universe sends me fabulous dreams! Early this morning I dreamed of a two-headed woman. Literally. A wise woman. Stout, graying, caramel-colored, with blue-grey eyes, wearing a blue flowered dress. Who was giving advice to people. Some white people, too, I think. Her knowledge was for everyone and it was all striking. While one head talked, the other seemed to doze. I was so astonished! For what I realized in the dream is that two-headedness was at one time an actual physical condition and that two-headed people were considered wise. Perhaps this accounts for the adage "Two heads are better than one." What I think this means is that two-headed people, like blacks, lesbians, Indians, "witches," have been suppressed, and in their case, suppressed out of existence. Their very appearance had made them "abnormal" and therefore subject to extermination. For surely two-headed people have existed. And it is only among blacks (to my knowledge) that a trace of their existence

is left in the language. Rootworkers, healers, wise people with "second sight" are called "two-headed" people.

This two-headed woman was amazing. I asked whether the world would survive, and she said No; and her expression seemed to say, The way it is going there's no need for it to. When I asked her what I/we could/should do, she took up her walking stick and walked expressively and purposefully across the room. Dipping a bit from side to side.

She said: Live by the Word and keep walking.[16]

In this brief pericope, a combination of folktale and ethical exegesis, Alice Walker captures the essence of what her convictions and our own convictions might mean and contain. For pastoral ministers seeking to maintain a balance between tradition and transition, this story and its concomitant hermeneutic can offer considerable sagacity as well as solidarity for all who are making strong efforts to address pastoral issues of change and renewal. Living by the Word is effectively radical evangelical praxis, as well as a type of affective methodology. This story and others like it can bring transformation into our church's theological, pastoral, liturgical life of community in the midst of what we claim and celebrate as cultural and social diversity.

In the ingenuous cultural world and belief system of Alice Walker, we are enjoined to "Live by the Word and keep walking."[17] She incorporates into her culturally contextualized fable a pastoral approach to change—indeed a biblical reply—to the ethically constructed question of "what I/we could/should do"[18] in a world that will survive only if our absolute attention is given to theological, liturgical, cultural and spiritual transformation.

I am arguing from a framework of a liberation-based model of pastoral ministry, which emphasizes its own particular social experiences in order to address issues of change and diversity in the face of unchanging universal claims. These universal changes are ones that often seem unjust or unduly arbitrary and unfair in a more contemporary society in which pastoral ministry and leadership require much more mutuality, humility, respect for multiple forms of diversity and difference as represented by the people, the local conditions and the global contexts of the church universal. I am asserting that liberational pastoral ministry must be both critical and deconstructionist

in its methodology. It focuses largely on providing healing and recon-
ciling experiences or "myths" that involve mastery of social analysis
and social justice, as well as spiritual direction and therapeutic intervention or "parables."[19]

A liberation-based pastoral approach to change in the church
can be theologically understood contextually only where liturgical
ritual, rite, proclamation, initiation and transformation are intentionally involved or sought. "Contextual theology is a method of the-
ologizing which is aware of the specific historical and cultural
contexts in which it is involved, and senses that it is directed to experiences and reflections of others."[20] A contextual theology, and by
extension a contextual form of religious transformation or change,
can proceed only from critical analysis of the social context that forms
our experience, our struggles and our emergent innovative projects.

Contextual change in religious, liturgical and pastoral practice
emerges from the painful and often lethal struggle against dominant
power positions and relationships. This means that no one who is not
at the least more than beginning to be involved in and committed to
the struggle for justice and liberation can write or participate, lead or
legally lobby for transformative liturgical renewal, which in effect is
a way of re-enacting and re-membering the resurrection from the dead
of our church and our diverse communities of faith.

Focusing on the words of Walker and utilizing the folk wisdom
of other mothers and fathers of the church that I know, this essay dealing with pastoral issues and strategies involved in renewal assumes
this understanding of contextuality and finds common cause with the
witness of texts such as *Living No Longer for Ourselves: Liturgy and
Justice in the Nineties*[21] because this kind of critical analysis urges a
kind of emergent transgressive praxis on the part of liberal people
who might verge even on becoming radical. It also calls for pastoral
ministers in liturgical renewal to act as prophetic "cultural workers"
in order to elicit the kind of transgressive restoration and resurrection conjured up by cultural critic bell hooks in her engaging studies
of transformative education[22] and advocated by Harvard educational
theorist Henry Giroux in his ongoing works.[23]

Liturgical renewal and, by extension, liturgical education provide
a location from which to challenge the mythic status quo. Liturgical

renewal and, by extension, liturgical education provide a moral authority and a moral imagination that has the ethical power to dispel a dominant "culture of disbelief"[24] through a public discourse that offers an explicit value system, an explicit claim to authority emanating from the community of faith's own cultural experience and analysis of what it must be and do in order to survive and to "succeed," and to live in right relation to others who do not entirely share its convictions and commitments.

I am positing that in the midst of a static culture of disbelief, epitomized by ennui and apathy, liturgical renewal holds the potential and the power to transform the stultifying discourse of secularism and of civil and institutional religion, in liberating and justice-orienting ways through the process of contextualization.[25] As Alice Walker contends, I argue that we are enjoined and empowered as wise persons, as provocative providers and pastoral purveyors of liturgical renewal, "to live by the Word and keep walking." That is, we are responsible and accountable to publicly articulate the content and cross-cultural context of our Judeo-Christian traditions on behalf of the universal church, as well as for the civic, racial ethnic, and socially diverse forms of community in which we are rooted and in which we live our daily lives.

In order to address with pastoral responsibility our American culture of comfort, rampant consumerism, classism, sexism, homophobia and all the other "isms' expressing ideologies of violence, dominance and maintenance of the social status quo, I posit that we must find a means of articulating counter-cultural views that enable change through the means of adopting transformative religious lifestyles.

I would describe this process as one of examining and embracing the role of diverse "downwardly mobile" cultures in American life. We must examine and embrace the place of cultures that are inextricably bound up in the dynamism of pro-justice and pro-liberation movements, which have transformed many of us from privatized Puritans to public prophets who have a dream of equality and mutuality, and who hold up a liberationally informed ethos of agape, inclusivity and solidarity with those who are most vulnerable, fragile and powerless. In order to move from tradition to transition, as pastoral ministers we must invoke and evoke in ourselves and others the power to live out the blessings of the "be"-attitudes, especially in their Lucan formulation (Luke 6:20–38).[26]

Invoking and evoking the beatitudes as a means of moving from tradition to transition is first of all, a cross-cultural embodiment and an incarnation of the New Testament Greek understanding of blessing or *makarios*.[27] Moreover, the liturgical action of blessing and being blessed at the end of our renewed eucharistic tradition occurs because we are invited to be in solidarity with the poor, the meek, the oppressed of the world.[28] It is a process and a worthy renewal in our process of movement from tradition to transition when this action of the liturgy is understood also as one symbolic means of actively advocating the contextualization and indigenization of cross-cultural experience into liturgical worship and rituals for the sake of a real renewal throughout all of the church.

I am convinced that in order to honor both tradition and transition, the community of faith must be empowered as pastoral ministers, liturgical or catechetical educators, to embrace and to enable the practice of renewed and renewing liturgical and pastoral rituals of justice-loving, believing and life-affirming peoples. We are enjoined to move from "Lord, have mercy!" to "Thank you, Jesus!" by intentionally addressing and redressing particularly those pastoral issues that have previously kept us ineffective and unenthusiastic for the faith that does justice.[29]

We are likewise enjoined to find liturgical expressions and ritual actions that allow us to more fully "live by the Word and keep walking" in the face and in the forms of a contrary culture of disbelief. This is the old and obstinate routinization of outmoded mythic rituals which have served to privatize and to de-politicize the radical ways in which we as a faithful believing people are called. We must begin to exercise anew the rights, responsibilities and forms of religious renewal and change which ought to extend a transforming praxis of liberation, peace and justice for all. This is the framework of a parable and praxis of justice, love and the peace that passes understanding for all.

Commitments

Having made my confession and named my convictions, I must attempt as a conclusion to offer some commitments that move toward effecting change. I believe that commitments, covenants and communities all develop best in the context of gratitude and thanksgiving for all that is and for all that might be in a future as well in a present that is full of hope (Jeremiah 29:11). In this final section, I will provide an outline of a method that can bring a committed praxis out of the myths and parables, out of the poetry and prophecy that have been expressed. I want ultimately to arrive at a modicum of meaning for the work of the people—the true expression of liturgical change in the context of what it means to belong to a believing Christian community shaped by the Exodus experience and the transforming paschal mystery which effectively does the work of justice and love.

As an overarching means of reaching and achieving the beatitudes and blessings that rejoice in renewal, rather than resisting forms of change, I want to suggest one final paradigm by which pastoral ministers might embody more the diverse and mutually enhancing roles of prophetic and pastoral leadership, education and moral agency within the experience and process of liturgical conversion and change.

This final section on commitments that foster transformative liturgical change examines the concept and metaphor of the "cultural worker"[30] as a category which might be useful to conceptualize the work of pastoral ministers who would wish to engage more practically in the process of *contextualization*[31]—a process that foundationally fosters strategies for achieving liturgical renewal and change. Contextualization is the liturgical successor to the topic of indigenization and inculturation in the liturgy.

Harvard educational theorist Henry Giroux has published extensively on issues of contextualization and education in recent years.[32] Giroux addresses educational change as well as contextualization by drawing upon a new paradigm in order to rewrite the meaning of pedagogy, education and their implications for a new acceptance of difference in the various forms in which it invites social transformation for justice and peace. I contend that this category has implications for our self-understanding as agents of liturgical change who would foster positive forms of renewal, not only in church, but in our other places where we experience community, such as in the larger secular civic society.

The concept of "cultural worker" has traditionally been understood to refer to artists, writers, "worker-priests," media producers and other liminal individuals. In Giroux's framework, he extends the range of cultural worker to people working in professions such as liturgy, law, social work, architecture, medicine, theology, education and literature. His intention is to rewrite the concept and practice of cultural work by inserting the primacy of political, pedagogical, ritual and therapeutic activities as strategies that can "deliver us from evil."[33]

He argues that a principal dimension of cultural work refers to the process of re-creating symbolic representations and the practices within which they are engaged. This includes a particular concern with the analysis of textual, aural and visual representations and how such representations are organized and regulated to encourage change within particular institutional arrangements. It also addresses how various people are to engage such representations in the practice of analysis and comprehension. His definition of "cultural worker" strongly parallels my own definition of what actually may constitute an authentic "liturgical renewal person" or an intentional agent of transformation.

The political dimension of Giroux's metaphor of the "cultural worker" empowers transformation and change through a process whose intent is to mobilize knowledge and desires that may lead to minimizing the degree of oppression in people's lives. What is at stake for Giroux as well as for pastoral ministers committed to engage in liturgical renewal is the acquisition of a moral imagination that extends the possibilities for creating new spheres of worship. What is at stake is the acquisition and engagement of a moral imagination in which the principles of community, mutuality, respect for difference and the desire to engage in liturgical praxis that can bring about justice and love and peace become the primary organizing principles for structuring relationships between the self and others.

This kind of habitual and liminal engagement in transformative liturgical renewal is a form of discursive praxis, an unfinished language and story. It is ritual interrogative call and response, a catechetical kind of questioning that is replete with possibilities. This exercise of the moral imagination has the potential to effect commitments that grow out of particular engagements and dialogues of "living by the Word" while we keep on with the journey of walking toward a future filled with hope.

This means arguing that pastoral issues and concerns about liturgical renewal must become an ongoing public discourse that should extend the principles and practices of human dignity, liberty and social justice by engaging in social criticism and social prophetic utterance and action. This kind of moral imagination means that we are always in the hiatus that exists between the expression and experience of "Lord, have Mercy!" and "Thank you, Jesus!"

Indeed, such a task of renewal is ultimately the liturgical work of *all* the people which demands both a rethinking and a rewriting of the meaning of religious ritual and rite itself. It means comprehending this kind of pastoral ministry as a reconfiguration of textual, verbal and visual practices that seek to engage the processes through which people understand themselves and the ways in which they engage not only their ecclesial community, but also their social and cultural environment.

What is at stake here is the development of liturgical worship forms capable of contesting oppressive traditional forms of symbolic and mythical intent. As a cultural praxis intentionally engaged in by committed cultural workers, the ongoing renewal of the liturgy is a form of transformative pedagogy which, in educator Roger Simon's terms, both contests and refigures the construction, presentation and engagement of various forms of images, text, talk and action.[34] This reimagining and reformulation of text, dialogue, reflection and action results in the production of renewed sacred activity and social forms of religious discourse and praxis that literally and symbolically have the potential to re-form the entire community of the faithful in regard to their individual and collective lives and vocations within the church.

Related to these pastoral realities is the issue of illuminating the role that pastoral ministers who may be willing to consider themselves cultural workers might play as engaged and transformative critics. This suggests a notion of leadership and pastoral and liturgical practice that combines a discourse of hope with forms of self and social criticism that do not require cultural workers to step back from church or society as a whole, or to lay claim to a specious notion of objectivity or authenticity, but rather to unlearn and to transform those practices of privilege that can only reproduce conditions of oppression and human suffering. It is to this point that the parable of Alice Walker speaks when she describes those cultural communities which have been driven to the brink of extinction while living by the Word and attempting to keep walking.

I argue that pastoral ministers in the business of liturgical and religious renewal and change, who may also understand themselves as cultural workers, need to reclaim and reassert the importance of public discourse and of the recognition of differences in social location. A working knowledge of these points recognizes how economics, education, history and ethics are inextricably intertwined so as to position, enable and limit their work within shifting locations of power. The radical nature of such discourse points to the roles of cultural workers as street-savvy religious and theological intellectuals who combine a sense of their own partiality with a commitment for justice and an attempt to "keep alive potent traditions of critique and resistance."[35]

Pastoral ministers invested in the process of enabling and empowering liturgical renewal and change, who see themselves through the metaphor of cultural workers and are dedicated to reformation in its best sense, also need to raise important questions of contextualization and its relationship to knowledge and power, learning and possibility, social criticism and human dignity and how these might be understood in relation to rather than in isolation from those practices of domination, privilege and resistance at work in many arenas of the religious communities in which we find ourselves identified and implicated.

Of primary importance for those who seek to utilize the benefits of liturgical renewal through the means of contextualization, indigenization and cross-cultural religious education is the need to resurrect traditions and social memories that provide a new way of reading religious and secular history and of reclaiming appropriate power and identity. Within this recovery of memory, which in the liturgy is expressed as our "great anamnesis,"[36] there is the distinct possibility of creating new social and religious practices that connect rather than separate liturgical renewal from other forms of cultural work entailed in everyday life.

It is in the reconstruction of our dangerous religious memories that the role of pastoral ministers acting as cultural workers and as transformative critics can offer the opportunity to retain and to realize the kind of renewal that bridges and heals the dichotomy experienced and expressed in efforts to balance between traditions and transitions. It is the prophetic and pastoral witness of working for liturgical renewal that stands in the interstices or gaps expressed by Mother Camille and so many others who find themselves somewhere struggling between the wide gaps of "Lord, have mercy!" and "Thank you, Jesus!" To this end and by this means I am committed to the renewal of all liturgical traditions and transitions that reinforce the work and witness of the universal faith community that does justice and love.

Thus we are enjoined and invited to participate in the ancient yet ever new liturgical call and refrain so readily available in every Sunday worship celebrated by the church — the resounding sound of *kyrie eleison,* and the words, actions and the dangerous memory of our eucharist. We are invited to gather and to celebrate together in myth and parable and with the profoundly diverse yet unified body of all God's people who are willing to risk everything to be present around the table of the One who invites us to solidarity, to live in holiness and wholeness, and to be finally at peace in the breaking of the bread and the sharing of the cup. Let the liturgical renewal and the ongoing cultural work of change, conversion, transformation, metanoia be for our good and that of all the church. "Lord, have mercy!" "Thank you, Jesus!"

1. Victor Turner, "Ritual, Tribal and Catholic," *Worship* 50 (November 1976): 504–26.

2. W. Robertson Smith, *The Religion of the Semites* (New York: Meridian, 1956). Originally published in 1889.

3. Mary Douglas presents a more historically nuanced critique of recent liturgical changes in general in *Natural Symbols* (New York: Random House/ Vintage, 1973), 19 ff. David Martin has also published several critiques of changes in the Anglican *Book of Common Prayer,* speaking both as a sociologist of religion and as a deacon in the Church of England.

4. See Edward Foley, "Liturgical Factions and Violent Reactions: Evolution or Revolution," in *Traditions and Transitions: Culture, Church and Worship,* Notre Dame Center for Pastoral Liturgy Conference, 1998. Foley indicates that

for Crossan, myth is about mediation and reconciliation . . . bridges the gap between apparently irreconcilable stances, individuals or situations, and demonstrates that mediation is possible. This is the point I am making in reviewing the first of two general approaches to addressing tradition and transition as pastoral issues for renewal in culture, church and worship.

5. Emile Durkheim's *The Elementary Structures of the Religious Life,* tr. J. W. Swain (New York: Free Press, 1965). Originally published in 1912.

6. Clifford Geertz, *The Interpretation of Cultures* (New York: Basic Books, 1973), 44–45, 48, 89, 113, 127 ff.

7. See Foley.

8. Catherine Bell, "Discourse and Dichotomies: The Structure of Ritual Theory," *Religion* 17 (1985): 95–118.

9. By definition, a "womanist" is a black feminist or woman of color who has appropriated Alice Walker's term to describe the liberative efforts of these women. The term, connoting strength, forthrightness and responsibility, emerges out of the language and experiences of African American communities of moral discourse. See Alice Walker, *In Search of Our Mothers' Gardens* (San Francisco: Harcourt Brace Jovanovich, 1983), ix.

10. See R. Scott Appleby, "Keeping the Faith in an Age of Extremes," in *Traditions and Transitions: Cultures, Church and Worship.*

11. Mary Helen Washington, "Zora Neale Hurston: A Woman Half in Shadow," introduction to *I Love Myself When I Am Laughing . . . And Then Again When I Am Looking Mean and Impressive: A Zora Neale Hurston Reader,* Alice Walker, ed. (New York: Feminist Press, 1979), 19.

12. See James N. Poling, *The Abuse of Power: A Theological Problem* (Nashville: Abingdon Press, 1991); also, Joanne Carlson Brown and Carol R. Bohn, eds., *Christianity, Patriarchy, and Abuse: A Feminist Critique* (New York: Pilgrim Press, 1989).

13. See Toinette M. Eugene, "Liberation: Gender, Race, and Class," in *The Globalization of Theological Education,* Alice Frazer Evans, Robert A. Evans, David A. Roozen, eds. (Maryknoll: Orbis Books, 1994), 185–202. For in-depth development of the infrastructures and workings of racism, sexism and classism, see Paula S. Rothenberg, *Race, Class, and Gender in the United States: An Integrated Study* (New York: St. Martin's Press, 1995).

14. The term "justice/love" is one I have appropriated and adapted for use from Carter Heyward in *Touching our Strength: The Erotic as Power and the Love of God* (San Francisco: Harper and Row, 1989).

15. These and other vocational and ministerial stories are recounted as models of change agents for the church as it expresses itself in the black Catholic community, from which I have received many lessons in how the liturgical work of one race can be a model for all people intent on the experience of liturgical, social and ecclesial renewal. See Cyprian Davis, OSB, *The History of Black Catholics in the United States* (New York: Crossroad, 1990) for further information and examples.

16. Alice Walker, *Living by the Word: Selected Writings, 1973–1987* (San Diego: Harcourt Brace Jovanovich, 1988), 1 ff.

17. Alice Walker, "Journal," *Living By the Word* (San Diego: Harcourt Brace Jovanovich, 1988), 2.

18. *Ibid.*

19. See for example, the extremely practical models of pastoral care offered by Edward P. Wimberley, *Pastoral Care in the Black Church* (Nashville: Abingdon Press, 1979), *Pastoral Counseling and Spiritual Values: A Black Point of View* (Nashville: Abingdon Press, 1982); *African American Pastoral Care* (Nashville: Abingdon Press, 1991).

20. Theo Witvliet, *The Way of the Black Messiah* (Oak Park, Illinois: Meyer-Stone, 1987), 97. For a good summary of contextual theologies, see Witvliet, *A Place in the Sun* (Maryknoll: Orbis, 1985).

21. See Kathleen Hughes, RSCJ, and Mark R. Francis, CSV, eds., *Living No Longer for Ourselves: Liturgy and Justice in the Nineties* (Collegeville: The Liturgical Press, 1991). This collection of essays by the faculty of Catholic Theological Union in Chicago attempts to recover the intrinsic relationship of worship and justice, once central to the liturgical movement, by demonstrating that the celebration of liturgy has social implications for the nineties and makes ethical demands on all who would call themselves members of the Body of Christ.

22. bell hooks, *Teaching to Transgress: Education as the Practice of Freedom* (New York: Routledge, 1994) and *Outlaw Culture: Resisting Representations* (New York: Routledge, 1994).

23. See Henry Giroux, *Border Crossings: Cultural Workers and the politics of Education* (New York: Routledge, 1992); *Living Dangerously: Multiculturalism and the Politics of Difference* (New York: Peter Lange, 1993); Henry Giroux and David Purpel, eds., *The Hidden Curriculum and Moral Education: Deception or Discovery?* (Berkeley: McCutchan, 1983).

24. I have appropriated and adapted the use of the term "moral imagination" from the formidable and challenging text of Edward Tivnan, *The Moral Imagination: Confronting the Ethical Issues of Our Day* (New York: Simon and Schuster, 1995). In addressing the reality that freedom breeds conflicting values, and by carefully mediating between opposing ideals, Tivnan arrives, as I do, at the conclusion that moral imagination has the ability to cleanse debate of hatred and moral arrogance when conservatives and liberals alike act as if there is only one

Toinette M. Eugene

way to think. See Stephen Carter, *The Culture of Disbelief: How American Law and Politics Trivialize Religious Devotion* (New York: Basic Books, 1993).

25. See Robert J. Schreiter, "Contextualization from a World Perspective," *Theological Education*, XXX supplement I (Autumn 1993): 63–86, for further development of this theme and prescriptive definition of contextualization as it relates to theological education and religious education.

26. See Segundo Galilea, *The Beatitudes: To Evangelize As Jesus Did* (Maryknoll: Orbis, 1988) for a rich reflection on the use of the Beatitudes as a radical means of addressing and engaging pastoral issues involved in the balancing of tradition and transformation required by liturgical renewal.

27. Friedrich Hauck, "Makarios," *Theological Dictionary of the New Testament*, ed. Gerhard Kittel, trans. G.W. Bromily (Grand Rapids: William B. Eerdmans, 1967), 4:369.

28. Michael Crosby's splendid text, *Spirituality of the Beatitudes* (Maryknoll: Orbis, 1984), 24, explains that every person, group or institution proclaiming a spirituality of the Beatitudes in its practice or profession can expect the world's rejection. But this very negation can become an affirmation of the effective power of God's reign and its blessing in our lives. "Furthermore, the experience of this blessing need not be anticipated in some future end time beyond our experience. The New Testament Beatitudes are not just imitations of the future or consolations in relation to it. They see the present in light of the future."

29. See John C. Haughey, ed., *The Faith That Does Justice: Examining the Christian Sources for Social Change* (New York: Paulist Press, 1977).

30. I draw heavily upon the analogy of "cultural worker" as a concept that describes pedagogues and other proponents of the teaching/learning process. This term is introduced by Harvard educator Henry Giroux and explicated in his work, *Border Crossings: Cultural Workers and the Politics of Education* (New York: Routledge, 1992).With this work Giroux names his desire to meet across boundaries, declaring his political solidarity with postmodern feminist thought, anti-racist theory and all who think critically about pedagogy. With clarity and insight he writes about the points of connection, expanding the scope of critical pedagogy and inviting us to engage in a broad political project that is fundamentally non-hierarchical and non-autocratic in the forms and styles of leadership for change and transformation from that which has been traditionally oppressive.

31. See Robert J. Schreiter, "Contextualization from a World Perspective," *Theological Education*, XXX, Supplement I (Autumn, 1993): 63–86 for a further development of this theme and prescriptive defintion of contextualization as it relates to theological education and liturgical renewal and education.

32. See Henry A. Giroux's work cited above. Also see his *Living Dangerously: Multiculturalism and the Politics of Difference* (New York: Peter Lang, 1993); Henry

Giroux and David Purple, eds., *The Hidden Curriculum and Moral Education: Deception or Discovery?* (Berkeley: McCutchan, 1983).

33. Giroux, *Border Crossings: Cultural Workers and the Politics of Education*, 5.

34. Roger Simon, *Teaching Against the Grain* (New York: Bergin and Garvey, 1992).

35. Cornel West, "The New Cultural Politics of Difference," *October* 53 (Summer, 1990): 108.

36. The "great anamnesis" or the practice of the great remembrance is the section of the liturgy so named by early Greek Christians, which was and is a time at worship wherein we are to recall the acts of redemption that renew us, reconcile us and put us in solidarity with all of God's people in all times and everywhere. We know that those who do not remember the past are doomed to repeat it in the future. The call to anamnesis or to remember is quintessential. May we never forget.

Authors

R. Scott Appleby is associate professor of history and director of the Cushwa Center for the Study of American Catholicism at the University of Notre Dame. He is the author of books on the relationship of religions, societies and policies, and is co-editor with Martin Marty of *Fundamentalisms Comprehended.*

Eleanor Bernstein, CSJ, is director of the Notre Dame Center for Pastoral Liturgy. Author and editor, she is president of the board of directors of the Liturgical Conference.

Mary Collins, OSB, is associate professor of liturgical studies in the department of religion and religious education at Catholic University in Washington, DC. She was honored by the Center for Pastoral Liturgy in 1995 with the Michael Mathis award in recognition of her contributions to the renewal of worship in the North American church. She is the author of *Contemplative Participation: Sacrosanctum Concilium Twenty-Five Years Later* and was co-editor for eight volumes of the *Concilium* series. She has been a consultor to the International Commission on English in the Liturgy (ICEL) and chaired ICEL's subcommittee for the translation of the Liturgical Psalter.

Godfried Cardinal Danneels is archbishop of the diocese of Mechelen-Brussels, Belgium, and cardinal primate of Belgium. Since 1990 he has been international president of Pax Christi. He has served on Vatican congregations and councils. In 1980 and 1983 he represented the Belgian bishops' conference at the Synod of Bishops in Rome; in 1985 he was named relator of the special Synod of Bishops marking the twentieth anniversary of the Second Vatican Council. He has been elected twice as a member of the Secretariate of the Synod. He has taught liturgy at seminaries in Belgium.

Catherine Dooley, OP, is associate professor in the department of religion and religious education at Catholic University in Washington. Her writings, including *To Listen and Tell: Introduction to the Lectionary for Masses with Children,* address liturgy, sacramental preparation and celebration, catechists and religious education.

Toinette M. Eugene serves as formation director for the pastoral leadership placement board and as director of the African-American Pastoral Center for the diocese of Oakland, California. Her writings on the integration of spirituality and social justice include *Lifting as We Climb: A Womanist Ethic of Care* and *Balm for Gilead: Pastoral Care for African-American Families Experiencing Abuse,* which she co-authored.

Edward Foley, OFM CAP, is professor of liturgy and music at the Catholic Theological Union in Chicago. He writes regularly on liturgy, music and ritual. He is the author of *From Age to Age: An Introduction to the History of Christian Eucharist.*

John G. Hibbard is a presbyter and pastor in the archdiocese of Kingston, Ontario, Canada. He is the former director of the National Liturgical Office, English Sector, of the Canadian Conference of Catholic Bishops. He is a regular contributor to the *National Bulletin on Liturgy* and the author of *Preparing to Serve at the Table.*

Alan J. Hommerding is music and text editor for World Library Publications of J. S. Paluch Company. A musician and liturgist, Alan is an author of hymn texts and of articles on music and liturgy.

Rosa María Icaza, CCVI, is professor of Spanish language and culture at the Mexican American Cultural Center in San Antonio, Texas, and a consultant for the Instituto de Liturgia Hispana. She is a member of the Hispanic subcommittee of the Bishops' Committee on the Liturgy and a translator of ritual books for the United States Catholic Conference.

Jan Michael Joncas is a presbyter of the archdiocese of St. Paul, Minnesota, where he is assistant professor of theology at the University of St. Thomas. His writings include *Preaching the Rites of Christian Initiation* and *From Sacred Song to Ritual Music: Twentieth-Century Understandings of Roman Catholic Worship Music.*

Richard P. McBrien is professor of theology at the University of Notre Dame, where he holds the Crowley-O'Brien Walter Chair in theology. Former chair of the department of theology at the university, he is general editor of *The HarperCollins Encyclopedia of Catholicism* and author of *Catholicism.*

John Allyn Melloh, SM, is director of the John S. Marten Program in Homiletics and Liturgics at the University of Notre Dame. He is a frequent workshop presenter for preachers and presiders.

Kathleen Norris, poet, essayist and writer, is best known for her best-selling works, *Dakota: A Spiritual Geography* and *The Cloister Walk.*

James M. Schellman is associate director of the International Commission on English in the Liturgy (ICEL), and co-editor of *Shaping English Liturgy Studies in Honor of Archbishop Denis Hurley.*

Bishop Donald W. Trautman is bishop of the diocese of Erie, Pennsylvania. As chair of the U.S. Bishops' Committee on the Liturgy from 1993 to 1996, he directed the preparation of a revised lectionary and sacramentary by the U.S. Catholic Bishops.

Victoria M. Tufano is editor of *Catechumenate: A Journal of Christian Initiation* and co-editor of the *Forum Essay* series. She is senior acquisitions editor at Liturgy Training Publications of the archdiocese of Chicago.

Richard S. Vosko is a presbyter of the diocese of Albany, New York. He is an award-winning designer and consultant for worship environments in the United States and Canada. He serves on the planning committee for Form/Reform conferences on church architecture.

W9-BYD-134

Dear Parent:
Your child's love of reading starts here!

Every child learns to read in a different way and at his or her own speed. Some go back and forth between reading levels and read favorite books again and again. Others read through each level in order. You can help your young reader improve and become more confident by encouraging his or her own interests and abilities. From books your child reads with you to the first books he or she reads alone, there are I Can Read Books for every stage of reading:

SHARED READING
Basic language, word repetition, and whimsical illustrations, ideal for sharing with your emergent reader

BEGINNING READING
Short sentences, familiar words, and simple concepts for children eager to read on their own

READING WITH HELP
Engaging stories, longer sentences, and language play for developing readers

READING ALONE
Complex plots, challenging vocabulary, and high-interest topics for the independent reader

ADVANCED READING
Short paragraphs, chapters, and exciting themes for the perfect bridge to chapter books

I Can Read Books have introduced children to the joy of reading since 1957. Featuring award-winning authors and illustrators and a fabulous cast of beloved characters, I Can Read Books set the standard for beginning readers.

A lifetime of discovery begins with the magical words "I Can Read!"

Visit www.icanread.com for information
on enriching your child's reading experience.

Ree Drummond and Diane deGroat gratefully
acknowledge the editorial and artistic contributions of
Amanda Glickman and Rick Whipple.

I Can Read Book® is a trademark of HarperCollins Publishers.

Charlie the Ranch Dog: Rock Star Text copyright © 2015 by Ree Drummond. Cover art copyright © 2015 by Diane deGroat. Interior art copyright © 2015 by HarperCollins Publishers. All rights reserved. Manufactured in China. No part of this book may be used or reproduced in any manner whatsoever without written permission except in the case of brief quotations embodied in critical articles and reviews. For information address HarperCollins Children's Books, a division of HarperCollins Publishers, 195 Broadway, New York, NY 10007.
www.icanread.com

Library of Congress Control Number: 2014949456
ISBN 978-0-06-234778-7 (trade bdg.)—ISBN 978-0-06-234777-0 (pbk.)

15 16 17 18 19   SCP   10 9 8 7 6 5 4 3 2 1   ❖   First Edition

CHARLIE
the Ranch Dog
ROCK STAR

based on the CHARLIE THE RANCH DOG books
by REE DRUMMOND, The Pioneer Woman,
and DIANE deGROAT

HARPER
An Imprint of HarperCollinsPublishers

Yawn. Stretch. Ahh . . .

Relaxing with Mama is the best

after a long day of ranch work.

Hey—check out that rock star dog!

Cool shades!

Everyone cheers for him.

His life is so easy!

I want to be like that rock star dog.

No more working my paws to the bone.

Good-bye to Charlie the Ranch Dog.

Hello, Charlie the Rock Star!

The next morning after breakfast,
Mama calls me out to the truck.

Nope. Not today!

Today I'm a new dog.

I need time to hunt

for the perfect outfit.

Look at my mess.

Somebody should clean this up.

Hello? Anyone?

Oh well.

Aha!

Now I'm fabulous.

Here come some of my biggest fans.
My sister and brother will get
all sweaty from ranch work.
But not me!

12

They say I'm the greatest.

Watch the ears, please!

They have to flop just so.

I'm looking sharp.

Now I need a pool,

with a big soft pillow

and a giant umbrella beside it.

I guess my picnic table will do.

Toss. Turn. Ouch!

This table has splinters.

What's that sound?

Oh right!

It's hay-hauling season.

Hay!

Hay isn't as soft as a pillow,

but a dog can dream.

I race out to the pasture.

Daddy is on top of the hay monster.

I hop on for a ride.

I have to try out every bale.

Ouch! This one is too scratchy.

Achoo! This one is too dusty.

Ahhh. This one is just right.

I see Mama in the vegetable garden.

The old me would be by her side,

working away.

But I'm a whole new Charlie.

I'm living the good life.

What's that noise?

Who dares disturb my beauty rest?

A dog can't get a lick of sleep

around this place!

I race around the garden.

Out, you sneaky squirrel!

Get slithering, baby snake!

And you!

Hiss . . .

Moo-moo.

This garden is for rock stars only.

I'll chase you out of here, cow!

Uh-oh!

My foot is all tangled up.

Wobble, wobble.

Crash!

25

Ugh, this scarf!

These shoes!

This stuff really gets in the way.

Hey, where did that cow go?

Finally some sweet silence.

I curl up on a hay bale.

Mama scratches my belly.

She says I chased away every critter

and saved all her vegetables.

Being a rock star isn't that great after all.

Helping Mama is much more fun.

Mama's got her camera.

One last photo shoot!

Hats are a good look for me.

Get my good side!

Put a piece of bacon in my mouth!

After dinner, it's snuggle time.

My family scratches me all over.

They thank me for my hard work.

The ranch couldn't run without me.

The rock star life
isn't as easy as it looks.

Tomorrow I'm back

to being a working dog.

My fans will miss me,

but the ranch life is the one for me.

Time for bacon!